Environmentally Induced Cancer and the Law

Recent Titles from Quorum Books

ENVIRONMENTALLY INDUCED CANCER AND THE LAW

Risks, Regulation, and Victim Compensation

Frank B. Cross

Foreword by John D. Graham

Quorum Books

New York • Westport, Connecticut • London

Library of Congress Cataloging-in-Publication Data

Cross, Frank B.
    Environmentally induced cancer and the law: risks, regulation,
and victim compensation / Frank B. Cross.
        p.   cm.
    Bibliography: p.
    Includes index.
    ISBN 0-89930-389-7 (lib. bdg. : alk. paper)
    1. Cancer--Law and legislation--United States. 2. Carcinogens--
Safety regulations--United States. 3. Pollution--Law and
legislation--United States. 4. Cancer--Environmental aspects--
United States. I. Title
KF3803.C3C76   1989
344.73'0436994--dc19
[347.304436994]   88-38295

British Library Cataloguing in Publication Data is Available.

Library of Congress Card Number: 88-38295
ISBN: 0-89930-389-7

First Published in 1989 by Quorum Books

Greenwood Press, Inc.
88 Post Road West, Westport, Connecticut   06881

Printed in the United States of America

The paper used in this book complies with the
Permanent Paper Standard issued by the National
Information Standards Organization (Z39.48-1984).

10   9   8   7   6   5   4   3   2   1

To my parents and my sisters

CONTENTS

EXHIBITS

FOREWORD
*by John D. Graham**

The winds of change are now becoming apparent to virtually every serious participant in America's process of environmental policy making. The institutions of the status quo have few intellectual allies. Command-and-control regulation is perceived as misdirected, economically inefficient, and largely ineffective. The current tort liability system seems too clumsy to grapple competently with the complexity of environmental pollution. Arbitrariness seems to be the salient feature of environmental tort litigation, both in terms of which pockets are socked and who gets compensated.

Elected politicians, Republican and Democrat, are beginning to sense the demand for reform of environmental policy. The presidential candidates of 1988 fought bitterly to capture the symbol of "environmentalism." George Bush is the first President in history to visit the Waterside Mall (the home of the U.S. Environmental Protection Agency) and the first President to appoint a card-carrying environmentalist to run EPA. Elected politicians are responding to what their polls say: "do something about the environment."

What precisely should public policymakers do to put environmental policy making on the right track? Two conflicting answers seem to be emerging, one radical (by the standards of American politics), and other moderate (or incremental). Radicals argue for a fundamental shift in the burden of proof: regulators and judges should *assume* that all pollution is unhealthy and that industry (primarily) is responsible for cleanup and compensation unless someone can prove otherwise with definitive science. Incrementalists argue that the growing body of environmental science needs to be put to better use ("risk assessment") as regulators and courts seek to target the most serious pollution problems. In the new environmental politics, the question is not whether change will occur but when it will occur and how dramatic it will be.

In this receptive intellectual and political climate, Professor Frank Cross explores the problem of environmental cancer in America: its causes, current responses, various reform proposals, and future directions. Drawing on both an impressive literature review and significant personal experi-

---

* Associate Professor of Policy and Decision Sciences, Harvard School of Public Health.

ence in environmental litigation, Cross presents a sobering analysis of the imperfections in current regulatory and judicial remedies.

A central finding of the book is that, in fact, there is no good reason to believe that America is facing an epidemic of environmental cancer. Public perceptions of risk from industrial chemicals seem to be out of proportion with what science has learned about the carcinogenic effects of such chemicals. At the same time, Cross sees sufficient evidence of environmental cancer in American life to justify vigorous regulatory and judicial responses. The largest sources of environmental cancer appear to be smoking, diet, radiation, indoor air pollution (especially radon), and occupational exposures to chemical carcinogens.

In the regulatory arena. Professor Cross recommends more sophisticated risk assessments that consider both "most likely" and "worst-case" scenarios. While recognizing the imperfections of risk assessment, Cross calls for federal agencies to regain control of the priority-setting process by following the prescriptions of comparative risk assessment. In standard setttings, however, Cross rejects both risk assessment and cost-benefit analysis in favor of a pragmatic form of feasibility analysis that considers both the technological and financial prospects of American industry. Taken together, these regulatory reforms are aimed at tackling the biggest sources of environmental cancer while fostering the ability of American businesses—both large and small—to remain competitive in a global economy.

Regardless of how well the regulatory process performs, Professor Cross sees a need for a vibrant tort liability system to compensate the inevitable victims of environmental cancer and to deter future pollution. To overcome the formidable impediments to successful lawsuits, Cross recommends that courts allow plaintiffs to recover from polluters if they can demonstrate a future health risk from contemporary exposures to chemical carcinogens. The amount of recovery would be related to both the amount of exposure and the potency of the chemical. An administrative mechanism could be established to standardize estimates of potency and to provide guidelines for exposure assessment. This new approach would circumvent two of the major obstacles to recovery under the current tort system: the statute of limitations and the burden of proving that a specific exposure was responsible for a specific cancer.

What Professor Cross has offered, in effect, is a careful analysis in favor of several profound, yet incremental reforms of American's environmental policy. His recommendations would strengthen (rather than replace) the risk assessment/risk management paradigm championed by William Ruckelshaus, former EPA Administrator. Underlying his recommendations is a sense of confidence that risk assessment, aided by scientific progress, can play a crucial role in rationalizing the apparent inconsistencies in both regulatory and common law approaches to environmental cancer.

PREFACE

Many Americans cynically believe that environmental pollution is responsible for hundreds of thousands of cancers suffered by citizens of our nation and that the government does little or nothing in response to this cancer, probably because of lobbying influence by industry. Synthetic chemicals are almost universally suspected as the responsible cause of this perceived cancer epidemic. Villains are found in big industry, in government, and, occasionally, among scientists, all of whom are sometimes regarded as self-serving and dishonest.

The perception of widespread environmentally induced cancer often manifests itself in action. Citizens arise to protest hazardous waste dumps, pesticides, food additives, and other chemical sources of exposure to risks of cancer. Strict regulations and warning labels are demanded. Many individuals eschew all modern chemical products in favor of "natural" foods and other more traditional or primitive products. Others more cynically assume that the present situation is hopeless, in an environment saturated with carcinogens, and that self action or government action is likely to be futile.

However understandable the above attitudes may be, they are demonstrably wrong as a matter of scientific fact. Most cancers are unrelated to what we commonly call pollution but are caused by personal lifestyle choices, especially tobacco smoking and dietary practices. Natural foods are often far more carcinogenic than the miniscule doses of pesticides or chemical additives typically found in some foods. The widely feared hazardous waste dumps present a far smaller hazard than ordinary exposures to indoor air in many households. Moreover, the greatest source of outdoor carcinogenic pollution may often be individuals or small businesses rather than the big industries that are typically blamed.

In short, public misperception of environmental cancer risks is widespread. Acknowledging this misperception need not exonerate all environmental chemical exposures, however. Some apologists for industry emphasize the tremendous cancer burden attributable to lifestyle choices and argue that most environmental pollutants have not been proven to cause cancer in humans. These individuals typically suggest that government is unfairly biased against industry and has done far too much regulation of chemicals already. In this view, society should have no fear for common exposures to even suspect toxic chemicals.

Yet there is more than a grain of truth in the public's fear of industrial chemicals. While such chemicals are not responsible for a majority of cancers, they doubtless contribute to thousands or even tens of thousands of preventable cases of cancer annually. And the federal government has done relatively little to stop the major sources of these avoidable cancers. Those who have suffered cancer face great difficulty in obtaining damages from whomever is responsible for their disease. The current governmental response to environmentally induced cancer is plainly insufficient.

The shortcomings of government action should not be ascribed to corruption, however. Cancer is a unique disease that presents tremendous difficulties to any organization charged with its prevention or with victim compensation. The present state of scientific knowledge about cancer is advancing but is still seriously incomplete and will likely remain so for the foreseeable future. Even scientific breakthroughs are unlikely to yield the information that is critically needed—it is impossible to identify the specific cause of any given cancer. This problem is compounded by a host of others, not the least of which is the fact that many common, economically essential substances may cause some risk of cancer. Part I of this book provides background context for the unavoidable problems of any government response to environmentally induced cancer.

While the special problems of environmental cancer prevent any perfect or precise solution, government cannot surrender to these problems but must do the best it can to respond in the public interest. Government's first task is to prevent environmentally induced cancer, insofar as possible, through such regulatory organizations as the Environmental Protection Agency. This responsibility is confounded by scientific uncertainty and conflicting values, but some measure of cancer prevention is possible. Part II describes the inadequate record of government regulatory action, the available approaches for regulation, and some future directions that offer promise for greater effectiveness.

Government also should provide for compensation of those individuals who unfortunately are victimized by environmental carcinogens. This task historically has been left to the court system and common law. Traditional judicial rules and procedures, however, have proved insufficient to compensate victims equitably. Part III analyzes these established legal standards for recovery, their serious limitations in the context of carcinogens, and promising future directions for compensating individuals who suffer from environmentally induced cancer.

There are no simple or guaranteed answers to the problem of the law's response to environmentally induced cancer. A primary objective of this book is to amplify the extraordinary and inherent legal problems presented by the special characteristics of cancer as a disease. The prevailing polarization of attitudes about environmental cancer contributes nothing to the development of constructive government policies, however. Both

sides are too facile, and neither offers an effective approach to environmental cancer. Promising action depends centrally upon an appreciation
of the innate complexity of the situation and a willingness to act pragmat-
ically in the absence of ideal information.

ACRONYMS

CPSC	Consumer Product Safety Commission
EDB	Ethylene Dibromide
EDF	Environmental Defense Fund
EPA	Environmental Protection Agency
FDA	Food and Drug Administration
FIFRA	Federal Insecticide, Fungicide, and Rodenticide Act
GAO	General Accounting Office
IRLG	Interagency Regulatory Liaison Group
MCL	Maximum Contaminant Level
MCLG	Maximum Contaminant Level Goal
MLE	Most Likely Estimate
MTD	Maximum Tolerated Dose
NCI	National Cancer Institute
NESHAP	National Emission Standard for Hazardous Air Pollutants
NPDES	National Pollutant Discharge Elimination System
NRDC	Natural Resources Defense Council
NSPS	New Source Performance Standard
NTP	National Toxicology Program
OMB	Office of Management and Budget
OSHA	Occupational Safety and Health Administration
OSTP	Office of Science and Technology Policy
OTA	Office of Technology Assessment
PCB	Polychlorinated Biphenyl
RMCL	Recommended Maximum Contaminant Level
SDWA	Safe Drinking Water Act
TSCA	Toxic Substances Control Act
UCL	Upper Confidence Limit
VOC	Volatile Organic Compound

PART I

CONTEXT OF ENVIRONMENTAL CANCER

Before proposing legal responses to environmentally induced cancer, policymakers need to understand the context of this public health problem. As will be seen, there is widespread public misunderstanding about the sources and characteristics of environmental cancer, and this misperception may reflect itself in government policies. When policies are grounded in false or incomplete information, however, they may do more harm than good.

Chapter 1 discusses the unique "cancer problem." For a variety of reasons, environmentally induced cancer presents special and particularly intractable difficulties for the legal system. Cancer incidence and fatality are extraordinarily high in our contemporary society, which commands effective government action against this disease. Developing effective government responses to cancer is not so simple as it might seem, however. Unique features of cancer as a disease complicate the government's duty.

Discussion of the cancer problem must begin by acknowledging the still very limited scientific understanding of this disease. Cancer occurs through a complex, multistage process that is only partially comprehended. This itself makes it hard for even expert bodies to determine the causes of cancer in the United States. Difficulties are compounded by cancer's latency—the disease may not be discernible for years or decades after the event that initiated the cancer. Government's task becomes even more difficult as it appears that there is no absolutely safe level of exposure to carcinogens. Cancer also strikes with apparent randomness, perhaps infecting only one of thousands of similarly exposed individuals. The combination of these features means that scientists have difficulty determining which substances cause cancer and have even more difficulty ascertaining how much cancer may be attributed to a substance. It is virtually impossible to say which substance caused any individual case of cancer.

Yet the public and the law demand that science answer these virtually unanswerable questions. If government is to prevent cancer, it must know the causes of cancer. If courts are to compensate cancer victims, they must be able to determine the parties responsible for the victims' suffering. The difficulty in achieving these goals underlies this entire book.

Action against cancer is not impossible, however, and chapter 2 identifies the leading causes of cancer in the United States today. While the number of cancers caused by any given source cannot be defined with precision, due to the shortcomings of current science, rough estimates are possible. This chapter estimates the degree of cancer attributable to external sources.

While many Americans seem to believe that industrial chemicals are responsible for an explosion of cancer incidence, the facts do not bear out this concern. The relative risk of cancer generally has not increased, once age and other factors are considered. Moreover, the substantial number of cancers that occur are primarily caused by tobacco and dietary practices, rather than environmental pollution.

While pollution of the environment by industrial chemicals is not responsible for a substantial proportion of cancer, such pollution should not be ignored. Toxic chemical exposures may well be responsible for thousands or tens of thousands of cancer deaths. Certain specific sources, such as indoor air pollution, may cause a significant number of potentially preventable cancers.

An understanding of the context of environmentally induced cancer will enable the law to better fulfill its preventive and compensatory role. Any policy must take account of the scientific uncertainty surrounding cancer, particularly regarding causation. Government policymakers can utilize the best available information, but they must allow for the uncertainty attendant to that data. Government can focus on the largest sources of environmental cancer risk in order to maximize public health protection. A more complete understanding of the problem can also enable greater accuracy and equity in assigning legal responsibility for cancer. Understanding the context of environmental cancer, as set forth in this part, contributes to all aspects of the law's response to environmentally induced cancer.

1

SOURCES OF THE "CANCER PROBLEM"

Cancer kills nearly 500,000 residents of the United States every year. At the present time, cancer is the second leading cause of death in the United States. Moreover, the total number of Americans who die from cancer has been steadily increasing. It has been projected that one out of every four Americans alive today will ultimately die of cancer. Virtually everyone now alive will lose a close friend or relative to this frightening disease. To date, cancer has frustrated nearly all government and private efforts at prevention or cure.

The disease known as cancer is not a simple or uniform public health problem. Cancer attacks many different sites in the human body. While all cancers share some of the same fundamental properties, significant differences can be seen between a blood cancer, such as leukemia, and a lung cancer. Exhibit 1-1 illustrates the frequency of cancer at various sites, in terms of diagnosed new cases and number of deaths per year. While many cancer sites are known to science, nearly half of all cancer deaths are attributable to malignancies of just three sites—the lung, breast, and intestinal tract. Over 200,000 U.S. deaths annually result from these cancers alone.

Given the magnitude of the public health problem posed by cancer it is unsurprising that citizens have called upon the legal structure for remedies. As citizens and voters, we may expect the federal government to take all necessary steps to prevent future avoidable cases of cancer. As victims, we may expect the courts to redress the costs and suffering of our injury, at the expense of whomever may be found responsible for causing a cancer.

The law, however, has struggled with these problems unsuccessfully. Regulatory efforts to prevent cancer have been both uncertain and costly. After more than a decade of these efforts, there is little evidence of progress. Nor has the judiciary been successful at compensating cancer victims. Occasionally, a plaintiff may recover compensation, but most individuals afflicted with cancer receive no legal redress. The source of these legal problems can be largely traced to special features of the disease itself. Consequently, some background discussion of cancer biology is necessary to understanding the law's difficulties in addressing cancer risks.

THE BIOLOGY OF CANCER

Cancer develops when a body's cell division process goes awry with uncontrolled multiplication of cells resulting in a tumor. Cancer is by no

Exhibit 1-1
Cancer Incidence and Mortality by Site (1985)

Style	New Cases	Deaths
Lung	144,000	125,600
Breast	119,900	38,700
Digestive Organs	215,200	119,800
Oral	28,900	9,500
Bone	2,000	1,400
Uterus	52,000	9,700
Prostate	86,000	25,500
Bladder	40,000	10,800
Brain	13,700	10,100
Leukemia	24,600	17,200
TOTAL	910,000	462,000

means a modern phenomenon. Fossil evidence indicates that dinosaurs suffered cancer. Human history contains thousands of years of records of this disease, yet scientists still lack essential information about how and why cancer occurs. Some aspects of the disease, however, are well established.

Cell division occurs normally and constantly in the healthy human body, at the rate of approximately 10,000,000 per minute. Unless disturbed, this process is an uneventful one with only beneficial consequences for humans. The cell's genetic material (DNA) replicates itself exactly and controls the nature and rate of cell division. In this carefully controlled manner, the body replaces old cells with essential new cells. A disturbance in the genetic material, though, may disrupt normal cell division, causing it to proliferate out of control and into a life-threatening tumor.

For our purposes, this carcinogenic process begins by exposure to an external substance, through direct dermal (skin) contact, inhalation, or oral ingestion. In most cases, the foreign substance does not immediately or directly attack a cell's DNA. When this substance enters the body, it is typically broken down and altered, or metabolized, by the body's enzymes into new substances, which may include a carcinogen (a substance capable of inducing cancer). The occurrence and extent of this metabolism is not an inexorable event, however; it may be affected by the simultaneous presence of other substances. Some other foreign substances may themselves directly induce cancer without any intervening metabolic activation.

When a carcinogen occurs, through metabolic processes or otherwise, that carcinogen may trigger the initial development of cancer by altering the normal genetic material of a cell. This alteration may take the form of deleting from, adding to, or breaking the chain of the cell's original DNA. Any of these consequences may ultimately yield a cancer. This process is called "insertional mutagenesis," because it involves the insertion of a mutation into a normal cell's DNA. Another theory suggests that all cells may contain the genetic information that causes cancer, known as an "oncogene," which is simply triggered by exposure to a carcinogen. Under either theory, the substance that first activates the cancer by altering genetic material is known as an "initiator" or genotoxic carcinogen. To the best of our current knowledge, *any* exposure to an initiator may commence the process of genetic damage ultimately leading to cancer. At least theoretically, a single molecule of such a carcinogen may create a mutation in a cell, thereby initiating a cancer that may ultimately spread throughout the body. This is sometimes referred to as the "one-hit" hypothesis.

Whether such initiation actually results from exposure to a carcinogen depends on various outside circumstances. The timing of exposure may be important, as the damaging cellular initiation is more likely to occur during the DNA synthesis stage of the cell's life cycle. Genetic factors may also influence the development of a cancer, as some individuals may be genetically more susceptible, or predisposed, to cancer. Different carcinogens may have greater or lesser likelihood of initiating cancer, which is called the substance's carcinogenic potency. The likelihood of cancer developing from exposure to an initiator may range from less than one in a million to as high as one in five.[1]

The occurrence of insertional mutagenesis is only the first step of a multistage process that leads to a malignant cancer, however. After insertional mutagenesis, the cell may "perceive" the internal disturbance and act to correct it. Some believe that the body's biochemical repair activities can sometimes reverse the harm done by the carcinogen. Other scientists, however, are convinced that the initiation step is functionally irreversible for at least some susceptible individuals. Even if repair fails, the simple existence of an "initiated" cell does not automatically lead to the destructive and often fatal replication of cells in a cancer. An initiated cell with altered genetic information may behave relatively normally for as long as a year or more. In a sense, these cells are "primed" to cause cancer but will not always do so.

What happens next is still not well understood. It appears, however, that another cancer-inducing substance may enter the cell and promote the growth of the malignant neoplasm of cancer. These latter substances, which are often called "promoters" or epigenetic carcinogens, do not directly alter the genetic information in the target cell. Promoters transform the initiated cell into a neoplastic cell, which is the defective source of a subsequent cancer. The precise manner in which promoters operate is not yet clear, but they somehow set the cancer process in motion, setting off the theretofore dormant initiated cell. The occurrence of promotion is also somewhat uncertain, and simple exposure to an epigenetic carcinogen will not always promote an initiated cancer. At minimum, promotion is affected by a host's hormonal and other characteristics. The promotion stage may be an extended one, requiring prolonged exposure to an epigenetic agent. And unlike initiators, promoters may have some threshold exposure level below which cancer does not develop. Many scientists believe that the "one hit" hypothesis does not apply to promoters. The promotion stage also appears to be a reversible one.

Apparently both initiation and promotion are prerequisite to the development of a cancer, but some substances may be "complete carcinogens," which act as both an initiator of genetic alteration and a promoter of subsequent tumorigenesis. Other substances may not initiate cancer, but may promote cancer in pre-initiated cells. Some promoters appear to act only with certain types of initiators or at certain sites in the human body. There may also exist antipromoters, which prevent cancer by somehow obstructing the creation of a neoplastic cell. Some promoters may be anti-initiators. These substances may prevent initiation of the genotoxic stage of a cancer but may still promote a cancer in already-initiated cells. Thus, the same substance may both prevent and cause cancer, depending upon the circumstances and timing of administration.

Once promotion is complete, a cancer becomes life-threatening by the progression of the neoplastic cell into a malignant tumor. Neoplastic progression may involve several distinct steps, but none of them are yet fully understood. Rapid cell division occurs during this stage of cancer. Such excessive cell replication creates what we know as a tumor. At this stage, dangerous progression may still be mediated by the body's immunological system. Even after both initiation and promotion, malignant cancer may never develop. The result may be a benign tumor that does not threaten the life of the host. Sometimes an early benign tumor may lie dormant for a time and then, somewhat inexplicably, reappear later in dangerous malignant form. At other times, even a malignant neoplasm may actually regress, perhaps spontaneously. External factors also stimulate or modulate the progression of cancer. Indeed, during the time from initiation to promotion to progression, various external or internal substances may intervene or combine synergistically to enhance or decrease the probability of the development of a malignant tumor. Unfortunately, in many cases progression leads to a malignant tumor.

Most malignant tumors become fatal through a process called metastasis. Malignant cells spread to other sites in the body, often via the lymphatic system or blood supply. While many of these malignant cells perish, others may take hold in tissues at various sites of the body. The factors causing fatal metastasis are still largely unknown. Like other steps in the development of cancer, metastasized cells may lie dormant for an extended period of time, before they are somehow "activated," and cancer spreads throughout the body. The multistage development of a fatal cancer is illustrated in exhibit 1-2.

In sum, cancer is a very complex, multistage process. Even the above discussion is a somewhat superficial description of carcinogenesis. The development of cancer usually takes quite some time, known as a latency period. This latency period may last from as few as five to as many as thirty years between initiation and metastasis, and twenty-year latency is common. The general belief that exposure to a toxic chemical automatically causes fatal cancer is misguided. Other factors are involved, such as genetic predisposition; and additional steps must usually take place, including metabolism of the chemical, interaction with other chemicals, overwhelming of repair mechanisms, progression, and other processes. When fatal cancer does result, the true cause is a "lethal synthesis" of factors. This knowledge should not be used to understate the potentially dangerous role of environmental chemicals in cancer causation, however. Humans are constantly exposed to innumerable substances which may contribute to the development of cancer, and any additional exposure may represent the "straw that broke the camel's back," actually causing the development of a fatal cancer.

THE TREATMENT OF CANCER

Billions of dollars have been spent on researching treatments for cancer. Notwithstanding this effort, many cancers remain largely incurable. It is encouraging to note that reported cancer survival rates seem to be steadily increasing. However, this fact may be largely due to earlier detection; and some particularly common forms of cancer show little improvement in survival rates.

Early detection may significantly enhance a patient's prospects. At an early stage, simple surgery or radiation therapy may excise the cancer. For advanced cases, however, treatment with chemotherapy may represent the

Exhibit 1-2
Stages of Cancer Development

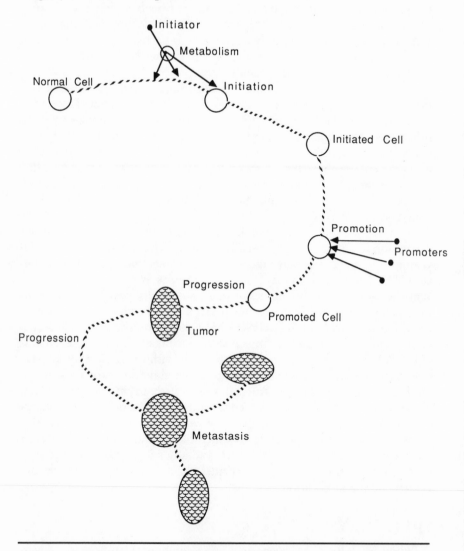

only hope. Advances in chemotherapy have dramatically improved the chances for victims of some cancers, such as acute lymphocytic leukemia in children. This cancer, which was usually fatal twenty years ago, is now survived by approximately 50 percent of those undergoing chemotherapy.

Continued efforts will be made to perfect the detection and treatment of cancer. We can expect future research advances and heightened survival rates for some cancers. Yet such a *post facto* treatment response to the disease offers very incomplete protection of public health. Many of the most common cancers, such as lung cancer, have resisted our best efforts at treatment. The five-year survival rate for lung cancer is only 11 percent, and the rate for pancreatic cancer is only 2 percent.[2]

Moreover, even with improved treatment, cancer will doubtless remain a major public health problem. Even an experimental breakthrough may take decades to develop for widespread use in patient treatment. A substantial majority of cancer patients do not currently receive even the National Cancer Institute's extant state-of-the-art treatment program.[3] Moreover, many advanced forms of cancer treatment have severe adverse side effects on the patient. In short, cancer treatment may ultimately save many lives, but there is little prospect for an effective cancer cure in the foreseeable future. Cancer prevention remains an essential part of the present war against cancer.

THE PSYCHOLOGY OF CANCER

Measured simply in sheer number of cases and fatalities, cancer obviously has an enormous impact. Yet the significance of cancer transcends even these millions of lives lost. Cancer is especially feared by many Americans and has been called the "dread disease." When it occurs, terminal cancer is an ugly, lingering death. Millions of Americans remain obsessed by fear of cancer, a word which now has become a broad metaphor for many other severe threats to our nation's health. Fear of environmentally induced cancer may be particularly profound, and former Environmental Protection Agency Administrator William D. Ruckelshaus observed that "many communities are gripped by something approaching panic."[4] Fear of cancer has given rise to large new industries in unproved quack cures for cancer and to some questionable cancer insurance schemes. Moreover, this fear and hopelessness associated with cancer may even increase the likelihood or severity of the disease.[5]

"Cancerphobia" is now recognized by psychiatrists as an established form of psychological trauma. As discussed in chapter 8, many individuals are suing for damages from their *fear* of future cancer. While concern has been somewhat displaced by the growing AIDS epidemic, cancer remains "the most feared of human diseases."[6] This fear necessarily colors any legal response to the cancer problem. Judicial decisions have acknowledged the difficulty of government regulation "where the matter involved is as sensitive and fright-laden as cancer."[7]

THE CANCER PROBLEM

Cancer obviously represents a public health problem of massive proportions. The magnitude of the public health threat from cancer, however, is not unique but roughly comparable to that presented by other hazards, such as heart disease or accidents. As a legal matter, though, cancer presents much more intractable and unique problems. Certain features of cancer as a disease raise great difficulties for the legal process.

Some of these difficulties are revealed by contrasting the chronic effects of cancer with the harmful effects of an acutely toxic substance. Consider the disastrous accidental leak of methyl isocyanate at Bhopal in India. The sudden exposure to high concentrations of this toxic gas almost instantly killed 2,700 people near Union Carbide's plant. While litigation over the Bhopal accident is factually complex, the theoretical legal response to this type of episode is not particularly difficult.

When government is called upon to regulate and prevent acutely toxic emissions of methyl isocyanate, the government can determine a level at which the substance endangers life. Relatively low levels of exposure to this chemical are not lethal, at least in the short term. These levels can be determined with reasonable accuracy from experimental data. The government can use this data to establish safety standards that permit the use of methyl isocyanate in pesticide production, while still protecting the public from fatal exposure levels.

Assigning liability for deaths resulting from the toxic leak of methyl isocyanate is also theoretically practicable. We can say with assurance how many people died and that these people unquestionably died from exposure to methyl isocyanate. No other chemicals are involved and the causal connection between methyl isocyanate and any given death is relatively clear. Nor is there any uncertainty about the particular source of the fatal chemical exposure. The deaths occurred almost instantly, when necessary evidence can still be readily accumulated. While the courts have struggled with various procedural issues in the Bhopal tragedy, most significant substantive issues, such as causation, are beyond reasonable dispute.

In contrast, cancer presents much more complex legal questions. Scientific uncertainty surrounding the development of cancer is far greater than for acutely toxic substances. Nor is the cause of an individual case of cancer ever clear. As a scientific matter, data are seldom available to demonstrate the particular cause of specific cancers. Indeed, it appears likely that nearly every cancer is the product of multiple influences, many of which cannot ever be traced. The scientific nature of cancer *qua* cancer creates unique legal problems.

The most intractable legal problems involve causation. Courts require proof of causation before assigning legal responsibility to a defendant. It appears random and unfair to impose liability on a person without first finding that the person caused the harm being remedied. Thus, proof of causation is virtually a universal prerequisite to civil recovery. Causation is also important to preventive regulation. Before controlling emissions of a carcinogen, the government should know whether and to what extent those emissions cause cancer. Otherwise the government may be wasting great effort and forcing the expenditure of great amounts of money, without any public health benefit. While demonstrating some degree of causation is therefore essential to the law's response to environmental cancer, such a demonstration is exceedingly difficult, because of the inherent complexity of cancer itself. The primary difficulties will now be summarized.

Scientific Uncertainty About Mechanisms of Cancer

Even after decades of study, our knowledge of cancer is still woefully incomplete. The role and importance of initiators, promoters, and other factors in cancer development may be known generally, but considerable dispute remains over key issues such as reversibility of damage, the nature of metabolic activation, and the significance of benign tumors, among others. One court decision complained that "[w]hat scientists know about the causes of cancer is how limited is their knowledge."[8]

The current lack of scientific knowledge regarding cancer is complicated by difficulties attendant to obtaining information. Various experimental procedures may be used to test hypotheses regarding the mechanisms of cancer. Yet there is no consensus regarding the ultimate significance of various types of experimental tests. While it is generally recognized that cancer experiments in other mammalian species are necessary, there is disagreement regarding the degree to which these experiments are fully applicable to humans. Even experimental breakthroughs, therefore, are unlikely to resolve scientific uncertainty about cancer.

Future experimentation is by no means futile, however, and recent history gives some encouragement about our ability to learn more about mechanisms of cancer. Were scientific uncertainty the only problem in cancer regulation, we could have some confidence in the future. Continued research will doubtless answer at least some of the important outstanding questions about cancer formation. But even if this research succeeds, other, more irresolvable problems exist in the very nature of cancer itself.

The Multistage Nature of Cancer

As described above, cancer is a relatively complex process that proceeds through various stages before becoming fatal. This fact raises a number of obvious legal questions. Exposure to methyl isocyanate alone was sufficient to cause death at Bhopal, which makes it possible to assign legal responsibility to the industrial source of the lethal methyl isocyanate. When a different disease, such as cancer, proceeds through many separate steps, each affected by both external and internal factors, the true "cause" of the harm is more difficult to define. Judgments must be made about whether any one stage of cancer development should suffice to qualify as a legal cause.

Should initiation of a cell, for example, be regarded as tantamount to causing cancer, even though actual cancer development will depend on subsequent events? Should promotion be considered equivalent to initiation as a cause of cancer? If promotion is indeed reversible, what significance should that fact carry in assessing causes of cancer? How should the victim's genetic susceptibility be considered in determining cancer causation?

The above questions all raise difficult problems of legal causation, since the process of carcinogenesis is more complex than the typical injuries with which courts and regulatory agencies must deal. Hypothetically, though, the government could make policy judgments regarding the causative significance of various steps in the process of cancer formation. While cancer is a synergistic process, each contributing step could be considered sufficient for legal causation. Yet even if these difficult judgments were made, other factors complicate the government's role in assigning responsibility for cancer.

Nontraceability

Even if government determines the theoretical significance of each step of cancer causation, it may be impossible to identify the substance responsible for this step in cancer development. If, for example, we decide that initiation of cancer is tantamount to its causation, we still must be able to identify the initiator before we can assign legal responsibility. Seldom is it possible to determine what substance initiated any given cancer.

A few relatively unusual cancers are linked to specific substances. Mesothelioma, for example, is uniquely caused by asbestos, a fact that has simplified a number of actual cases. Unfortunately, the vast majority of cancers, and the most common cancers, may be caused by scores of different chemicals. When these cancers develop, it becomes virtually impossible to say with confidence which substance "caused" the cancer. It is even more difficult to determine that a certain substance played a given role at a specific stage of cancer development. Causes of cancer leave no "marker" in the body identifying the nature of their lethal role.

Sometimes, however, we may be able to say that a certain substance has caused a cancer. An individual may have been exposed to only one cause of the cancer that he or she suffered. Alternatively, one source of cancer may overwhelm other possible causes. Smoking cigarettes is such a major source of lung cancer that if a smoker dies of lung cancer, we can have some confidence in assigning causation to the cigarettes. It may be possible to say that it is more likely than not that smoking caused the lung cancer. For environmental pollutants, however, this procedure is of little help. Most individuals are exposed to innumerable carcinogens, none of them in quantities large enough to overwhelm other suspect causes. This difficulty is further complicated by other features of carcinogenesis.

Latency

If cancer happened as suddenly as the Bhopal deaths from methyl isocyanate, it would be much easier to find the cause of certain cancers. Cancer, however, typically takes decades to develop from initiation to metastasis. Determining the source of any specific cancer therefore requires a historical search into exposures long past.

As a practical matter, latency exacerbates the difficulty of determining causation. Few individuals will have a sound recollection of their activities twenty years ago, much less the various substances to which they may have been exposed. Even if a person recalls drinking what seemed to be polluted water, it will generally be impossible to determine what chemicals were present in that water and in what quantity. Even if the chemical exposures could somehow be accurately identified, it might be equally difficult to ascertain the source of the pollution twenty years past. The evidence, assuming that it was even collected so long ago, will often be unavailable at the time that cancer strikes.

Apparent Randomness

Science has revealed certain factors that contribute to cancer, ranging from environmental pollutants to genetic susceptibility. Yet it appears that none of these factors is certain to cause cancer, and it is very unusual that any factor even appears to make cancer more probable than not. Rather, exposure to current environmental cancer-inducing factors typically may create a 1 in 10,000 (1×10^{-4}) risk of cancer or less. Thus only about 1 out of 10,000 similarly situated persons will get cancer because of a given exposure. The very expression of this risk, in terms of odds, implies the seeming randomness of the cancer risk.

This is not to suggest that those individuals who actually contract cancer are simply unlucky. Cancer may one day prove to be entirely deterministic, with our present probabilities explained by the numerous biological interactions of the cancer development process or defined genetic characteristics of the cancer victim. Scientific knowledge, however, is decades away from establishing cancer causation with such deterministic precision. For now and the foreseeable future, the law must respond to a disease that strikes individuals with apparent randomness.

The unpredictability of cancer presents perplexing problems for any legal structure of response. Exposure to toxic doses of methyl isocyanate will evoke adverse health effects with great reliability, and with relatively slight human variation in resistance. Such acute toxic harms caused by methyl isocyanate, therefore, are easy to identify and trace to a given causative source. When cancer occurs, however, the victimized individual has almost certainly been exposed to scores or even hundreds of possible causes, each of which has been associated with a (typically low) probability of cancer.

Consider a person who contracted a cancer and was exposed to only four possible carcinogens at the site. Even this case is almost irresolvable. Suppose that the exposures created risks of 4 in 1,000, 3 in 1,000, 2 in 1,000, and 1 in 1,000 (1, 2, 3, & 4 x 10^{-3}), respectively. We can say that it is slightly more likely that the first substance caused the cancer than did any other individual substance; yet we must acknowledge that it is even more likely that the cancer was not actually caused by the first substance but by some one of the other three carcinogens. Rather obviously, establishing causation in this unusually simple case is still quite difficult.

Absence of a Known Threshold

At the present time, it appears that exposure to even a single molecule of carcinogen presents some probabilistic risk of causing or contributing to cancer. This statement is yet only a hypothesis, and some individuals postulate the existence of thresholds for at least some carcinogenic modes of action. There appears to be no prospect, however, of demonstrating known thresholds for individual carcinogens. Dr. Bernard Weinstein of the Columbia University School of Public Health, thus explained in congressional testimony:

Although the response to various types of carcinogens is likely to be dose dependent, I know of no evidence that clearly establishes a threshold level for any carcinogen. Furthermore, even if this were established in a given experimental system, it would be difficult to predict with confidence the threshold level in a heterogenous human population.[9]

For the time being, virtually all expert entities operate under the no-threshold hypothesis.

The absence of a threshold makes it all but impossible for any person to disprove a contention that a given carcinogen caused an individual cancer. In addition, the absence of a threshold means that exposure must be reduced to zero in order to eliminate the risk of cancer entirely. In an unfortunate number of circumstances, total elimination of exposure is practically impossible. Even when theoretically possible, zero exposure is inordinately costly. One court thus opined:

[Past] cases demonstrate the inevitable tension attending regulation of carcinogens. Frequently, such regulations have severe economic impact. Indeed, ... such regulations may jeopardize plants or whole industries, and the jobs depending on them.[10]

For an acutely toxic substance, such as methyl isocyanate, indentifiable thresholds typically exist, at least for the most adverse health effects. Feasible control technology can keep human exposure at a level where these effects will not occur, barring breakdowns such as the disaster at Bhopal. Indeed, technology can typically keep exposures well below the hazardous level, preserving a margin of safety for the potentially exposed population. For cancer, however, the problem is much more difficult, because absolutely zero risk means zero exposure to carcinogens. At this time, "it is not possible . . . to manufacture, store or use potentially hazardous substances without some release to the environment, however, small."[11] Indeed, technology may never be able to entirely eliminate exposure. Even if we could, a traditional margin of safety is illusory, because we cannot go below the zero exposure necessary to ensure simple safety. The only way to attain this zero exposure level for some carcinogenic substances would be to shut down all of America's manufacturing industry.[12]

The absence of thresholds therefore presents serious problems for government's effort to prevent cancer through regulation. The no-threshold hypothesis also exacerbates courts' problems in individual cases, by making it difficult to narrow the number of potential causes of a given cancer.

The six reasons highlighted above are not the only difficulties presented by carcinogenesis. Government action is complicated by the special psychological response evoked by cancer, the difficulties of monitoring exposure to carcinogens, the considerable costs of cancer and of its control, and other factors. These factors, especially those detailed, make traditional definitions of causation impossible to meet in cancer litigation or regulation. Consequently, the law must establish creative approaches for defining legal causation. This need presents scientific, practical, political, and jurisprudential questions.

Persons have responded to the above questions in very different ways. The scientific uncertainties of cancer have polarized much of society into two extreme camps. One risk-averse group emphasizes the lack of a carcinogenic threshold and calls for the elimination of any and all environmental exposure to potentially cancer-causing chemicals. A second group emphasizes the societal economic value of these chemicals and argues against regulation of carcinogens, unless the hazard can be conclusively proved by science. Much of the conversation about regulating environmental carcinogens is driven by proponents of these two extreme positions, but society's optimal response to the problem lies between these two poles.

The remainder of this book focuses primarily on how government has responded to the cancer problem and makes suggestions for future responses. Before embarking upon this study, however, chapter 2 explores the nature and degree of various leading environmental sources of cancer.

Our judicial and regulatory responses to cancer must be colored by the overall picture of environmental cancer portrayed therein.

NOTES

1. Henry Pitot, Goldsworthy, and Moran, "The Natural History of Carcinogenesis: Implications of Experimental Carcinogenesis in the Genesis of Human Cancer," *Journal of Supramolecular Structure and Cellular Biochemistry* 17 (1981): 137.

2. Claudio Nicolini, *Biophysics and Cancer* (New York: Plenum, 1986), 159.

3. U. S. General Accounting Office, *Cancer Treatment 1975–1985: The Use of Breakthrough Treatments for Seven Types of Cancer* (January 1988).

4. William D. Ruckelshaus, "Science, Risk, and Public Policy," *Science* 221 (1983): 1026.

5. Goodkin, Antoni, and Blaney, "Stress and Hopelessness in the Promotion of Cervical Intraepithelial Neoplasia to Invasive Squamous Cell Carcinoma of the Cervix," *J. Psychosomatic Research* 30 (1986): 67.

6. Michael Shimkin, *Science and Cancer* (Washington, D.C.: Silvergirl Inc., 1980), 1.

7. Environmental Defense Fund v. Environmental Protection Agency, 510 F.2d 1292, 1298 (D.C. Cir. 1975).

8. Environmental Defense Fund v. Environmental Protection Agency, 598 F.2d 62, 89 (D.C. Cir. 1978).

9. *Hearing on Control of Carcinogens in the Environment Before the Subcommittee on Commerce, Transportation, and Tourism of the House Committee on Energy and Commerce*, 98th Cong., 1st Sess., 1983, 16.

10. Environmental Defense Fund v. Environmental Protection Agency, 598 F.2d 62, 88–89 (D.C. Cir. 1978).

11. Congressional Research Service, *Hearing on EPA's Air Pollution Control Program Before the Subcomm. on Oversight and Investigations of the House Comm. on Energy and Commerce*, 98th Cong., 2d Sess., 1984, 134.

12. Frank Cross, "Section 111(d) of the Clean Air Act: A New Approach to the Control of Airborne Carcinogens," 13 *Boston College Environmental Affairs Law Review* 221 (1986).

2

ENVIRONMENTAL CAUSES

The development of sound and effective legal standards governing environmental carcinogens requires some knowledge of the relative sources of this hazard. A substantial controversy now rages over the degree to which environmental pollution is responsible for deaths from cancer. A considerable segment of the population believes that industrial emissions are responsible for a "cancer epidemic" in which hundreds of thousands are dying of the disease. This belief is largely founded in the following two facts. First, the number of cancer deaths in the United States has steadily and dramatically increased over the twentieth century, simultaneous with a great increase in the production and use of chemicals. Second, studies have indicated that 60 to 90 percent of all cancers are "environmentally" caused by external exposures. The concatenation of these facts has led to great fear of pollution, additives, and other by-products of our industrial economy as causes of cancer. As it happens, both the above facts are strictly true, but these facts are sometimes used in misleading ways. Americans' fear of industrial chemicals is not wholly pointless, but the magnitude of cancer risk from these chemicals has been exaggerated considerably.

The first fact, that overall cancer deaths have risen, is indisputable. The number of Americans who annually die from cancer has increased by hundreds of thousands over the past several decades. Population increases do not fully explain this increase. In the year 1950, about 11 of every 10,000 American males died from cancer. By 1980, over 20 out of 10,000 male Americans would die from cancer.[1] The numbers for women are less dramatic but also reveal a steep growth in cancer death rates. Much of this increase is intuitively perceived by citizens, who everyday confront an increasing number of their friends and family suffering from cancer. Even *Jane Fonda's Workout Book* has warned "that we are in the midst of a cancer epidemic."[2]

This remarkable increase in cancer death, so often ascribed to industrial chemicals, can be almost exclusively attributed to another factor—age. When cancer death rates are adjusted for the age of the population, the increase all but disappears. The American population has aged significantly over the past four decades, and the incidence of cancer increases with age. Cancer incidence rates were lower in the 1940s because Americans of that decade tended to die of other causes first, before the latency period for most cancers might have concluded. As science brought these other causes under control and extended our longevity, cancer rates increased correspondingly. Age-adjusted cancer rates have inched up very slowly, and this tiny increase is entirely a consequence of lung cancer. The incidence at most cancer sites has actually declined.

In a dramatic editorial, Philip Abelson, a deputy editor of *Science* magazine, declared:

> For more than 10 years, the public has been subjected to a media barrage leading to widespread, misinformed fear of chemicals. Through the use of questionable evidence, many major substances have been labeled carcinogens. If data are adjusted to eliminate effects of cigarette smoking, there has been no overall increase in cancer due to other factors. The highly publicized cancer epidemic that was predicted earlier has not materialized.[3]

Indeed, there is "some evidence that, as a result of underreporting in the past, age-adjusted mortalities from many types of cancer (except lung cancer) have been declining significantly for decades."[4] Exhibit 2-1 reveals the pattern of reported cancer incidence in the years since 1930.

Even if the perceived increase in cancer is largely an artifact of increased longevity, there is still the perception that environmental pollution causes most of the hundreds of thousands of cancer deaths that occur each year in the United States. There is a widespread belief that 60 to 90 percent of cancers are avoidable or "environmental" in nature. Indeed, this figure traces back to the work of John Higginson, the founding director of the prestigious International Agency for Research on Cancer. Dr. Higginson, however, used the word "environmental" in a very broad sense, including such sources as smoking, diet, and cultural practices.

The claim that "60 to 90 percent of cancer is environmentally-caused" may be strictly true, but the meaning of the statement has been seriously misunderstood. Dr. Higginson himself has expressed frequent concern that his conclusion has been "misinterpreted."[5] No scientific studies have suggested that chemical pollution of the environment causes anything approximating a majority of human cancers. When the National Cancer Institute established priorities and goals for the year 2000, the NCI did not even mention pollution, but focused on preventing smoking and bad dietary practices, increasing early cancer screening, and improving the use of advanced treatments.[6] Recent statistical analysis reveals that cancer rates are declining for individuals under 55 and that increases among older Americans are due to lung cancer, which is overwhelmingly attributable to smoking.[7] Thus, widespread beliefs about the hazards of industrialization have tended to be hyperbolic. Cancer is primarily caused by sources other than environmental pollution.

The fact that industrial chemicals probably do not cause hundreds of thousands of annual cancer deaths, of course, does not mean that these

Exhibit 2-1
Age-Adjusted Cancer Death Rates

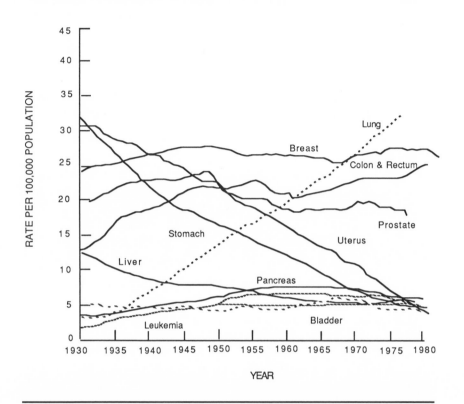

chemicals are innocuous. Hundreds of these chemicals are known to be potentially carcinogenic. For the vast majority of chemicals in use, the government has no safety data. Some significant number of cancer deaths may indeed be due to such pollution. The remainder of this chapter discusses the best estimates of the sources of cancer in America today.

The most comprehensive source for identifying the significance of environmental sources of cancer is probably a study by Richard Doll and Richard Peto of Oxford, conducted for the United States Office of Technology Assessment.[8] Doll and Peto utilized a variety of available sources, assessed the validity of their conclusions, and proposed their own best quantitative estimates of the numbers of cancers that may be traced to various environmental causes. While available data does not permit certainty, Doll and Peto suggested that environmental sources such as pollution, additives, and occupational exposure may account for approximately 10 percent of contemporary cancer incidence in the United States. This relatively small percentage accounts for some 40,000 cancer deaths annually. Doll and Peto are probably the most-cited and authoritative source on causes of cancer, but their estimates are by no means universally accepted.

The remainder of this chapter will review the number of cancers attributable to various sources, using the Doll and Peto results, as well as those from other reliable studies. Of course, the difficulties in assigning causation to cancers discussed in Chapter One considerably complicates any effort at assessing the sources of cancer in the United States today. The figures given below are at best rough estimates of the percentage of cancer cases and deaths that may be traced to various different causes.

TOBACCO

Tobacco use, particularly smoking, is an overwhelming source of cancer in the United States. One representative source estimated that smoking was responsible for 34.5 percent of all cancers in men and for 82.8 percent of lung cancers in men.[9] The respective figures for women were 5.4 percent and 43.1 percent. The significance of smoking as a source of cancer in women, however, is steadily increasing along with the percentage of women who smoke.

Smoking is securely established as the largest source of cancer in the United States. The only major form of cancer that has significantly increased in recent years is lung cancer, and studies confirm that the substantial majority of lung cancer cases can be attributed to smoking. Tobacco use may also be responsible for cancers of the lip, mouth, larynx and esophagus. Indeed, cigarette smoking has been linked to cancer at relatively unexpected sites. Twenty-five to fifty percent of bladder and pancreatic cancers in the United States appear to be caused by cigarettes.[10]

The above figures, though shockingly large, may actually understate the number of cancers caused by smoking. These estimates were derived by comparing cancer rates between smokers and nonsmokers. Some nonsmokers, however, may suffer cancer from inhaling sidestream or passive smoke produced by nearby smokers. The extent of cancer from such passive smoking is less certain than the direct harm to smokers. Cancer from passive smoking may be substantial, however. A series of studies have shown that the spouse of a smoker has roughly twice the risk of lung cancer as the spouse of a nonsmoker. Under the one-hit theory of cancer causation, we may expect even less extensive exposures to passive smoke to cause some number of lung cancers among the nonsmoking population. Current, somewhat uncertain estimates are that approximately 2,000 Americans may die annually from exposure to smoke from other people's tobacco use.[11]

In short, smoking is now established as the largest source of cancer in the United States today. One can make a strong case that the predominance of government's anticancer efforts should focus on the prevention of tobacco use. Fortunately, the percentage of persons who smoke has begun to decline, especially among males, although smoking-caused cancer may continue to climb due to latent effects of past smoking.

While smoking prevention may yield the greatest reduction in cancer, environmental sources of cancer should not be overlooked. The importance of an antismoking campaign should not obscure the attack against other sources of cancer. Tens of thousands of cancers cannot be attributed to smoking. Moreover, the connection between cancer and smoking is now well known, and smoking is thus a largely voluntary risk assumed by the smoker. Environmental sources of cancer may be unavoidable by individuals and involuntary, and therefore a greater concern of government.

DIET

Diet is now recognized to be a major source of cancer in Americans, second only to smoking. Many persons would be surprised, however, to discover which characteristics of diet are linked to most cancers. Public attention has tended to focus upon chemical food additives, such as saccharin or artificial coloring, as dangerous carcinogens. The available evidence indicates that other, seemingly innocuous, characteristics of food and drink are responsible for far more cancers than are additives.

Dietary Makeup

Eating certain foods may have a great effect on cancer incidence. The clearest evidence for the linkage of diet to cancer is probably related to consumption of fats. Numerous studies comparing different populations with different eating habits have found an association between total intake of dietary fat and cancers of the breast, the bowel, and, to a lesser degree, the prostate. Animal experiments largely confirm this effect. High dietary fat intake may be responsible for one-fourth of all cases of breast cancer in women (or about 30,000 cancers and 10,000 deaths) and over 40 percent of colorectal cancer (or about 50,000 cancers and 23,000 deaths).

Other features of dietary intake are also correlated with cancer. The evidence for particular sources of cancer is ambiguous, however. Some studies indicate that high levels of cholesterol may promote cancer, while others have suggested that cholesterol may actually prevent cancer. High protein intake appears to induce cancer of the bowel, but the significance of this association is yet unclear. High fiber intake may help avoid cancer, but once again the evidence is inconclusive. Diet plainly is linked to the incidence of cancer in the United States, but the precise source of the hazard is not well defined.

Food Preparation

The cooking process itself may produce potent carcinogens in food. Broiling, smoking, or frying foods in fat produces benzo(a)pyrene and other established carcinogens. Particularly when food is charred or pyrolyzed, carcinogens may be produced on the surface of the food. One review suggests that the "total amount of browned and burnt material eaten in a typical day is at least several hundred times more than that inhaled from severe air pollution."[12] Some evidence directly links the form of food preparation and gastric cancer rates. This evidence is not strong, however, and food preparation is probably not responsible for a significant percentage of cancer in the United States.

Natural Carcinogens

There is a tendency for people to view nature as healthy or benign and to perceive chemical additives with suspicion. Yet natural, organically produced foods contain various carcinogens. Plant cells may produce toxic compounds, which are found in some of the most common vegetables that have become integral in the diet of even health-conscious Americans.

Mycotoxins, for example, are toxic products resulting from the metabolism of molds found in foods. A very hazardous carcinogenic mycotoxin, known as aflatoxin, is commonly found in foods such as corn and peanuts. Exposure to some level of aflatoxin is unavoidable for those who eat these food products. Strong evidence links aflatoxin consumption to cancer of the liver and other internal sites.

Other identified carcinogens are found in mushrooms, certain edible ferns, nuts, and some berries. Carcinogens may even occur in such vegetables as broccoli and cabbage. The evidence on the carcinogenicity of these substances is not yet conclusive, and these natural carcinogens are responsible for an unknown proportion of cancer in the United States.

A significant natural source of carcinogens may be found in the minerals occurring in foods and water. Zinc, which is found in vegetables grown in high zinc soils and taken by many as a health supplement, has been associated with gastric and esophageal cancer. Copper is another essential nutrient that may cause cancer, and iodine intake has been associated with thyroid and breast cancer. Arsenic, a well-known carcinogen, is found in small amounts on fruits and potatoes. Selenium, found in cereals, meat, and seafood, is particularly confusing. Some major studies have shown that selenium induced cancer development, while others have found a protective anti-cancer effect for this mineral. The overall contribution of these minerals to cancer is uncertain, but many such minerals have been identified as suspect carcinogens. One leading scientist, Dr. Bruce Ames of the University of California, believes that natural dietary carcinogens exceed all exposures to synthetic chemicals as a contributor to cancer in the United States. Dietary deficiencies in certain vitamins and minerals may also contribute to cancer.

Alcohol

Alcohol is known to contribute to cancers of the liver, mouth, esophagus, and other sites. Pure alcohol itself may not be a carcinogen, but consumption of alcoholic beverages may facilitate the transport of carcinogens or metabolize substances into carcinogens. A powerful synergistic effect has been found between tobacco and alcohol in inducing cancer. Sufficient study has been done on alcohol to estimate its contribution to overall cancer at 3 percent (or 25,000 cancers). This substantial figure is somewhat misleading, however, because most of these cancers could be avoided by cessation of smoking in combination with alcohol consumption.

Food Additives

The food processing industry adds a variety of chemicals to food, to preserve it or to modify its color or flavor. There is a widespread belief that consumption of these food additives is hazardous, perhaps because of carcinogenicity. Some such additives have been identified as carcinogens, but it seems clear that food additives represent at most a miniscule source of total cancer incidence in the United States.

Fear of food additives has been at the source of some of the best-known controversies over environmental cancer. A family of artificial sweeteners known as cyclamates was removed from the market in 1969 due to suspected carcinogenicity. Evidence that saccharin could cause bladder cancer spawned another public health controversy in the late 1970s.

The saccharin episode is instructive. One study first indicated that substantial consumption of saccharin could increase the risk of bladder cancer by 60 percent in males. Large scale animal studies confirmed the potential carcinogenicity of saccharin, and there is little doubt that saccharin may cause cancer. Yet a series of studies have revealed that saccharin makes very little contribution even to bladder cancer alone. Large, well-controlled studies have found no increase in bladder cancer among users of saccharin, and most of these studies have shown that saccharin users have a lower rate of bladder cancer than comparison populations. These studies cannot be sensitive enough to identify a small increase in cancer, but it appears that saccharin is responsible for, at most, 500 to 1000 cancers a year. It is very possible that the true figure is much lower. Extensive epidemiological studies have failed to find any excess of cancer among saccharin users.

Saccharin, the best-studied and most-consumed of food additives, is responsible for only a fraction of a percentage of cancer incidence. With the possible exception of nitrites used to preserve meat, other food additives are responsible for less risk than saccharin. In short, food additives are a trivial source of cancer in the United States today.

Overview

By scientific consensus, diet is the largest source of human cancer other than smoking. As many as 35 percent of all cancers appear to be diet-linked, based on studies comparing various populations with different diets. A major survey by the National Academy of Sciences refused to assign specific percentages to diet's role in cancer but gave credibility to estimates that ranged as high as 40 percent in men and 60 percent in women.[13] The precise dietary causes of this high cancer risk are not yet clearly established. Virtually all of this diet risk, however, derives from natural food products, and chemical additives are responsible for a negligible percentage of cancers.

REPRODUCTIVE AND SEXUAL BEHAVIOR

A material percentage of cancer in the United States may be attributed to reproductive behavior. Pregnancy and childbirth play a significant role in the incidence of cancers of the endometrium, ovary, and breast (which account for nearly 30 percent of all cancers in women). Early pregnancy has a protective effect on such diseases, particularly breast cancer. Waiting five years for a first child might increase the risk of breast cancer by 30 percent. Cancer of the cervix, which accounts for more than 1 percent of all U. S. cancer deaths, appears to be closely related to the number of sexual partners a woman has had. Doll and Peto estimate that 7 percent of all cancers are attributable to reproductive and sexual behavior.

Cancer may also be caused by oral contraceptives used to prevent pregnancy. Early sequential contraceptives, since abandoned, were linked to increases in endometrial cancer. Considerable dispute revolves around the carcinogenic effects of the current combination pill. Oral contraceptives have been studied extensively, with some investigations showing an increase in breast cancer and others finding a decrease. Similar inconsistency appears in studies on other cancer sites. At the present time, it appears that very few cancers are caused by use of oral contraceptives.

CHEMICAL POLLUTION OF THE ENVIRONMENT

As previously indicated, many people believe that industrial chemicals in the environment are a cause of a significant percentage of cancer cases. Our air and water seem to be saturated with suspect carcinogens, which has given rise to this fear of pollution. The evidence, however, does not support the notion that chemical pollution causes a large fraction of cancer incidence in the United States. It seems likely, however, that chemical pollution is responsible for some meaningful number of cancer cases annually.

Air Pollution

Of all routes of exposure to industrial chemicals, air pollution probably presents the greatest risk. The one cancer that has increased dramatically is lung cancer, which raises greater concern for chemicals that are inhaled, rather than otherwise ingested. Much of the increase in lung cancer, however, is explicable through reference to smoking, and the evidence on air pollution's role in cancer induction is somewhat ambiguous.

Air pollution presents special measurement difficulties. In assessing the effects of tobacco, or alcohol, or many aspects of diet, scientists can practically compare consumers with a control group of individuals who abstain from the substance being studied. It is much more difficult to separate groups of those exposed to air pollution from those not exposed. As a rule of thumb, investigators tend to compare cancer rates in urban areas (presumably polluted) with those in rural areas (presumably unpolluted) to measure the pollution factor in cancer. Thus, we can measure the "urban factor" in cancer, which may be a proxy for air pollution effects. This procedure may serve as a rough indicator, but the great mobility of the American population suggests that the current urban dweller may have spent much of his or her life in a rural area and vice versa. The long latency of cancer magnifies the distortions created by such mobility. The key question is pollution exposure twenty years ago, but this is more difficult to trace.

Reliance on the urban factor in assessing air pollution risk has other serious limitations as well. Many other factors besides pollution may exist in the urban environment, and these other factors may be responsible for any difference in cancer rates found. Rates of smoking, alcohol consumption, dietary fat consumption, and stress may be higher in urban areas. Use of the urban factor has been the source of misleading oversimplification. Environmentalists may point to high levels of cancer in certain urban areas as "proof" that air pollution causes hundreds of thousands of cancers. This just feeds their opponents, however, who may "prove" air pollution harmless by observing that "the lung cancer death rate in some of the more polluted areas of New Jersey is about the same as it is in Rutland, Vermont, where the major industry is tourism."[14] In reality, too many confounding factors undermine use of the urban factor as a direct proxy for air pollution harms, particularly when infected by selective comparison of regions.

Notwithstanding this difficulty in measurement, the effect of air pollution on cancer rates is a source of reasonable concern. Dozens of suspect carcinogens are commonly present in the ambient air. To measure the significance of air pollution as a cause of cancer, we must attempt to eliminate the effects of the other confounding factors in the urban environment.

Many studies that have attempted to isolate the effects of air pollution have found no detectable effect. A major study for the American Cancer Society surveyed men who had lived in the same neighborhood for at least ten years, and sought to eliminate biases due to occupation, age, and smoking. This study also sought to compare urban areas with varying levels of pollution in the air. This study found "little or no differences in mortality ratios by urban-rural place of residence . . . [or] by whether they lived in cities with high, medium or low air pollution levels."[15] Several other population studies have also failed to find any carcinogenic effect of air pollution.

We should not become too sanguine, however, about the safety of breathing urban air. The limited statistical sensitivity of these population studies would not uncover relatively small percentage increases in cancer incidence. Furthermore, some other studies have found an increase in cancer mortality linked to air pollution. An analysis of population data prepared for the Natural Resources Defense Council suggested that 10 percent of all lung cancers (10,000 to 20,000 cases per year) were caused by air pollution.

The primary carcinogenic suspect among air pollutants is a byproduct of fuel combustion, called benzo(a)pyrene. This clearly carcinogenic substance has been heavily studied. Based on studies of the urban factor, extrapolations from times of very high exposure, and animal studies, several investigators concluded in the 1970s that this substance was responsible for 10 percent of all lung cancer. This conclusion found widespread support, but was based upon exposures during the previous three decades. Exposure to benzo(a)pyrene has decreased by over tenfold, and the resultant cancer incidence should be correspondingly lower. Thus, the most prominent airborne carcinogen may now be responsible for less than 1 percent of lung cancer (0.1 percent of all cancer).

The Environmental Protection Agency (EPA) has recently surveyed the available data on air pollution as a source of cancer, including benzo(a)pyrene and various carcinogenic metals found in the air. EPA found that about 1,500 cancers per year were caused by air pollution. This represents about 0.2 percent of total cancer incidence in the United States. Moreover, many of these deaths may be due to synergism between air pollution and smoking, and could be prevented by elimination of either risk.

In addition, EPA found that most of these air pollution−caused cancers were not caused by the major sources of chemical emissions. Less than half the cancer incidence was traced to major industry plants. Air emissions from wood stoves in individual homes may present the greatest carcinogenic risk of all airborne pollution. These stoves are the primary source of benzo(a)pyrene and other incomplete byproducts of combustion in the ambient air. Automotive emissions, especially from diesel engines, may also cause a significant proportion of the cancer attributable to air pollution.

Water Pollution

Many suspect carcinogens are also found in the water that we drink. These carcinogens find their way into the water through direct discharge, by deposition from air pollution, and through runoff from the surrounding land. Like air pollution, the risk of cancer from water pollution is a major fear of much of the American population.

Data on the risk from water pollution rely primarily on population studies, with all the consequent uncertainties described in the preceding discussion on air pollution. In addition, reliable information on water quality are often lacking. These limitations complicate any attempts to assign a certain percentage of cancer incidence to water pollution.

The data are adequate, however, to draw some conclusions. It appears that very little cancer can be traced directly to industrial effluents in drinking water. Many of these effluents may be carcinogenic and may bear monitoring, but they appear to contribute little to the incidence of cancer in the U.S. For example, extensive EPA regulation of numerous volatile synthetic organic chemicals in water was estimated to prevent only thirty-two cancer cases per year.[16] Ironically, some significant waterborne cancer may be caused by water chlorination, a practice initiated long ago to destroy other waterborne diseases.

Chlorine interacts with synthetic organic chemicals already in the water to produce a class of substances known as trihalomethanes. Various population studies have found that exposure to relatively high levels of these trihalomethanes may significantly increase the risk of rectal, colon, and bladder cancer. The results of these studies have been disputed, however, for failure to consider other possible variables that might explain the association with cancer. Most experts assign very few cancer cases to water pollution of any kind. Doll and Peto thus concluded that it "is not plausible that any material percentage of the total number of cancers in the whole United States derives from this source."[17] A material localized risk may exist, however, from highly polluted wells.

Hazardous Waste Disposal

In the 1980s much public attention has focused on the unsafe conditions at hazardous waste disposal sites. These sites frequently contain carcinogenic wastes, and most dumps are in relatively poor condition. Leakage of hazardous wastes is common. This circumstance naturally gives rise to

concern over the risks of such unsafe dump sites. Citizens living near hazardous waste disposal sites have alleged that exposure to chemicals has
caused cancer among their population.

To the best of our knowledge, hazardous waste disposal sites do not
presently cause a large number of cancers, however. Initially, the harms of
unsafe waste disposal occur through pollution of the water or air, and
most risk from waste disposal should be captured by the relatively low estimates for air and water pollution. People are unlikely to be exposed to
chemicals from this source unless hazardous wastes leach into water or
blow into the air near the site.

There is little evidence that hazardous waste sites create such high levels
of exposure to chemicals as to increase the cancer risk significantly. While
localized problems may occur, the national health problem does not appear to be great, relative to other sources of cancer. Love Canal in New
York was one of the most publicized and hazardous waste sites discovered.
Yet Environmental Protection Agency and New York State Department of
Health investigations have found no identifiable increases in cancer among
those living near Love Canal. Even when wells have been closed due to
chemical contamination, the polluted water has been found to present a
cancer risk less than that of chlorinated tap water or common natural
foods.[18]

Pesticides

Considerable public concern exists over exposure to agricultural pesticides. Exposure to some level of pesticides may occur either in drinking
water or on food products treated with the pesticides. Some individuals
refuse to eat foods that have been grown with the assistance of chemical
pesticides. Once again, much of this concern relates to cancer risk.

Ample studies have shown that several pesticides are in fact carcinogenic. Animal tests have repeatedly confirmed the cancer-causing potential
of various chemicals used to destroy pests or unwanted vegetation. Yet human exposures to these chemicals remains quite low. The concentration of
pesticides on foods sold to the public or in most drinking water supplies is
much lower than the concentration of several comparable natural carcinogens discussed above.

Studies of farm workers indicate that occupational pesticide exposure
may cause an elevated cancer risk. Pesticide residues in food may be responsible for some human cancer, but the significance of this source appears to be quite low. The number of cancers that can be ascribed to agricultural chemicals is probably undetectable with current methods. Surveys
of cancer incidence typically do not even mention pesticides as a material
risk factor.

RADIATION

While radiation is not one of the most potent carcinogens, the cancer-causing properties of exposure to radioactivity are long known and well established. Most Americans have a healthy fear of radiation. Yet there is general misunderstanding regarding the most significant sources of exposure to radiation. There is widespread concern about nuclear power plants, but this source produces only trivial exposures to radioactivity, especially when compared with other sources.

Natural Radiation

The largest source of radiation exposure in the United States is from natural sources. Natural radiation exposure comes from the radioactive components of the earth's crust, such as uranium and thorium. In addition, humans receive some ionizing radiation from our sun's cosmic rays. Exposure to this radiation increases with altitude. While natural radiation occurs at a relatively low level, it is both constant and pervasive.

Estimates of cancers caused by exposure to radiation rely upon extrapolation from high doses, such as those found in the wake of the bombing of Japan during World War II. Consequently, there are uncertainties and some dispute over the actual cancer burden caused by radiation. A substantial body of scientific evidence, though, suggests that exposure to natural ionizing radiation is responsible for 1 to 2 percent of all cancers in the United States. In any event, there is little disagreement that natural radiation is the largest source of exposure for United States residents, representing about half of the total radiation dose for the population.

Natural exposures are also responsible for cancers caused by a different, non-ionizing, ultraviolet radiation. The ultraviolet rays of the sun that reach the earth are known to cause cancer in exposed human skin. The vast majority of skin cancers, as well as lip cancers, are caused by exposure to ultraviolet sunlight. This source accounts for 1 to 2 percent of all cancer deaths in the United States and an even higher proportion of nonfatal cancers. The progressive reduction of the protective stratospheric ozone layer, which screens out a portion of ultraviolet rays, will almost certainly lead to a future increase in cancers due to exposure to ultraviolet radiation.

Medical Radiation

Another large source of radiation exposure comes from approved medical uses of radiation, such as X-rays. The mammography used to diagnose breast cancer at an early stage may itself contribute to cancer in exposed women. Particular concern has been raised about in utero exposures from X-rays of pregnant women. Although these medical procedures have established benefits, they also carry a risk of cancer. In many applications, the health benefits of medical radiation substantially exceed the risks, but the risk may still be substantial. Approximately 0.5 percent of all U.S. cancers are probably due to medical uses of radiation.

Nuclear Power Plants

Nuclear power has become quite controversial politically, primarily due to health concerns on the part of nearby populations. This health concern is largely the fear that cancer may be caused by the radiation emitted from nuclear power plants. The concern may be for the most part misbegotten, however, as nuclear power produces only miniscule radiation exposure in normal operation.

Radiation exposure is measured with a unit called the millirem, and an average American might receive approximately one hundred millirems of radiation from natural sources, perhaps eighty millirems from various medical procedures, and much less than one millirem from nuclear power plants. Nuclear power is such a small source of cancer risk that many sources do not even mention it. Ironically, a typical coal-fired power plant produces more population exposure to radiation than a nuclear power plant, because of radioactive particles in the coal being burned. Low-level radioactive exposures from nuclear power may present an undetectably small cancer risk.

Nuclear power production may still raise some concern, however. The risk of a major accident that disperses high levels of radiation is omnipresent. The Chernobyl accident in the U.S.S.R., for example, created a substantial cancer risk in surrounding regions and may ultimately be responsible for hundreds or thousands of cancers. The well-known accident at Three Mile Island in Pennsylvania may eventually result in one or two excess cancers.

One final source of significant exposure to radiation is from high radon levels in private homes and other buildings. This substantial risk is discussed in the following section.

INDOOR POLLUTION

When most people consider pollution, they think of outdoor exposures. Little consideration has been given to pollution that may occur inside homes and office buildings. Yet these indoor pollution exposures may present a far greater cancer risk than outdoor pollution. Exposure levels inside are frequently much higher than outdoors, a problem magnified by the fact that most individuals spend 80 to 90 percent of their time inside structures. A number of different carcinogenic agents may present a hazard from indoor pollution.

Radon

Many individuals would be shocked at the cancer risk presented by exposure to indoor radon. The risk from this exposure can dwarf that from all outdoor sources of pollution. While indoor radon is getting increased attention, the problem remains relatively little known.

Radon is a radioactive gas that enters homes and other structures from the ground underneath or from building materials. As homes become more tightly closed for weatherization purposes, indoor radon levels build up. Given the number of houses affected and the amount of time people spend indoors, the cumulative radiation exposure is enormous. Some homes, of course, have considerably higher radon levels than others.

The overall cancer risk from these radon exposures are extrapolated from other sources, particularly studies on the exposure of uranium miners to radon. Based upon this data, the best estimate is that 10,000 to 20,000 lung cancer deaths annually can be ascribed to indoor radon exposure. This represents up to 5 percent of all cancer deaths. Moreover, the quality of the underlying data is such that investigators have particular confidence in the estimate. Radon clearly represents a serious and often overlooked source of cancer.

Asbestos

Of all forms of indoor pollution, asbestos has received the greatest publicity. Ironically, indoor exposures to asbestos are relatively small, compared to other hazards. The hazards of asbestos exposure are well known, and asbestos is clearly responsible for a large number of occupational cancers from past exposures. Indoor asbestos exposures, however, are much lower than those responsible for past cancer in workers.

Asbestos was used in many buildings for floor or ceiling tiles or combined with cement in structural sections. Most buildings that contain asbestos release very little asbestos into the indoor air to be inhaled, and these building consequently present very little risk. Studies have shown that many buildings containing asbestos have no higher indoor exposure levels than the ambient outdoor asbestos levels. One major Canadian study of the risk from indoor asbestos concluded that this source "almost never poses a health hazard."[19] An exception to this conclusion exists when indoor asbestos is exposed and crumbly ("friable"), releasing fibers into the air. In this circumstance, individuals may be exposed to very hazardous levels of asbestos dust. Some of the most serious risks may occur when asbestos is removed from buildings without proper precautions being taken.

In most cases, however, indoor asbestos presents little risk of cancer. The Environmental Protection Agency has recently estimated that indoor asbestos exposure is responsible for approximately one hundred cases of cancer and fifty deaths per year.[20] Although worthy of concern, this represents only a small fraction of a percentage of the overall cancer burden of the United States.

Other Indoor Carcinogens

Americans are exposed to a frightening number of carcinogens from indoor sources. Gas cooking stoves and furnaces produce ordinary products of combustion by-products, including various carcinogenic volatile organic compounds. Other carcinogenic chemicals are given off by paints, solvents, and many other products used in the home. Wall coverings and insulation may yield carcinogenic formaldehyde.

Not only are people exposed to a wide diversity of indoor carcinogens, but their concentrations may be quite high, exceeding any risk from outdoor pollution. The Environmental Protection Agency recently sponsored a major study, known as the Total Exposure Assessment Methodology, or "TEAM" Study.[21] This study placed personal exposure monitors on more than 600 people, to measure the source of their exposures to hazardous substances. These substances included many of those for which outdoor emissions are strictly regulated. In virtually all instances, indoor concentrations of the substances were greater, often much greater. This conclusion has been confirmed by other studies as well.

The overall cancer incidence that may be assigned to indoor exposures to carcinogens has not been authoritatively estimated. The data suggest, however, that the number of cancers from these indoor exposures are likely to exceed the number from ambient air pollution by a considerable amount.

OCCUPATION

For the sources of cancer discussed in the preceding sections, there is general agreement about the incidence ascribable to each. Few scientifically credible sources differ much from the figures cited. For occupational exposures to carcinogens, however, a battle has raged over the number of cancers caused by the workplace. The estimates of occupationally caused cancer vary substantially. Published figures range from less than 1 percent to more than 20 percent of all cancers assigned to occupational exposures.

One side of the debate over the workplace contribution to cancer is represented by a 1978 study conducted by researchers at the National Cancer Institute, the National Institute for Occupational Safety and Health, and the National Institute of Environmental Health Sciences. This paper focused on only six known carcinogens—asbestos, arsenic, benzene, chromium, nickel, and petroleum fractions. The authors made no estimates of occupational cancer in 1978, but projected that the future incidence of past exposure to these six carcinogens would represent from 23 to 38 percent of all cancers in the United States.[22] Asbestos alone represented about half of this incidence.

The report that as many as one-fourth of all cancers derived from occupational exposures created quite an impact. This figure was much higher than prior estimates. Yet the researchers were respected, and a subsequent presidential task force reexamined the study and largely accepted its conclusions.[23]

Not all reviewers were convinced by the government estimates, however. Doll and Peto, for example, suggested that the government figures were gross overestimates of the incidence of cancer traceable to workplace exposures to carcinogens.[24] Much of Doll and Peto's criticism alleged inaccurate estimation of occupational exposure levels to carcinogenic substances. Moreover, Doll and Peto noted that the government study implied that 10,000 workers would be dying each year from mesothelioma (an unusual cancer caused by asbestos exposure), whereas mesothelioma actually was occurring at a rate of less than 1,000 cases per year. For these and other reasons, Doll and Peto claimed that the government estimate had no validity and was put forth for political rather than scientific reasons.

Doll and Peto do not deny, however, that occupation is a significant source of cancer in the United States. Any estimate of occupationally caused cancer is probably questionable due to uncertainties over past exposure levels and inaccurate death records. Doll and Peto's analysis of the data tentatively attributed 4 percent of all U.S. cancer deaths (or about 17,000 annually) to occupational causes. Of this, workplace exposures to asbestos account for 1 to 2 percent of all deaths. The authors concede, however, that the true number of cancers caused by the workplace could possibly be as high as twice their estimate.

Other scientists have roughly agreed with the general range of estimates provided by Doll and Peto. A series of well-regarded studies have yielded figures ranging from 1 to 8 percent of all cancers attributed to occupational carcinogens. While uncertainty remains, the best evidence now suggests that occupation is a major source of cancer in the United States, but the government estimate of one-fourth of cancer from the workplace is almost certainly exaggerated.

RISK MISPERCEPTION

The public misperceives the nature of many societal risks, including cancer risks. Many individuals believe that relatively safe activities are highly

hazardous, and vice versa. Scientists have suggested that "people's perceptions of probabilities are frequently in gross error."[25] Public fear of the carcinogenic impact of industrial chemicals, as opposed to other sources, is
but one example of risk misperception.

Claims of public misperception of risk are not simply scientific arrog-
ance—they are verifiable fact. The number of deaths due to auto accidents, heart disease, cancer, and other causes is readily demonstrable, with
only marginal disagreement. Yet when people are asked which of two such
risks causes the greatest mortality, they frequently respond incorrectly.
People consistently overestimate the number of deaths caused by cancer in
general and underestimate the mortality from other causes.

Surveys demonstrate how wildly inaccurate risk perception may be.
When students were asked how many annual deaths are caused by smoking, their estimates averaged 2,400. A sample of the League of Women Voters guessed that 6,900 deaths were annually attributable to smoking. The
correct number is approximately 150,000 deaths. These study groups also
significantly underestimated the risks from alcoholic beverages, motor vehicles, handguns, electric power production, X-rays, and other sources.[26]
The survey produced equally dramatic results when it asked individuals to
rank ninety sources of risk. Surveyed individuals ranked DDT as the third
greatest risk we face, ahead of crime, smoking, alcoholic beverages, and
motor vehicles.[27]

The possible causes for risk misperception are numerous. Some blame
is surely due the media, which tends "to present information about risks
in a manner which frightens laypeople and overwhelms them with predic-
tions or descriptions of undue consequences from exposure to chemicals."[28] People also may possess an inherent fear of the new or unknown,
and technology thus becomes frightening. Furthermore, people have some
reason to be cynical about claims of safety emanating from industry or
government sources. Experience with asbestos, the Dalkon Shield, and
other products suggests that these institutions are not always trustworthy
guides to risk information. The tobacco industry still maintains that its
product does not cause cancer.

Reasonable cynicism about industry has overwhelmed reality, however.
The dangers of some new technologies need not condemn all technological
advances. At present, the public exaggerates the risk of death from environmental pollutants. This misperception of risk is itself hazardous. In our
democracy, government is at least somewhat responsive to public demands. Public misperceptions will translate into regulatory misdirection.
As a consequence, more substantial risks will be overlooked while limited
societal and regulatory resources are aimed at relatively insignificant hazards.

Perhaps it is unrealistic to expect individuals to take the time required
to possess a precise understanding of relative risks in our society. Some
rough understanding, though, is important to optimal control of risks.

Exhibit 2-2
Percent of Cancers Attributable to Environmental Causes

Cause	Doll & Peto	Others
Tobacco	30	24-40
Alcohol	3	2-5
Total Diet	35	25-60
Food Additives	<1	<1
Reproductive & Sexual Behavior	7	7-13
Air Pollution	1-2	0-5
Water Pollution	<1	0-3
Hazardous Waste	<1	- -
Industrial Products	<1	0-2
Indoor Radon	- -	2-6
Natural Radiation	3	2-4
Occupation	4	1-20

Greater knowledge on the part of both the public and government agencies can contribute to the prevention of risks from cancer.

OVERVIEW

Science can shed considerable light on risks of cancer present in the United States today. Science can also dispel certain concerns founded in emotion rather than data. This chapter has attempted to identify and quantify the major contributors to cancer. The results of this assessment are summarized in exhibit 2-2.

Exhibit 2-2 presents estimates of the causes of cancers that are common in this country. While the estimates are necessarily only approximate, certain conclusions can be drawn. For instance, the environmental sources of most cancers in the U.S. appear to be primarily natural or voluntarily assumed. Among involuntary environmental exposures, certain sources of significant risk appear to be consistently underestimated, particularly indoor air pollution.

The ability to draw such conclusions on sources of cancer has value in preventing disease and death. Once the primary contributors to cancer are known, government priorities can be set or revised so as to address the greatest and most preventable causes of cancer. Misperception of which of the known carcinogens are most responsible for disease incidence can only lead to misallocation of control resources and, in all likelihood, a greater overall risk of cancer.

On these grounds, some of the most zealous environmentalists may be criticized. For example, suggesting that food additives or pesticides are responsible for a cancer epidemic is incorrect, irresponsible and ultimately self-defeating. If environmentalists are effectively to save us from cancer, they may be properly concerned about food additives and pesticides, but they should be more concerned about other sources, such as indoor and occupational exposures to carcinogens. Furthermore, the apocalyptic decrying of all industrial chemicals eventually undermines the credibility of the environmental community. The wages of crying wolf are well known. This may already be seen in the inaccurate and cavalier attitude of persons who "don't care" about cancer, because "after all, everything causes cancer." Meanwhile, others scrupulously avoid all chemicals, while blithely exposing themselves to a plethora of natural carcinogens.

Having argued for realism in the environmental protection community, one must be careful not to assume a Pollyanna's approach to industrial chemicals. Concluding that natural and voluntary sources of cancer are paramount does not deny that thousands of cancer deaths are caused by involuntary environmental exposures of one form or another. Industry has pointed to natural causes of cancer almost as a justification for killing more people with new toxic by-products. Government can do little about cosmic rays, for example, but it can control and prevent chemically induced cancer. This objective is a worthy one for government. So long as administrators and courts do not consume their time by chasing after trivial risks, they may save lives from exposures to environmental carcinogens. The following chapters address government's approach to preventing environmental cancer.

NOTES

1. Wrynn Smith, *A Profile of Health and Disease in America: Cancer* (New York: Facts on File Publications, 1987), 15.

2. Jane Fonda, *Jane Fonda's Workout Book* (New York: Simon & Schuster, 1981), 238.

3. Philip Abelson, "Cancer Phobia," *Science* 237 (1987): 473.

4. Chris Wilkinson, "Being More Realistic About Chemical Carcinogenesis," *Environmental Science & Technology* 21 (1987): 844.

5. Interview in Elizabeth Whelan, *Toxic Terror* (Ottawa, Illinois: Jameson Books, 1985), 26.

6. National Cancer Institute, U.S. Department of Health and Human Services, *Cancer Control Objectives for the Nation: 1985–2000* (1986), 9.

7. Lester Breslow and William Cumberland, "Progress and Objectives in Cancer Control," *Journal of the American Medical Association* 259 (1988): 1690.

8. Richard Doll and Richard Peto, "The Causes of Cancer: Quantitative Estimates of Avoidable Risks of Cancer in the United States Today," *J. Nat. Cancer Inst.* 66 (1981): 1191.

9. E. C. Hammond and H. Seidman, "Smoking and Cancer in the United States," *Preventive Medicine* 9 (1980): 169.

10. National Cancer Institute, U.S. Department of Health and Human Services, *Cancer Control Objectives for the Nation: 1985–2000* (1986), 17.

11. J. Repace, *Risks of Passive Smoking,* (1983): 5.

12. Bruce Ames, Renae Magaw, and Lois Gold, "Ranking Possible Carcinogenic Hazards," *Science* 236 (1987): 271.

13. National Research Council, National Academy of Sciences, *Diet, Nutrition, and Cancer,* (1982): 14.

14. Elizabeth Whelan, "Chemicals and Cancerphobia," *Society* (March/April 1981): 6.

15. E. C. Hammond and L. Garfinkel, "General Air Pollution and Cancer in the United States," *Preventive Medicine* 9 (1980): 206.

16. 50 *Fed. Reg.* 46926 (1985).

17. Doll and Peto, 1249.

18. Ames, Magaw, and Gould, 272.

19. Ontario Royal Commission on Asbestos, *Report of the Royal Commission on Matters of Health and Safety Arising from the Use of Asbestos in Ontario,* 1 (1984): 13.

20. U.S. Environmental Protection Agency, *EPA Study of Asbestos-Containing Materials in Public Buildings,* Appendix 6 (February 1988).

21. U.S. Environmental Protection Agency, *The Total Exposure Assessment Methodology (TEAM) Study* (June 1987).

22. U.S. Department of Health, Education and Welfare, *Estimates of the Fraction of Cancer in the United States Related to Occupational Factors* (1978).

23. Toxic Substances Strategy Committee, *Toxic Chemicals and Public Protection,* (May 1980), 153–160.

24. Doll and Peto, 1305–1308.

25. Chauncey Starr and Chris Whipple, "Risks of Risk Decisions." In *Risk in the Technological Society* (Boulder Colo.: Westview, 1982), 217, 222.

26. Baruch F. Slovic, Paul S. Fischhoff, and Sarah L. Lichtenstein, "Facts and Fears: Understanding Perceived Risk." In *Societal Risk Assessment,* ed. R. Schwing (NY: Plenum, 1980): 193.

27. Ibid., 203.

28. Paulette Stenzel, *The Need for a National Risk Assessment Communication Policy,* 11 HARV. ENV. L. REV. 381, 391(1987).

PART II

FEDERAL REGULATION OF CARCINOGENS

A significant number of cancers are caused by preventable environmental sources. A number of federal agencies have been commissioned with the responsibility of preventing some portion of these cancers. This part discusses the difficult decisions facing the agencies.

Chapter 3 addresses the scientific techniques available for identifying cancer-causing substances and measuring the degree of risk caused by individual substances. Studies of human populations are ideal for identifying carcinogens, but accurate human studies are hard to come by. Consequently, regulators have relied heavily upon studies of rodents and other animals. Laboratory *in vitro* studies and comparisons of chemical structure may also inform the decision regarding whether a substance has the potential to cause cancer in humans.

While some question remains about carcinogen identification, a much greater controversy persists over attempts to quantify the carcinogenic risk presented by a substance. Quantitative risk assessment requires measures of human exposure to a substance and an estimate of the carcinogenic potency of a substance (its probability of producing cancer). The latter step is particularly disputed. The proper means for extrapolating results from animal tests are unresolved. Proper extrapolation procedures cannot be resolved by scientists but necessitate policy assumptions. Some groups, particularly environmentalists, want conservative assumptions that give a "worst case" risk level. Others, particularly industry, prefer the "most likely" assumptions that typically yield a lower level of risk. Indeed, some commentators believe that the entire quantitative risk assessment process is too fraught with uncertainty and should not be relied upon by regulators. As a practical matter, however, some degree of risk assessment is necessary, and the extrapolative procedures described in chapter 3 are the best we currently have.

Once a carcinogenic risk is identified and measured, some direction is needed in determining the necessity and extent of control of the carcinogen, called risk management. Chapter 4 describes the four leading risk management approaches: zero risk (preventing all carcinogenic risk), significant risk (permitting some small residual carcinogenic risk), cost/benefit (balancing the benefits of carcinogen control against its costs), and feasibility analysis (reducing carcinogenic risk as far as technologically possible).

Each of these risk management approaches have their supporters and detractors, and none is ideal. Zero risk must be ruled out *ab initio,* pending scientific proof of a carcinogenic threshold. At the present time, zero risk requires zero exposure, which would necessitate abolition of virtually the entire United States economic base. Such an outcome of carcinogen regulation is neither wise nor likely.

Among the three remaining paradigms for risk management, none is distinctly preferable in the abstract. Significant risk and cost/benefit analysis rely heavily on highly uncertain data. Feasibility analysis has somewhat greater certainty but ignores highly relevant concerns, including the absolute level of risk presented by a carcinogen to be regulated. The choice of risk management approaches is best left to practical experience.

Chapter 5 summarizes the experience of federal regulatory agencies in cancer prevention. Past regulations of the Occupational Safety and Health Administration, the Environmental Protection Agency, the Food and Drug Administration, and the Consumer Product Safety Commission are reviewed. This summary permits analysis of the evolution of carcinogen regulation and its effectiveness.

As shown in this chapter, federal carcinogen regulation to date has too often been insufficient, slow, and inconsistent. The factors influencing regulation (or the lack thereof) can be identified, to some degree. Political inclinations of the party in power have very little to do with the extent of carcinogen controls. When regulations have been issued, they can be explained by the substantial risk presented by a substance and by the relative cost of its control.

Using this experience as a guide, chapter 6 sets forth an outline of future directions for more effective federal regulation of carcinogens. I propose that agencies assess risks more honestly, with full acknowledgement of the uncertainties associated with contemporary quantitative risk assessment. Then agencies should assume control of their own priorities for regulation, focusing first on the most significant hazards. Resultant regulation should be moderate, neither imposing extreme costs on industry nor ignoring significant risks to human health. Use of feasibility analysis, when possible, is preferred, simply because it has proved more effective than competing risk management paradigms. Carcinogen control policies should be integrated both within and among agencies, to provide more efficient and effective targeting of carcinogens for control and regulation. Finally, judicial review of regulations should be prevented or restrained, insofar as possible.

I do not claim that my proposed directions are comprehensive, nor do I assert that they will ensure widespread and effective carcinogen control. The carcinogen problem described in part I is too complex for any panacea. The redirections suggested in chapter 6 should, however, incrementally improve federal regulation of carcinogens, and may contribute to life saving in a politically and economically practical manner.

3

CARCINOGEN IDENTIFICATION AND RISK ASSESSMENT

Effective government action to reduce the incidence of environmentally caused cancer depends on a reliable scientific determination of the substances that are responsible for the cancer. Such a determination can be a complex and difficult one, as described in chapter 1. At the outset, government must identify those substances that are capable of causing cancer. This step is obviously an essential prerequisite to controlling environmental cancer. Knowing that a substance is carcinogenic, however, does not indicate the measure of public health risk from current exposure to that substance. Consequently, it is helpful to ascertain the degree of risk to the public presented by the carcinogens so identified. Determining which carcinogens and which routes of exposure are responsible for the greatest number of environmentally caused cancers enables the government to focus its efforts on the most significant carcinogenic hazards faced by its citizenry. The first step, carcinogen identification, is a qualitative assessment, while the second step of risk assessment attempts to quantitate the risk from specific carcinogens.

CARCINOGEN IDENTIFICATION

The first step in any regulatory policy for cancer prevention is to identify those chemicals or other substances that are carcinogenic. Although this might seem to be a rather simple procedure, it unfortunately is not. Science has not progressed to the point where carcinogen identification is easy or clear-cut. Scientists have developed certain study protocols, however, that are generally accepted tools for identifying those substances that have carcinogenic potential. The most widely accepted methods involve studies on laboratory animals and epidemiologic comparisons of human populations. In addition, evidence of carcinogenicity may be found in comparisons of chemical structure and "short-term tests" on cells *in vitro*. These tests and their respective significance are addressed in the following discussion.

Before evaluating the various tests for carcinogenicity, it is critical to bear in mind the different purposes for carcinogen identification. Scientists tend to be wary of claiming unambiguous carcinogenicity, because current test methodologies are not precise enough to remove all doubts. For scientific purposes, considerable evidence of carcinogenicity may be demanded before positive conclusions are reached. To scientists, misidentifying a substance as carcinogenic is an error, while waiting for further evidence is usually not a scientific error. Consequently, science strives to avoid inaccurate affirmative conclusions of carcinogenicity and may be somewhat reluctant to take a firm position on carcinogenicity. Government regulatory purposes are different. A government commissioned with public health protection should not await conclusive evidence before acting. Such a delay may condemn thousands to cancer. Government must also fear failure to identify carcinogens promptly. Thus, the tests for carcinogen identification should be relatively less rigorous for government regulatory purposes.

Animal Bioassays

Studies on chemicals administered to laboratory animals provide the most frequent source of carcinogen identification for regulatory purposes. Investigators administer a test chemical to laboratory animals and observe whether these animals eventually suffer a greater than expected rate of cancer (statistically more than a control population of unexposed animals). If a substance is shown to cause cancer in test animals, scientists hypothesize that the substance also has the potential to cause cancer in humans. Reliance on animal bioassays is occasionally controversial and is disputed by some, but these animal studies are widely accepted by regulators as predictors of carcinogenicity in humans.

For an animal bioassay to be reliable predictor, however, the study must follow certain methods. The most frequently used animals for carcinogenesis bioassays are mice, hamsters, and rats. These species have the benefit of short natural life spans, and they have been studied extensively for use in carcinogen identification. The specific test animal to be chosen may depend on the type of cancer suspected and the background incidence of this cancer in a particular strain of animals. Within each species, investigators may use different inbred strains, with different susceptibilities to tumorigenicity.

Once the test species has been selected, the investigator must choose the number of individual animals that are to be studied. A comparable control group, unexposed to the test substance, must also be set up. As few as fifteen animals might be used, but such a small sample size permits detection of only massive increases in cancer incidence. A larger number of test animals allows the detection of relatively smaller increases in the cancer rate. Ideally, hundreds or thousands of animals would be tested, but practical concerns, such as cost and space, usually prevent such large-scale tests. A representative test might involve fifty-five animals. If a 5 percent background cancer rate is expected, a test of this size is generally capable of detecting a 20 percent cancer rate with the confidence of 95 percent statistical significance (meaning a 95 percent probability that the increase is due to the test chemical and not due to random chance).[1] Scientists now recommend that animal bioassays include at least fifty animals of each sex in both the test and control groups.

The next significant investigative judgment is the route of administration of the test chemical. The carcinogenicity of a substance may vary depending upon whether it is administered through inhalation, ingestion in diet, or skin application. Ideally, the route of administration in the experiment will match the manner in which humans are likely to be exposed to the substance being tested. Practical considerations, however, may require that a different route of administration be employed. Unfortunately, use of routes of administration different from those typical in humans considerably complicates efforts to assess the risk that a substance presents to public health.

Investigators also must choose dose levels to apply to test animals. Typically, the highest experimental dose level vastly exceeds the probable human doses of a substance, and this practice has caused animal tests to be ridiculed in the mass media. There are good and substantial reasons, however, for using such unrealistically high doses of test chemicals. Even a good sized animal test will be unable to detect cancer increases of much less than 15 or 20 percent. A dose of a substance that increases cancer rates by 1 or 2 percent will go unobserved in animal tests, but this exposure level in humans could represent thousands of deaths. To detect this circumstance, investigators must increase the dose sufficiently to cause a substantial, detectable increase in cancer among test animals. Most animal bioassays use the Maximum Tolerated Dose (MTD), which is the highest dose of a substance that does not cause significant noncarcinogenic toxicity in the test species. In addition to MTD, an animal bioassay should include two or three lower doses, to determine whether carcinogenic effects appear to increase with the dose of the test chemical. These lower doses are frequently one-half and one-fourth of the MTD, depending upon what was already known about the substance.

Once the preceding judgments are made for an animal bioassay, the experiment must follow rigorous procedures. The study must control many variables that may interfere with results. Organizations such as the National Cancer Institute have complex standards for the conduct of animal bioassays.[2] Factors such as diet, indoor air quality, bedding, and other housing conditions must be stringently controlled, or the experiment may be skewed. These conditions must be maintained for the duration of the study, usually about two years in rodents. After the study term is complete, the surviving animals are sacrificed, and their tissues are subjected to microscopic examination by pathologists to identify tumor incidence. Accurate pathologic examination is essential to reliable results. Pathologists must examine slides of experimental animal tissue to diagnose tumorigenicity in the test animals. This step is not simple but requires professional diagnostic judgment in assigning tumor incidence rates. Completion of an animal bioassay takes several years and requires considerable effort and expense.

The final step in animal tests for carcinogenicity is evaluation of the significance of the results. An increase in tumor rate among animals exposed to the test substance is measured by standard tests for statistical significance. Typically, a 95 percent confidence level is required for positive results. A well-conducted animal bioassay that provides this level of statistical significance is strongly suggestive of a carcinogenic effect of the test substance, but even this bioassay is less than conclusive. By definition, these results leave a 5 percent probability of a "false positive"—that the observed increases in tumorigenicity are simply due to random chance. There is an even greater probability of a "false negative," where even a carcinogenic substance yields no positive results in an animal bioassay. False negatives may be due to chance or to insufficient sensitivity in test instruments.

Animal bioassays are central to carcinogen identification, but they indisputably have limitations. Obviously, rodents differ from humans in size, life span, metabolic processes and other important characteristics. The risk of false positives and false negatives is omnipresent. Some scientists also object to certain widely used procedures. Employing high, MTD exposures to a substance is sometimes questioned. Theoretically, such high doses may alter metabolism or overcome defense mechanisms and produce carcinogenesis, when lower doses, more typical of human exposure, might not induce cancer. Nevertheless, such high doses are essential in animal bioassays or the tests would be unable to identify the vast majority of carcinogens with the confidence demanded for statistical significance. In order to identify a 1 in 1,000,000 cancer risk, an animal bioassay would require at least 6,000,000 rodents. Use of lower doses in animal bioassays also helps avoid the potential bias of total reliance on the MTD.

Other scientists have also questioned the applicability of carcinogenesis in test animals to human carcinogenicity. Rodents typically used in animal bioassays metabolize substances differently than humans. Most of these metabolic differences appear to be quantitative, rather than qualitative, however, and use of test animals as a proxy for human carcinogenicity is generally accepted. More perplexing problems may result when, for example, a substance causes cancer in the zymbal glands of rats. Humans have no zymbal glands.

Some leading cancer researchers, such as Gio Gori, have questioned whether animal tests can ever "provide meaningful data for extrapolation of human risk."[3] The use of MTD applied to inbred sensitive animal strains and other features of animal bioassays "frequently introduce deliberate bias in order to enhance the probability of a positive response and ... ignore a number of sources of variability that cannot be controlled or are difficult to control with available technology."[4] Whatever merit may reside in Gori's criticism of reliance on animal data, these bioassays remain the best available source of data for conclusions regarding the carcinogenicity of many substances in humans.

In short, while MTD animal bioassays are presently necessary for carcinogen identification, their limitations must be acknowledged. A single positive result in a small bioassay is generally not considered sufficient to find a substance to be carcinogenic. The National Cancer Institute seeks results in both sexes of at least two species before drawing conclusions from such bioassays. Further judgment about these tests is required before affirmatively identifying a chemical as a carcinogen. A positive bioassay is more convincing if it reveals a dose-response relationship—that is, if greater doses yield greater tumor incidence.

We have considerable practical experience in reliance on animal bioassays. The widespread belief that "everything causes cancer in animals" does not stand up to the evidence, even at high level MTD exposures. For example, a broad bioassay of 120 pesticides suspected as possible carcinogens found clear positive results for twelve substances, some positive evidence for twenty-three substances, and no evidence of carcinogenicity in eighty-five substances.[5] The Occupational Safety and Health Administration's expert contractor evaluated 2,400 substances that had been tested by various means and concluded that 570 of these had sufficient evidence of carcinogenicity for regulatory purposes.[6] Not every chemical is carcinogenic in animal bioassays. Nevertheless, it is important to remember that even negative results in animal tests do not provide strong evidence of noncarcinogenicity. It is exceedingly difficult if not impossible to "prove" that a substance does *not* cause cancer.

Some risk of false positive results also remains. The commonly accepted test for statistical significance admits an inevitable 5 percent chance of a false positive. This chance is magnified if investigators examine multiple possible sites for carcinogenesis and apply the statistical significance test independently to each site. Depending upon the test species and background probability of tumors, this procedure may increase the likelihood of a false positive to 20 percent or more.[7] Consequently, a single positive result from an animal bioassay is not dispositive evidence of carcinogenicity even for regulatory purposes. Nevertheless, animal bioassays "have, in general, proved to be reliable indicators of carcinogenic properties and will continue to play a pivotal role in efforts to identify carcinogens."[8]

Epidemiology

The best positive evidence of carcinogenicity can be produced by certain epidemiologic studies. These studies compare two distinct human populations that are largely alike except for their respective exposure and non-exposure to a given substance. If the exposed population has a significantly higher rate of a given cancer, a strong inference is created that the substance is responsible for the cancer. Complementary biological evidence explaining the carcinogenic effect identified through epidemiology creates convincing evidence of carcinogenicity. Strong epidemiologic evidence demonstrates the carcinogenicity of smoking, as cigarette smokers have a much higher incidence of lung cancer than do nonsmokers of the same age, sex, and race. Epidemiology has the strength of identifying carcinogens in humans, rather than some other species.

There are two different types of analytical epidemiologic studies, known as cohort studies and case-control studies. In cohort studies, the investigator first identifies two populations that are similar except for exposure to a given substance. These groups are then followed to find any increases in cancer incidence. For example, an investigator might compare cancer rates between construction workers using asbestos products and workers doing similar construction work but using no asbestos products. Cohort studies were important in identifying tobacco smoke, asbestos, vinyl chloride, and other chemicals as carcinogenic.

In case-control studies, the investigator begins by taking a population that suffers from a given type of cancer. Then, he or she takes a group of people of similar age, sex, and race who do not have cancer. The investigator can then seek out unique exposures in the group with cancer that may explain their disease. For example, one study compared hospital patients with pancreatic cancer with another group of patients suffering from other digestive diseases. The investigators found a pattern of higher coffee consumption in the patients with pancreatic cancer and hypothesized that coffee might contribute to this form of cancer.

Cohort studies are more difficult than case-control studies to conduct but are generally considered more reliable. The coffee study described above is instructive. The positive association of pancreatic cancer with coffee may simply be due to the fact that patients with other digestive diseases may be advised not to drink coffee. Rather than coffee causing cancer, the investigators may have only discovered that other digestive diseases preclude coffee consumption. This experience illustrates a common problem of case-control studies, and agencies are reluctant to rely exclusively on such studies. Both types of epidemiology are used, however, and usually demand 95 percent statistical significance for positive results to be reported.

Although epidemiology is useful for identifying some carcinogens, this test is insufficient by itself. First, it may be difficult to find good comparison groups that are alike except for exposure to a given substance. For example, epidemiology demonstrates that cancer is more prevalent in many urban areas, but the technique cannot prove what characteristic of the urban environment is responsible for this excess of cancer. Thus, reliable epidemiology requires good evidence of the degree of exposure to the chemical in question, and to other factors that may be alternative causes of any cancers discovered in the test. The longer latency of cancer in humans further delays the usefulness of epidemiology as a test for carcinogenesis. Epidemiology provides no evidence until decades after the initial exposure to a substance.

Epidemiology is a relatively insensitive tool and can detect only gross increases in cancer rates. The ability of a method to identify relatively small increases in cancer rate with statistical significance is called statistical power, and epidemiologic studies usually have relatively weak statistical power. Few epidemiologic studies with statistical significance are large enough to detect any less than a 30 percent increase in cancer rates. Somewhat greater precision is possible with very large study populations and when relatively rare types of cancer are being studied. Epidemiologists, however, must take the populations as they find them, and ideal circumstances with good statistical power are relatively rare. Consequently, this methodology will miss carcinogenic exposures that cause smaller increases in cancer. The relative insensitivity of epidemiology further means that negative results have little significance. Failure to find a statistically significant increase in cancer rates as part of an epidemiologic study may simply mean that the increase was too low to be detected. Epidemiology is generally unable to detect increased cancer rates of less than 1 in 100, or 1 in 1,000. These "smaller" increases may still be responsible for tens of thousands of cancer deaths, however. Some epidemiologic investigation has produced negative results even for asbestos, a well-known and significant cause of cancer.

Negative results of epidemiology cannot demonstrate lack of carcinogenicity. The lack of a statistically significant association between a substance and cancer may simply be due to test insensitivity. The expert Interdisciplinary Panel on Carcinogenicity observed that "[i]n epidemiology, as in other disciplines, it is impossible to prove a negative."[9] Negative results from epidemiology may have some value, though, as they may place an upper bound on the risk presented by a substance, as recognized in the Environmental Protection Agency carcinogen guidelines.[10] For example, a large epidemiologic study of saccharin and bladder cancer provided evidence that the total cancer risk to humans was not so great as some animal studies suggested possible.

Positive results from well-controlled epidemiologic investigations provide strong evidence of carcinogenicity. These results are not common, however, due to the limitations of the methodology. The International Agency for Research on Cancer has identified eighteen substances for which epidemiology provides sufficient evidence to identify them as carcinogenic in humans.[11] For hundreds of other substances of suspect carcinogenicity, evidence from animal bioassays of other sources must be used. Even aflatoxins, which are generally accepted as very potent carcinogens, have only very limited epidemiologic evidence of carcinogenicity.

Epidemiologic testing for carcinogenicity is highly instructive and should be encouraged. Shortcomings of this approach, however, render it an incomplete tool for carcinogen identification. Epidemiology must be supplemented by other tests, or scores of harmful carcinogenic substances will go unidentified and uncontrolled.

Short-Term Tests

A variety of different types of laboratory experiments go under the name of "short-term tests." These tests share in common the characteristics of brevity and inexpensiveness. Some of the short-term tests may take as little as one day and cost only a few hundred dollars (as compared to several years and hundreds of thousands of dollars for a quality animal bioassay). Short-term tests typically apply a subject chemical to certain isolated bacteria or other cells growing in culture in the laboratory. The investigators then observe the cells to discover any alterations of DNA or other neoplastic cell transformation that might reveal a mutagenic effect of the test chemical. Such mutagenic effects are then considered a proxy for carcinogenic effects.

Over one hundred short-term test systems exist, but probably the best known of these is called the Ames test, after its developer, Dr. Bruce Ames. This procedure combines the test chemical with a bacterial culture and then counts the number of mutated bacteria that are produced. Different bacteria may be used to broaden the test. Thousands of substances have been evaluated using the Ames test.

One potential inaccuracy in short-term tests, including the Ames test, involves metabolic activation. Most test cultures lack the complete systems for metabolism extant in living animals, so investigators must supplement the test chemical with a metabolic activation system, to metabolize the chemical into its potentially carcinogenic products. These additional metabolic activation systems, however, cannot precisely parallel those found in humans. This inability to mimic human metabolism can yield erroneous test results, in the form of both false positives and false negatives. Medical experts at the Occupational Safety and Health Administration concluded that short term tests still yield "a large number of false positives and false negatives."[12]

For the above-described reason among others, the reliability of all short-term tests as identifiers of carcinogens is still disputed. Strictly speaking, these tests do not measure carcinogenicity, but rather they test for mutagenicity in cell DNA. Fundamentally, scientists disagree whether the mutagenic effect identified by these tests provides an accurate proxy for carcinogenicity. Ames has argued for the accuracy of the test, noting that 90 percent of known carcinogens show evidence of mutagenicity identifiable in short-term tests.[13] In addition, nearly 90 percent of substances that lack carcinogenicity in animal tests also lack mutagenicity in the Ames test. Some have viewed this high correlation with skepticism, however. The investigators knew the established carcinogenicity of the substances being tested and may have manipulated the short-term test protocols until the desired results were reached. Other examinations have suggested lower correlations between short-term test results and those of animal bioassays, in the range of 50 to 70 percent.[14]

At least some short-term tests appear to be reasonably accurate predictors of carcinogenicity. While these tests may produce incorrect results, no methodology, including animal bioassays and epidemiology, can guarantee perfect accuracy. Short-term tests can offer persuasive evidence of a substance's carcinogenicity and can also provide some useful evidence of noncarcinogenicity. Once again, however, negative results are not dispositive, as short-term tests only test for initiators and cannot identify substances that act as promoters.

Short-term tests contain one additional serious limitation. Even if such tests can identify cancer-causing substances, the tests are not accepted for assessing the magnitude of the risk resulting from a given exposure. Thus the risk assessment discussed later in this chapter may require additional studies on live animals or human epidemiology. Short-term tests at present are more useful for identifying candidates for further study than for conclusively identifying carcinogens. Positive results in a short-term test should raise a strong suspicion of carcinogenicity. These tests have obtained positive results for thousands of chemicals, which require further study in better-demonstrated carcinogenicity assays. A group of experts from the federal Office of Science and Technology Policy and the National Institute of Environmental Health Sciences has concluded that it "seems prudent to treat in vitro tests (either individually or as a battery) as screening tests only."[15] Carcinogen identification requires additional testing in animals.

Structure-Activity Tests

Structure-activity tests compare the molecular structure of a subject substance with the structure of known carcinogens. If the two substances possess similar molecular structures, there is some reason to suspect that both may be carcinogenic. For example, a number of coal tars are known to be carcinogenic, so structure-activity relationships would suggested that an heretofore untested coal tar is also a probable carcinogen.

There is some basis for ascribing credence to structure-activity testing. Numerous carcinogens share similar structural features. Structure-activity comparisons provide a very rough guide to carcinogenicity, however. Even closely related chemicals are known to differ in carcinogenicity. Structural comparisons provide only very weak evidence of carcinogenicity. These tests provide even less evidence for risk assessment. Consequently, structure-activity tests are seldom used to identify carcinogens and are more properly employed to choose candidates for animal bioassays. The "general consensus of the scientific community appears to be that chemical structure has limited value in identifying carcinogens and is to be used in carcinogenesis hazard assessment only as corroborative supporting evidence."[16]

Overview of Carcinogen Identification

No single type of test can be relied upon for carcinogen identification. The carcinogenic effects of tobacco smoking, which are obvious from epidemiology, have not appeared in numerous animal bioassays. Each form of test is certain to overlook some number of carcinogenic substances. Moreover, some positive results may be unreliable. In addition to statistical significance, investigators should scrutinize the study for errors in conducting the study, internal consistency of results, reproducibility of results, and other biological evidence consistent with carcinogenicity of the test substance.

Difficulties in identifying carcinogens are compounded by the complex features of the disease. Some tests may identify initiators of carcinogenesis, but not promoters. The synergistic effects of combined exposure to two or more substances may induce greater carcinogenesis than the two considered separately. With thousands of chemicals yet untested and numerous synergistic combinations of concern, the prospect for evaluating any significant degree of synergistic carcinogenesis remains slim.

Carcinogen identification requires the use of scientific judgment based upon the results of a variety of different types of tests. Each source of data should be critically evaluated. Expert scientific organizations have struggled for decades in the attempt to define what is necessary to identify a substance positively as carcinogenic. These organizations have not reached a consensus, but many investigators seek clear positive results in both sexes of two animal species, or strong epidemiologic evidence, before positively identifying a substance as carcinogenic in humans. For example, the International Agency for Research on Cancer has declared that "sufficient evidence" of carcinogenicity is provided by bioassays showing positive results in multiple species or strains, and/or in multiple experiments, and/or to an unusually positive degree, with further consideration given to evidence of dose-response effects, mutagenicity and molecular structural analysis.

Even positive results in two species must be considered in context, however. Positive results may be more or less conclusive. In some bioassays, the evidence is clear, as most of the exposed animals die quickly from cancer, while in other bioassays the statistical significance may be borderline. Furthermore, positive results at two very different cancer sites (e.g., lung and colon) in different species are not so convincing. Further difficulties arise when a test shows a significant increase in tumors at one site but a significant reduction at some other site. For example, a chemical known as Yellow 14 appeared to cause an increase in liver tumors in rats accompanied by a decrease in leukemia/lymphoma.[17] No simple formula can be employed for identifying carcinogens; at best, we can employ guidelines tempered by judgment in individual instances. An expert from the National Cancer Institute has thus observed that "[d]etermining that an agent is capable of causing a neoplastic response is therefore the outcome of a complex judgmental activity involving evaluation of many different factors, such as knowledge of the chemical and biological systems under consideration, determination that the conditions of observation were adequate, and evaluation of the morphology and function of the observed organisms and of their target issues from a qualitative and quantitative point of view."[18]

Simply calling for good professional judgment contributes little, however. Generalized conclusions about tests for carcinogenicity can be drawn. Strong positive results from epidemiology or animal bioassays should usually suffice to identify chemicals as carcinogenic for government regulatory purposes. Weaker results, combined with positive evidence from short-term tests or structure-activity tests, should also suffice for this purpose. This approach risks some false positives, but this problem can be minimized by further testing, and safeguards built into risk assessment and risk management.

Even negative results should not override significant positive data for carcinogen identification. Refusing to rely on negative results is not warranted because society should have some presumption against chemical exposures, as frequently argued. Many chemicals are too valuable economically or otherwise to indulge such a presumption. Rather, the presumptive reliance on positive results simply acknowledges the high probability of false negatives under any of the methodologies discussed above. Negative results simply do not demonstrate noncarcinogenicity. Although positive results will seldom prove carcinogenicity conclusively, such evidence from animal bioassays and epidemiology raises sufficient concern to warrant some level of government action.

The preceding discussion focuses on accurate carcinogen identification. Yet society must also worry about adequate carcinogen identification. There are over 100,000 known chemicals, nearly 50,000 in common use, and over 1,000 new chemicals are introduced every year. Investigators have tested only a small fraction of these, and we fall further behind every year. Complete reliance on animal studies and epidemiology is too expensive and too slow. We must make increased use of short-term tests as a guide to carcinogenicity, if not as conclusive evidence.

RISK ASSESSMENT

Risk assessment is a term that covers a broad array of procedures intended to measure the relative human health consequences of exposure to various carcinogens. The assignment of significance to various carcinogens described in chapter 2 is a form of risk assessment, particularly for tobacco and alcohol. The descriptive population comparisons in chapter 2, however, are too broad and general for useful risk assessment. We do not simply want to know the number of cancers resulting from air pollution, we need to know the cancer risk attributable to specific air pollutants that are amenable to control.

In usual application, risk assessment yields a quantitative estimate of risk from a given substance. This estimate may be expressed in total number of deaths attributable to the substance or in terms of average probability of suffering cancer among the exposed population. This probability is usually expressed in terms such as a 1 in 1,000 chance of cancer (1×10^{-3}) or a 1 in 1,000,000 chance of cancer (1×10^{-6}). Conducting such a risk assessment enables us to compare the relative hazard presented by various substances and thereby assess the relative need to control exposure to these substances.

Risk assessments are based upon the same types of studies described in the preceding discussion on carcinogen identification. Epidemiologic studies may yield direct evidence on the risk to humans. Animal bioassays must be extrapolated to human exposures through one of a varied set of scientific procedures, based on varying hypotheses about cancer and the applicability of animal data to human conditions. The first and most controversial aspect of quantitative risk assessment is evaluating the carcinogenic potency of the substance in question. Potency means the probability that a given level of exposure to a substance will cause cancer.

Potency Assessment

Assessment of the carcinogenic potency of a certain substance is a crucial prerequisite to quantitative risk assessment. While any exposure to a carcinogen could theoretically cause a cancer, the probability of cancer causation varies widely among known carcinogens. Exposure to some carcinogens is many times more likely to cause cancer than exposure to oth-

Exhibit 3-1
Relative Carcinogenic Potency

Substance	Potency Index
Aflatoxin B_1	32,000
Methylnitrosurea	2,000
Dimethylnitrosamine	430
Benzo[a]pyrene	190
Cyclophosphamide	99
Benzidene	13
2-Naphthylimine	0.54
Aniline	0.078

ers. Indeed, available evidence suggests that the carcinogenic potency of different substances may vary by a factor of 10,000,000.[19] Exhibit 3-1 lists the relative potency of some selected carcinogenic chemicals. Obviously, information about the relative potency of carcinogens is useful knowledge. Society should be far more concerned about the carcinogenic substance that is 10,000,000 times more potent than another carcinogen. Potency assessments, supplemented by assessments of current population exposure levels, can also provide an estimate of the actual cancer burden created by a chemical.

Potency assessment is not a simple matter, however. Necessity frequently demands that potency assessment be based upon animal bioassays. Yet such a procedure requires two major extrapolations. First, the assessor must extrapolate the effects at the very high maximum tolerated dose in the typical bioassay to the much lower exposure levels to which humans are likely exposed. Second, the assessor must employ interspecies extrapolation, translating the dose in animal experiments to humans. Both these extrapolative procedures rest upon assumptions and hypotheses, rather than established scientific fact. Not surprisingly, the choice among the various extrapolation methodologies has become a controversial one. Fortunately, there is some scientific evidence to support certain potency assessment methodologies.

Several different methodologies have been proposed for conducting the above extrapolations. The choice among these methodologies will have a substantial effect upon the results of the potency assessment. One method may offer a potency assessment many times higher than that estimated by a competing method.

As an initial matter, most extrapolation methodologies accept the "no-threshold" hypothesis discussed in chapter 1. There is no known totally safe level of exposure to any carcinogen. Moreover, the limited sensitivity of our test procedures makes it unlikely or impossible ever to prove that such a safe level exists for any substance.

Occasionally a scientist suggests the presence of a safe threshold for a carcinogen. This is especially true if a substance's metabolite is carcinogenic and if a threshold can be demonstrated for the relevant metabolic processes. Bodily repair mechanisms also provide some support for a threshold. While theoretically logical, there is seldom if ever convincing scientific evidence of such a metabolic threshold for any specific substance. Dr. Arnold Brown thus declared that he believes that thresholds do exist for carcinogens but conceded that "no empirical approach is available to demonstrate a threshold."[20]

Moreover, important theoretical analysis supports the absence of a threshold for at least some categories of carcinogens. Consequently most risk assessment procedures operate on the assumption that no such safe threshold can be shown for any given substance. Nevertheless, some models have been developed that provide for a safe threshold dose for carcinogens, should sufficient evidence of such a threshold ever be found.

In addition to generally assuming that there is no safe threshold for carcinogens, investigators must make certain assumptions regarding the relationship between varying doses of a substance and cancer induction. Such assumptions are necessary to translate carcinogenic findings in the high MTD exposures of test animals into the much lower exposures typically found in the human environment. Elaborate models have been created to perform this extrapolation from high-level exposures in animal bioassays to lower-exposure levels in man.

One common extrapolation model is known as the linear, or one-hit, model. This model takes the no-threshold assumption that any single, even minute exposure may theoretically cause cancer and further assumes that each such exposure has an equivalent probability of causing cancer. Thus the risk is directly proportional to the exposure. Graphic depiction of this model yields a straight line running directly from the cancer rates and doses determined experimentally to the origin.

The linear model for dose-response risk assessment is usually described as conservative, meaning that it produces the largest low-level human risk estimates from a given animal experiment. Other models usually produce somewhat lower risk estimates. Because the extrapolation usually must rely upon assumptions, rather than data, there is a natural tendency to be conservative in assumptions. Thus the linear model is a popular one. Even critics of this model acknowledge its value for setting an upper bound of possible risk at low exposure levels. Moreover, extensive evidence on exposure to radiation is generally supportive of linear extrapolation models.

Some investigators contend that the linear model does not accurately describe either the available data on carcinogenic dose-response relationships or the known biological effects of cancer. These investigators suggest that very low-level exposures may be less than proportionally less hazardous than high-level exposures. This may be due to the existence of repair mechanisms, metabolic thresholds, the assumption that multiple "hits" of carcinogens are prerequisite to cancer, or other factors. To respond to this concern, several quadratic sublinear models have been developed. Rather than drawing a straight line to the origin, these models usually yield a concave line curving downward to meet the origin.

These sublinear models take several forms. One form is the multihit model, assuming that multiple exposures are required before cancer develops. While this model has scientific support, some evidence suggests that it may underestimate true risk levels. A second form is the multistage model, which acknowledges the various stages in the carcinogenic process and considers the probability of cancer progression at each stage. This model can assume varying forms, some of which approach the linear one-hit model with certain conservative assumptions at certain doses. A third form is known as the log-probit model. This model assumes that the probability of cancer development is largely a feature of differing individual human susceptibilities to carcinogens. The model further assumes that human susceptibilities are normally distributed (on a "bell curve"). As doses become lower, therefore, proportionally fewer individuals will suffer cancer.

The sublinear models all produce lower risk estimates at low exposure levels than does the linear model. Consequently, these models tend to be favored by industry representatives who seek to downplay the risk of a substance. Significantly, these models usually do not suggest the presence of a safe threshold dose. These models all accept the no-threshold assumption, at least in an environment where numerous other carcinogens are present. Supporters of the sublinear models acknowledge that even a single minute exposure may result in cancer but suggest that the probability is less than that implied by a linear model. Still other models attempt to incorporate metabolic rates or the varying times before tumor incidence found in animal experiments.

The three generalized categories of sublinear models each produce different results for individual cases, but all these models yield roughly the same type of concave curve (under certain assumptions, however, the multistage model may approach linearity).

The sublinear models now recognize and identify the uncertainty surrounding their projections. Confidence intervals are placed around the curve, indicating the 95 percent probable range of effects. The extrapolations yield results in terms of the most likely estimate (MLE) and the upper confidence limit (UCL), which is the highest reasonable estimate in light of uncertainty. The latter figure provides a conservative approximate upper bound to possible risk from a carcinogen.

Some investigators have posed yet another possibility, that dose-response may be supralinear at low levels. This theory suggests that high-level exposures may be inefficient at inducing cancer, as the test animal becomes saturated with the carcinogen dose. Thus low levels may yield a proportionately higher cancer incidence per unit, producing a supralinear convex dose-response curve. With the exception of a few substances, however, the supralinear theory is not generally accepted. Exhibit 3-2 graphically displays the distribution of cancer risk under the varying dose-response extrapolation models for potency assessment.

The choice among these various models assumes very significant practical importance. Using an identical animal bioassay, the models may produce widely varying estimates of risk at lower human exposure levels. In some circumstances the linear model may estimate a risk that is more than 1,000 times higher than that found by a sublinear model. A supralinear model will carry even greater disparity. Obviously, the choice among extrapolation models carries great importance in risk assessment.

Scientists have yet to develop a dose-response extrapolation model that is universally acceptable to a consensus of experts. Many scientists believe that various carcinogenic substances have different characteristics and that different models may be appropriate to specific substances in question. Unfortunately, experts have been unable to agree upon what criteria should be used for selecting an extrapolation model based upon any given set of positive animal data.

An apparently logical approach would simply examine the experimental data and determine which model best fits the results from the animal test. Extensive experience with animal bioassays reveals that the sublinear

Exhibit 3-2
Dose–Response Models

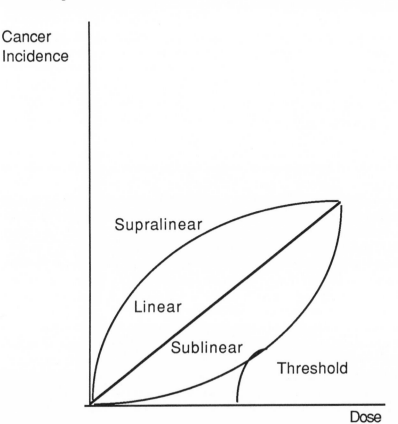

models will ordinarily fit the animal results better than the linear extrapolation, as illustrated above in exhibit 3-1. Many experts dispute this procedure, however. Animal bioassays are not so sensitive that great reliance can be placed upon a few limited data points. The Environmental Protection Agency carcinogen guidelines conclude that "[g]oodness of fit to the experimental observations is not an effective means of discriminating among models."[21] Hence many scientists prefer a more conservative option and argue that the linear model presumptively should be used for dose-response extrapolations from animal bioassays. Few scientists believe that the supralinear model describes the dose-response curve for carcinogens.

Regulators longingly seek assurance from scientists regarding proper extrapolation in risk assessment. Yet this hope is largely futile. Scientific information does not permit undisputed conclusions about dose-response extrapolation models. Nor is the future likely to bring the desired scientific consensus. The Harvard Scientific Conflict Mapping Project has observed:

Scientists face profound and perplexing challenges in trying to answer questions that are sometimes only partly scientific and are often of a sort that transcend current knowledge of carcinogenesis. Genuine technical disagreements may arise from differences in professional training, disciplinary orientation, intellectual style, and professional intuition and judgment. And in some cases it appears that scientists, like other people, operate at least in part under the conscious or subconscious desire to influence downstream policy results.[22]

Scientific knowledge can inform risk assessment, but science cannot provide all the answers for dose-response extrapolation or other stages of risk assessment. There is increased scientific support for the use of the MLE produced through sublinear extrapolation procedures, but this estimate should be accompanied by some measure of UCL, to illustrate extrapolative uncertainty and provide an upper bound on the estimate of human risk.

Nor does does-response extrapolation resolve all questions surrounding potency assessment. Interspecies extrapolation between test animals and humans must still be conducted. The very nature of interspecies extrapolation is a controverted one. Even among the closely related species of mice and rats, carcinogenicity testing has produced inconsistent results.

Employing interspecies comparisons is unavoidable, though, if animal bioassays are to be employed for risk assessment. Before applying experimental results to humans, however, the dose in the bioassay must be adjusted to the dose received by humans. Because test animals are much smaller than humans, a smaller dose is required to produce carcinogenicity. Animal results must be adapted for the different sizes and rates of human metabolism. This adjustment is ordinarily based upon body weight or surface area.

Differential characteristics among species may also be considered in determining the delivered dose or biologically effective dose of the test substance. The delivered dose is the fraction of the applied dose that actually reaches the cells where carcinogenic effects are found. Metabolic or other differences among species may prevent much of the applied dose from reaching these cells and may result in different delivered doses for a given exposure level. Thus, a carcinogen may be metabolically deactivated in its path through the human body. Delivered dose may also vary disproportionately at high and low dose levels, which may be considered for purposes of selecting a dose-response extrapolation model.

For whatever reason, some animal bioassays appear to overestimate the carcinogenic potency of substances in humans. Comparing animal data with human experience reveals that aflatoxin, for example, appears to be ten times more carcinogenic in rodents than in humans. For other substances, however, the correspondence between animal and human carcinogenic potency is quite close. Studies on cigarette smoking and asbestos, for which there is substantial human evidence, have found that extrapolation from animal bioassays is quite an accurate predictor of cancer in humans. In still other cases, a carcinogenic substance may attack different species at different sites. For example, formaldehyde causes nasal cancer in rats but may cause lung cancer in humans.

Notwithstanding the above uncertainties, extrapolation from test rodents to humans is both necessary and defensible. In some but not all cases, this extrapolation may overstate risk at low-level exposures to humans. Until we know which circumstances cause such overestimation, however, investigators cannot simply assume that humans are more resistant than test animals to any given cancer risk. Further study of metabolic processes may enable us to determine differences between test animals and humans, but our current knowledge is deficient for this purpose.

Although potency assessment is essential to risk assessment, this step presently relies upon numerous unprovable assumptions. Scientists and other decisionmakers vigorously fight over which extrapolation model is best, expending considerable time and effort; yet this fight is seldom resolved. Perhaps it is best to consider all the possible extrapolation results to define risk assessment uncertainty, bearing in mind that no individual model provides dispositive risk estimates.

Exposure Assessment

Although most risk assessment attention has focused upon potency assessment procedures, which are scientifically controversial, exposure assessment is equally critical to an overall human risk assessment. Potency assessment only tells us the carcinogenicity of a substance at a given exposure or dose, and further information about prevailing human exposures is essential to define the risk levels confronted in real-life situations.

Comprehensive exposure assessment must account for the broad diversity of routes through which an individual may be exposed to a chemical or other substance. These include ambient outdoor air and water pollution, indoor air pollution, occupational ambient levels, consumer product exposures, and other routes. Discovering the routes through which persons are exposed is patently precedent to controlling exposures to any substance found to be carcinogenic.

Exposure assessment also must quantify the exposures from these various routes. While personal exposure monitors provide an ideal method for exposure assessment, this procedure is expensive, time-consuming, and seldom used. Furthermore, personal monitors cannot clearly identify the original source of the chemical to which an individual is exposed.

Exposure assessment methods depend significantly upon the exposure route being measured. Exposure assessment for air pollution relies largely on computerized models of pollutant dispersion. Emissions from a given source at a given site are measured and then an atmospheric model is applied to determine where the substance goes and at what concentrations. Then local ambient levels (and presumably exposures) of the substance may be estimated. Occupational exposure assessment is somewhat simpler and merely requires ambient measurements in representative workplaces. Dietary exposure assessment is slightly more complex, depending upon data about the typical range of Americans' diets and the concentration of the substance in various foods. Consumer product exposure assessment requires a similar assessment. For pesticides, investigators may need an estimate of bioaccumulation of a substance in the food chain, as well as information on the human diet. Accepted data bases are presently available for each of these exposure routes.

The tools described in the preceding paragraph may be applied to particular circumstances to define human exposures to a substance. Usually exposure assessment requires several different estimates. Assessors ideally will provide the exposure levels of the average exposed individual and also the levels confronted by any subset of that population facing significantly higher exposures than the average. The latter group reflects the maximally exposed individuals, and the size of this group is also relevant to overall risk assessment.

Exposure assessment, like potency assessment, depends on assumptions as well as scientifically verifiable data. For example, exposure assessment must assume certain characteristics about human diet or the amount of time spent in a particular location. While these assumptions cast some uncertainty on exposure assessments, the measures of exposure are much more certain than most potency assessments.

Risk Assessment from Epidemiology

The preceding discussion elaborates on assessing human risk from the results of animal bioassays, which are the source for most risk assessments. When epidemiologic data is available on human risk, this too may be used for risk assessments. Such epidemiologically based risk assessments seem preferable because they are grounded in the risk of actual human exposures.

Risk assessments from epidemiology are by no means simple, however. Potency assessment requires some estimate of the number of cancers caused by some unit of exposure. Newly discovered increases in cancer are founded in exposures that are several decades past. To assess the potency of a substance, we must know the past exposure levels that produced the epidemiologically identified increase in cancer. Unfortunately, exposure measurements in the past tended to be highly imprecise.

Quantitative risk assessment of benzene illustrates this difficulty. Studies of workers exposed to high levels of benzene conclusively demonstrated an association with leukemia incidence. Careful measurements were not taken in these workplaces, however. Suppose that one investigator assumed that the identified excess of leukemia in these past workers was produced by an average exposure of 400 parts per million (ppm) of benzene, while another estimates that past exposures averaged 100 ppm. The latter investigator will estimate that benzene has four times greater carcinogenic potency than the estimate of the former investigator. Additional disputes may result from extrapolation of the risk to current exposure levels, which are approximately 1 ppm. As in animal bioassays, this extrapolation may employ linear or sublinear methods, which can yield very different results. Risk assessment from epidemiology is further complicated by certain necessary assumptions about the age of exposed individuals and other potential obscuring factors to which the study population is exposed.

In short, even clear positive results from epidemiology will not provide an unambiguous risk assessment. Epidemiology avoids the problems of interspecies extrapolation but retains the uncertainty of dose-response extrapolation and carries the additional problem of uncertainty about past exposure levels and confounding exposures to other substances that cannot be controlled as with laboratory experimentation.

Although epidemiology is not a panacea, the actual evidence of cancer in humans provides somewhat more certainty for risk estimates. Negative epidemiologic results may also be used in combination with animal bioassays to add accuracy by placing an upper limit on the incidence of cancer in humans. For example, studies on formaldehyde in animals found an increased incidence of nasal cancer. Extrapolation of these results in a risk assessment for humans, using very conservative assumptions, produced an estimate of formaldehyde-caused nasal cancers that exceeded the entire incidence of nasal cancer in the United States population. In this instance, human data rather clearly demonstrates the inaccuracy of an assessment based on animal bioassay results.

Results of Risk Assessment

A complete risk assessment simply takes the potency assessment (yielding a cancer risk per unit of exposure) and marries those results to the exposure assessment (yielding average or maximum units of exposure) to provide an estimate of prevailing risk. The resulting estimate is usually expressed in terms of probability of cancer, as in 2 chances in 10,000 of cancer (2×10^{-4}). Risk assessment may also be employed to estimate the total number of cancers caused by the cumulative exposure of the entire population.

Risk assessments have now been performed for hundreds of substances or activities that may cause cancer. Risk assessment may also be used for noncarcinogenic hazards, such as heart disease or automobile accidents. Exhibit 3-3 lists assessed risks for a variety of human exposures and activities, both carcinogenic and noncarcinogenic. The probabilities expressed are for the average individual exposed to the hazard in question. Results are expressed in terms of a lifetime risk of acquiring cancer, based upon a seventy-year life.

Exhibit 3-3 reveals that environmental exposures to carcinogens are relatively small, as compared to many noncarcinogenic risks. Moreover, these risks are generally much less than certain voluntarily accepted risks of cancer. Yet the environmental involuntary risk of cancer is not negligible and should be avoided if possible. Prevention of this source of cancer would prolong thousands of lives. This risk must be placed in context, however, as it hardly provides grounds for panic.

Criticism of Risk Assessment

Quantitative risk assessment is not universally applauded. The primary criticism of risk assessment is its inherent uncertainty. One author thus noted:

Toxic risk assessment suffers from fundamental uncertainties about causal mechanisms and other hazards, extrapolative relationships between high-dose and low-dose responses and between animal test data and human risks, latent effects and latency periods, special sensitivities in exposed subpopulations, synergistic or co-carcinogenic effects of various substances, past and present exposure levels, dispersion patterns for contaminants, and virtually every other area of required knowledge.[23]

Even defenders of risk assessment must concede much of this uncertainty indictment.

The attack on risk assessment initially was led by the environmentalist community, which feared that the procedure would be manipulated by industry to avoid regulation. Regulators and industry might present assessed risks for carcinogens that were so low that they would claim that regulation was unnecessary. Given the many assumptions latent in any risk assessment, an unscrupulous risk assessor could produce a very low estimate for any environmental carcinogen. The critics accepted quantitative risk assessment in principle but argued that the tool was yet too primitive for regulatory use.

Thus the uncertainty or inaccuracy of risk assessment formed the basis for criticism. The most commonly cited example of uncertainty was found

Exhibit 3-3
Relative Lifetime Risks of Death

Cause	Risk of Death

Smoking 1×10^{-1}

Passive Smoking 5×10^{-4}

Natural Background Radiation 1×10^{-4}

Lightning 4×10^{-5}

Drowning 2×10^{-3}

Home Accidents 7×10^{-3}

Auto Accidents 2×10^{-2}

Police Officer 1×10^{-3}

Farming 5×10^{-3}

Hunting 1×10^{-4}

Historic Asbestos Work 2×10^{-2}

Alcohol (one beer per day) 1×10^{-3}

Saccharin (one diet can per day) 6×10^{-4}

Formaldehyde from Mobile Home 1×10^{-4}

Vinyl Chloride Air Pollution 1×10^{-5}

Food Additive D&C Red No. 6 1×10^{7}

High Radon Home 2×10^{-2}

Average Radon Home 3×10^{-3}

10^{-7} 10^{-6} 10^{-5} 10^{-4} 10^{-3} 10^{-2} 10^{-1}

in the risk assessment for saccharin. Risk assessors applied several different models to the data on cancer resulting from saccharin exposures in
rats. These models yielded risk estimates ranging from 1,200 cancers per
million exposed humans to .001 cancers per million exposed humans.
Thus, a factor of 1,000,000 separated the highest from the lowest risk assessment. Given this disparity, environmentalists questioned the usefulness of quantitative risk assessment for carcinogens.[24]

Some representatives of environmental organizations took a more cynical view that risk assessment could be counterproductive. Given the range
of uncertainty inherent in all carcinogenic quantitative risk estimates, industry representatives attempting to stave off regulation could always produce a risk estimate that was very low. Cooperative regulators could seize
upon such numbers as an excuse for inaction. Even regulators committed
to carcinogen control might have difficulty demonstrating the superiority
of a higher risk estimate, and industry might be able to strike down regulations in courts judicially reviewing an agency's action. On occasion, this
feared scenario has come to pass, frustrating regulation of carcinogens.

Even industry representatives have had some second thoughts about risk
assessment. Cautious agency regulators have tended to use a series of conservative assumptions in risk assessment, to avoid underestimating the
true risk of a carcinogen. These assumptions have resulted in agency risk
estimates that are significantly higher than what industry considers to be
accurate. Given an institutional tendency to employ such conservatism in
risk assessment, industry representatives fear that the procedure causes
cancer risks to be overstated and may promote unnecessary regulation.
While industry representatives generally support risk assessment, skeptics
remain.

In short, quantitative risk assessment offers no conclusive scientific solution to carcinogen regulation. Even defenders of the procedure acknowledge that it is still beset with irresolvable uncertainties. One expert group
suggested that "it is likely that no responsible scientist would even try to
make (or take much interest in) such numerical estimates were it not for
the pressure to do so for policy reasons."[25] Extensive reliance on quantitative risk assessment may be deemed unscientific and unreliable for use in
government regulation of carcinogens.

Defense of Risk Assessment

The defense of risk assessment frequently begins by conceding much of
the attack on the procedure. Quantitative estimates of cancer risk remain
uncertain, and no immediate prospect for great improvement appears on
the horizon. Nevertheless, quantitative risk assessment provides *some* evidence, albeit uncertain, of the magnitude of a cancer risk. Having some
evidence should be preferred to no evidence, in the absence of such risk
assessment.

The National Academy of Sciences observed that even uncertain quantitative risk estimates for carcinogens "would represent a significant advance" over the "intuitive, ad hoc, unsystematic, and often frantic methods now used."[26] Dr. Lester Lave concluded that "[i]f regulation is to be lifted out of the currently unsatisfactory state of visceral reactions and political judgments, [risk] analysis must play a more central role."[27] The Environmental Protection Agency declared that quantitative risk assessment represents "a significant step toward the objective of achieving real benefits in improved public health. . . . "[28] Virtually every expert government body and independent scientific organization in the field supports the conduct of quantitative risk assessment for carcinogens.

The uncertainty attendant to current quantitative risk assessment is thus acceptable, so long as it is acknowledged. Even uncertain estimates are preferable to no estimates. Moreover, the uncertainty is often exaggerated. Returning to the saccharin example illustrates this principle. The highest risk estimates were inconsistent with epidemiologic results. The lowest risk estimates were so low that disparities were insignificant. (There is a tenfold difference between .001 and .01 cancers, but as a practical policy matter, the two estimates are equivalent.) Quantitative risk assessment indicated that saccharin was probably responsible for at most 1,000 bladder cancers annually. This estimate permitted policymakers to understand the magnitude of the problem and to respond accordingly. Surely rational policy was furthered by this knowledge. Saccharin, of course, was restored to the market with a warning. Had the risk been much greater, it is likely that the federal government would have banned saccharin altogether.

The danger that risk assessment will be abused to promote a political agenda is a real concern. Yet risk assessment is but one of many methods to avoid regulation, and is at most a symptom of a powerful underlying problem. Even in the total absence of quantitative risk assessment, obstructionist elements have a plethora of tools to avoid action. Potential misuse of risk assessment is no reason to forgo the tool entirely. Indeed, risk assessment may be employed to illuminate a lack of regulatory action, as in the case of indoor air pollution.

Indeed, risk assessment has typically been a tool for prompting regulation. A tendency to rely upon conservative upper confidence limits may have overstated the risk from carcinogens. Commentators thus note that "risk assessment can be used to protect the public health because it approaches the assessment of potential human risk in a manner designed to err on the side of overstating the potential risk—the actual risk, if any, is likely to be substantially less than that projected."[29]

An Alternative—Qualitative Risk Assessment

Some scientists, troubled by the suspect scientific assumptions underlying present quantitative risk assessment policies, have proposed an alternative involving the use of qualitative risk assessment for carcinogens. Current programs first make an "all-or-nothing" conclusion about a substance's carcinogenicity and extrapolate estimates of human risk, occasionally based upon very limited and sometimes questionable experimental data. This process itself implies a much greater degree of scientific certainty than is warranted.

Proponents of qualitative risk assessment typically eschew conclusive determinations of carcinogenicity or potency, in favor of some carcinogen "score," dependent upon the strength of the underlying experimental evidence of carcinogenicity. One such leading scoring system was based on the number of different species with positive results, the different types of cancer induced, the sensitivity of test species, evidence of a dose-response relationship, the malignancy of induced neoplasms, and genotoxicity as found in short-term tests.[30] Application of this system produced exemplary relative carcinogenicity scores of 100 for aflatoxins, 90 for vinyl chloride, and 36 for saccharin.

Any numeric scoring in qualitative risk assessment is necessarily somewhat arbitrary, but the process acknowledges experimental uncertainties, unlike some present practice with quantitative estimation. Qualitative risk assessment may therefore inform the regulatory practice more completely. Unfortunately, qualitative risk assessment does not estimate the actual human risk from environmental exposures to carcinogens, which ultimately is the critical information necessary both for regulation and for assigning civil liability. For example, a substance might have a low qualitative score but still present a significant human risk due to substantial human exposure. Some quantitative risk assessment is still necessary for both legal and practical reasons.

Overview of Risk Assessment

Quantitative risk assessment is assuming a central role in carcinogen regulation. It is pointless to take a position "for" or "against" conducting such assessments. The procedure is a means, not an end. The key question involves the integrity of assessment and the uses to which risk assessment is put.

Risk assessment is essential to establishing priorities for carcinogen control. Quantitation can define the relative risks of various substances and thereby enable regulatory agencies to address the greatest hazards faced by their constituency. Public health will receive more protection from targeting the major risks rather than chasing carcinogens willy-nilly.

Using risk assessment to define the degree of regulation is somewhat more controversial. Theoretically, regulators might use quantitative risk assessment to decide that some risks were so small that they were unworthy of any attention. When setting a standard, these regulators would not

impose controls against very low-level sources of risk. Although this judgment is simply another form of prioritization of resources, it may be beyond the scope of quantitative risk assessment. With uncertainties ranging
up to and in excess of a factor of 1,000, risk assessment seems an imprecise
tool for limiting regulation. If the most conservative assumptions are
made, providing an upper bound on total risk, regulators may be able to
use risk assessment in establishing regulatory standards.

Quantitative risk assessment for carcinogens is now entrenched in regulatory practice. The procedure provides essential information to regulators. A danger remains, however, that the inherent uncertainty of risk assessment will be overlooked and point estimates of risk will receive undue
deference. Risk assessment uses science and seems "scientific," but the
process necessarily involves unverifiable assumptions and policy judgments. Thus the procedure is called "trans-scientific." Continued recognition of the procedure's uncertainties and their importance is vital to any
responsible use of quantitative risk assessment. Risk assessments must
make their assumptions explicit and quantify uncertainties insofar as possible. Qualitative risk assessment may also contribute to a more complete
and accurate recognition of uncertainty involved in carcinogen identification and risk assessment.

NOTES

1. Report of the Interagency Regulatory Liaison Group, "Scientific Bases for Identification of Potential Carcinogens and Estimation of Risks," reprinted in *J. Nat. Cancer Inst.* 63 (July 1979): 241, 249.

2. National Cancer Institute, *Guidelines for Carcinogen Bioassays in Small Rodents* (1976).

3. Gio Gori, "The Regulation of Carcinogenic Hazards," *Science* 208 (1980): 257.

4. Ibid., 258.

5. Robert Barnard, "The Emerging Regulatory Dilemma," *Annals of N.Y. Acad.
of Sciences* 363 (1981): 89, 90 (analyzing the results of the study).

6. Office of Technology Assessment, *Technologies for Determining Cancer Risks
from the Environment* (June 1981), 130.

7. Office of Science and Technology Policy, *Chemical Carcinogens: Notice of Review of the Science and Its Associated Principles,* 49 Fed. Reg. 21593, 21639 (May 22,
1984).

8. National Research Council, National Academy of Sciences, *Risk Assessment in
the Federal Government: Managing the Process* (1983), 22.

9. Interdisciplinary Panel on Carcinogenicity, "Criteria for Evidence of Chemical
Carcinogenicity," *Science* 225 (August 17, 1984): 682, 683.

10. 51 *Fed. Reg.* 33995 (1986).

11. Office of Technology Assessment, 141.

12. Yodaiken, Jones, Spolnicki, and Deitchman, "Regulators and Workplace Carcinogens," *Occupational Medicine* 2 (1987): 204.

13. Joyce McCann, Edmund Choi, Edith Yamaski, and Bruce Ames, "Detection of Carcinogens as Mutagens in the Salmonella/Microsome Test: Assay of 300 Chemicals," *Proceedings of the National Academy of Sciences U.S.A.* 72 (1975): 5135.

14. Interdisciplinary Panel on Carcinogenicity, 684.

15. D. R. Calkins, R. L. Dixon, C. R. Gerber, D. Zarin, and G. S. Omenn, "Identification, Characterization, and Control of Potential Human Carcinogens: A Framework for Federal Decision-Making." *J. Nat. Cancer Inst.* 64 (January 1980): 169, 172.

16. Umberto Saffioti, "Identification and Definition of Chemical Carcinogens: Review of Criteria and Research Needs," *J. Toxicol. Environ. Health* 6 (September–November 1980): 1043.

17. Weinberg and Storer, "Ambiguous Carcinogens and Their Regulation," *Risk Analysis* 5 (1985): 151.

18. Saffioti, 1029, 1037.

19. Gori, *Carcinogen Regulation*, Council on Scientific Affairs, JAMA (July 17, 1981): 253, 254.

20. Arnold Brown, "The Meaning of Risk Assessment," *Oncology* 37 (1980): 302, 303.

21. 51 *Fed. Reg.* 33998 (1986).

22. John D. Graham, Laura Green and Mark J. Roberts, *Seeking Safety: Science, Public Policy and Cancer Risk* (to be published by Harvard University Press).

23. Howard Latin, "Good Science, Bad Regulation, and Toxic Risk Assessment," 5 YALE J. REG. 89, 91 (1988).

24. *Hearings on Comparative Risk Assessment Before the Subcomm. on Science, Research and Technology of the House Comm. on Science and Technology,* 96th Cong., 2d Sess., May 14, 1980, 316 (statement of David Doniger of the Natural Resources Defense Council).

25. Graham et al.

26. National Research Council, National Academy of Sciences, *Decision Making for Regulating Chemicals in the Environment* (1975), 45.

27. Lester B. Lave, *Quantitative Risk Assessment of Toxic Substances,* Working Paper: Carnegie-Mellon University (March 1981): 9.

28. U.S. Department of Health, Education & Welfare, *EPA Health Risk & Economic Impact Assessment of Suspected Carcinogens.*

29. Joseph Rodricks and R. Taylor, "Application of Risk Assessment to Food Safety Decision Making," *Reg. Toxicol. & Pharmacol.* 3 (1983): 275, 280.

30. Robert Squire, "Ranking Animal Carcinogens: A Proposed Regulatory Approach," *Science* 214 (1981): 877.

4

CARCINOGEN RISK MANAGEMENT

Having identified an environmental substance as carcinogenic and assessed the extent of its risk, government next must decide how to prevent this risk, through risk management. Regulatory agencies are commissioned to prevent cancer risks, but such prevention is not simple. Of course, agencies may ban products or activities, mandate emission control devices, or establish maximum permissible exposure levels. Some regulatory plan or paradigm is required, however, to determine which of these steps to adopt in any given regulatory case. Furthermore, if exposure is to be controlled, agencies must still choose some maximum permissible level of exposure, at zero or higher. Given the complex nature of the cancer problem, adopting a risk management plan is difficult.

At least four different carcinogen risk management paradigms are available. The four leading approaches are: (1) "zero risk" or the abolition of all cancer risk; (2) "significant risk" or the acceptance of some small, *de minimis* level of residual cancer risk; (3) "cost-benefit analysis" or the balancing of the costs of regulation against the benefits to determine if controls are worthwhile; and (4) "feasibility analysis" or use of the best available technology to reduce cancer risks as far as technically or economically possible. Federal regulatory agencies have at times used each of these approaches under different laws for carcinogen regulation. This chapter will discuss these four paradigms in turn, considering both the advantages and disadvantages to each approach.

ZERO RISK

Many environmentalists favor taking regulatory actions to eliminate all risk from carcinogens. Surely society should strive to prevent all avoidable suffering and death. This approach is analogous to other forms of public health protection; for example, standards for noncarcinogens are typically set at a level that is intended to eliminate all hazard to human health. The public will feel much safer in the knowledge that the government is taking steps to abolish all carcinogenic risks.

The zero risk approach appeals for a number of reasons. Philosophically, zero risk recognizes the sanctity of human life and avoids the need to "sacrifice" some individuals. Practically, zero risk management largely avoids the need to assess risks quantitatively, obviating the complex and expensive processes described in chapter 3. A zero risk paradigm also avoids difficult judgments about acceptable risk levels or unacceptable cost levels in regulation. Rhetorically, zero risk is a powerful persuasive approach to individuals fearful of the cancer hazards present in our technological society.

Notwithstanding these merits, use of a zero risk paradigm for carcinogen control presents serious problems. Because any minute level of carcinogen theoretically presents *some* risk, the elimination of all risk requires the elimination of all exposure to carcinogens. The latter task is daunting, if not impossible. A reliable adherent to the zero risk paradigm would shut down the United States economy. The ultimate benefits of zero risk are also debatable.

Economic Impossibility of Zero Risk

Zero risk may be practical and desirable for many acutely toxic substances, but for carcinogens, zero risk is literally impossible. Furthermore, any regulatory program approaching zero risk for carcinogens must eliminate most sectors of our economy.

The problem of zero risk arises out of the following circumstances. As we have seen, any exposure to a carcinogen carries some risk. Thus, zero exposure is necessary for zero risk. Our ability to detect substances has improved dramatically, to the point where parts per trillion can be identified. Technology is unable to capture every part per trillion of a carcinogen, however. It is simply impossible to manufacture, store, or otherwise use a carcinogen without some minimal release of the substance. Consequently, the only method for eliminating all carcinogen exposure is to prohibit the use of any carcinogens or substances containing carcinogens.

Prohibiting the use of any substances containing carcinogens would eliminate virtually every economic activity in America. A report by the Harvard Energy and Environmental Policy Center has observed that "[t]o prohibit the release of any carcinogen would be to ban most industrial activity."[1] The most compelling example is the production of electricity. Coal-burning power plants release radiation from tiny amounts of uranium in the coal. Nuclear power plants release some small amount of radiation as well. Oil and natural gas combustion unavoidably produces volatile organic compounds that are known to be carcinogenic. Perhaps hydropower would be noncarcinogenic, but new evidence suggests that the transmission of electricity itself produces some carcinogens. Strict application of the zero risk paradigm would prohibit electricity. Most transportation, using gasoline for fuel, would also be banned. Virtually all food products would become illegal. Even if these extreme steps were taken, whatever substitutes might be found could well be carcinogenic themselves.

The zero risk paradigm thus appears somewhat ridiculous. Do environmentalists really want to ban electricity, motor vehicles, and most foods? Rather obviously, environmentalists and other proponents of zero risk do not desire this extreme result. These advocates apparently want a zero risk legal standard for use as leverage in regulatory disputes with government and industry. Assuming that no regulatory agency would literally apply a zero risk standard for carcinogens, the environmentalists recognize that the threat of zero risk may be employed to pressure government and industry into greater control of carcinogens than otherwise might result. The threat of a lawsuit can produce beneficial compromises by industry. Zero risk is never reached, but lower risks may result. Other environmentalists simply argue that zero risk should be the ultimate objective of government regulation, even if this objective is unattainable in the foreseeable future.

Thus zero risk from carcinogens is not necessarily so ridiculous as it initially might seem. Nevertheless, the zero risk paradigm suffers serious flaws. First, the approach is intellectually dishonest and misleading. Politicians may mouth a commitment to zero risk, while tacitly realizing that there is no prospect of actually using such a standard. Second, a commitment to zero risk insofar as possible may actually undermine maximum effective control of carcinogens. Given limited resources for carcinogen control, devoting great energy and expenditure to small risks may divert control efforts from greater carcinogenic hazards. Third, use of zero risk as a bargaining tool may actually backfire. Fear of costly or politically unpopular overregulation can cause agencies to sit on their hands and avoid taking any regulatory action.

Ineffectiveness or Counterproductiveness of Zero Risk

Striving to abolish all danger with a zero risk paradigm may, paradoxically, increase the overall risk level in society. There are at least three reasons why the zero risk approach can be counterproductive. First is a psychological reason, that obsession with absolute safety can stifle technological and other advances that contribute important safety benefits to society. Second is a practical resource reason, that attempts to eliminate all risks divert limited resources from greater hazards. Third is a political reason, that the economic impracticality of zero risk will freeze regulators into inaction.

The psychological reason recently has been explicated by Aaron Wildavsky, a Professor of Political Science and Public Policy at the University of California, Berkeley. Wildavsky argues that "seeking safety may increase danger," while "accepting risks may increase safety."[2] Risky activity, including that using carcinogens, carries opportunity benefits for both the quality and quantity of life. Hyperconcern with safety leads to the great fear of societal errors of commission, whereby a hazardous chemical is permitted to endanger life. The absence of any balancing check on the zero risk paradigm, however, means that errors of omission may be overlooked, and the opportunity benefits of risky activity are ignored. Another author has suggested that "to avoid all risk would lead to the ultimate risk of stagnation and 'rotting in a dungeon of security.' "[3] Former Chief Justice Warren Burger wrote that "[p]erfect safety is a chimera: regulation must not strangle human activity in the search for the impossible."[4] Illustrative is the imaginary zero carcinogenic risk world without motor vehicles, electric power, and most foods. Psychological obsession with complete safety can endanger actual safety.

Even more compelling is the practical resource case against zero risk. Society has limited financial resources to commit to cancer prevention, and government regulatory agencies have limited budgets. People also have limited attention or "worry resources" to concern themselves with hazards. Regulatory effectiveness demands that these resources be focused on the greatest preventable hazards. Attending to every hazard, however small, can leave greater risks unattended, thereby expanding the overall societal risk level. There is an inexorable trade-off between depth and breadth of regulation. The more energy devoted to regulatory depth—that is, strictness of controls—the less commitment can be devoted to regulatory breadth—that is, the number of substances controlled. Dr. Bruce Ames thus has contended:

We must ignore the trivia if we are to deal effectively with the important causes of cancer. We might possibly eliminate every trace of man-made carcinogens from our water or food supply, but it would cost an enormous amount, be of minimal relevance to the causes of human cancer and distract health workers from real, more important health risks.[5]

Until we have limitless time, money and attention to respond to carcinogenicity, we must direct regulation to significant risks. In 1979, Dr. Roy Albert of the Environmental Protection Agency Carcinogen Assessment Group expressed concern that a no-threshold, zero risk approach for carcinogens created a "real danger that the Federal Regulatory Program will bog down in ineffectiveness."[6] Dr. Albert's prediction has at least partially come to pass.

The third argument against the safety of zero risk is a political argument. I have suggested that the true basis of the seemingly impractical zero risk paradigm is a political one. Environmentalists may consider the threat of zero risk regulation as a lever for compromise. The threat is so great, however, that it may paralyze action. Regulators may fear initiating regulation, if zero risk rules will compel action that is economically and politically disastrous. The regulated community may fight controls vigorously, out of a fear that zero risk rules may force action that will bankrupt their businesses. Zero risk also presents the danger that an unrealistically risk-averse risk management paradigm may drive agencies to adopt extremely risk-tolerant procedures for carcinogen identification or risk assessment.

For example, reliance on a zero risk paradigm could push government into defining false and artificial thresholds for environmental carcinogens in order to implement regulations. As a consequence, the commitment to zero risk may either prevent regulatory action against cancer or force regulation to be based upon erroneous risk assessment. Even if zero risk regulation was implemented, political pressure could prevent effective enforcement of these rules.

Indeed, striving for zero risk is contrary to human nature. Although individuals may seek to avoid many risks, these same individuals readily accept others in exchange for perceived benefits from risk-taking behavior. Automobiles present one of the greatest risks in contemporary society, yet Americans continue to drive, often simply for pleasure. The greatest causes of cancer today are voluntarily accepted risks. Obviously people are willing to accept risks under some circumstances.

The zero risk paradigm for carcinogen control still has rhetorical appeal and doubtless will continue to be invoked on behalf of environmental causes. For some limited topics of regulation, zero risk may even be workable. For the great bulk of carcinogenic hazards, however, zero risk is unreasonable. Because attaining zero risk is so unreasonable, the practical effect of a zero risk standard is likely to undermine the effective control of environmental sources of cancer.

SIGNIFICANT RISK

The significant risk paradigm for carcinogen regulation addresses only those substances that create a risk so great as to be "significant" and worthy of government attention. Smaller risks, conversely, are labeled *de minimis* or acceptable and are ignored by regulators. The significant risk paradigm thus restricts carcinogen regulation to dangers surpassing some defined level of significance.

Possible reliance on the significant risk paradigm was dramatized by the decision of the United States Supreme Court in *Industrial Union Department, AFL-CIO v. American Petroleum Institute*,[7] sometimes referred to as the "*Benzene* decision." In this case, the Court reviewed an occupational health standard for benzene and ruled that the Occupational Health and Safety Administration (OSHA) must "find a significant risk of harm and therefore a probability of significant benefits before establishing a new standard."[8] In effect, the Court mandated that OSHA conduct a quantitative risk assessment prior to regulating carcinogens and issue regulations only for those substances that present a significant risk that can be significantly reduced by the regulations.

In *Benzene*, however, the Court chose not to define the level of carcinogenic risk that is significant enough to merit regulation. Rather, the Court merely suggested that the significance threshold should fall somewhere between a one in a thousand risk of cancer and a one in a billion risk. Before the significant risk standard can be employed, regulators must somehow define what risk levels will be deemed significant.

The *Benzene* decision applied only to occupational health regulation, but the principles enunciated could apply to virtually any carcinogen control program. Significant risk has appeal for overcoming some of the difficulties of the zero risk paradigm. Significant risk has its critics, however, who contend that the approach is unrealistic or even immoral.

Uncertainty and Significant Risk

Contemporary visions of significant risk standards must rely upon quantitative risk assessment to identify those substances presenting a significant risk and to define the level of control required to eliminate the significant risk. As addressed in chapter 3, however, quantitative risk assessment can provide only uncertain estimates of the true risk from a substance or activity. The quantified risk measure may vary by a factor of thousands. This uncertainty offers a rather unstable foundation for any risk management paradigm.

Under current principles of administrative law, the regulatory agency will bear the burden of proof that a substance or activity presents a significant risk. Given the inherent uncertainty of quantitative risk assessment, agencies face a difficult task in meeting this burden. Justice Thurgood Marshall, dissenting in *Benzene*, feared that the significant risk standard would "place the burden of medical uncertainty squarely on the shoulders of the American worker"[9] and make effective carcinogen regulation impossible.

The uncertainty of quantitative risk assessment is indisputable. Such uncertainty necessarily undermines the accuracy of significant-risk-based regulation and compromises its effectiveness. Defenders of significant risk, however, can still persuasively argue that uncertain information about risk is better than no information at all. The most compelling point made by critics involves the burden of proof on agencies. Given inherent uncertainty, a strict burden of proof could preclude all carcinogen regulation. Government can never conclusively demonstrate the significance of a risk at prevailing exposure levels. Reliance on a significant risk paradigm demands that considerable deference be given to agency judgments of risk significance, lest regulation become impossible.

Still further uncertainty attends the significant risk paradigm. This approach necessitates some definition of what risk levels are considered significant enough to warrant regulatory action. Yet no scientific or policy evidence can definitively establish such levels. Furthermore, the levels of significance may be cynically manipulated to further ulterior motives of regulators. Uncertainty regarding minimum risk significance levels remains irresolvable. Care must be taken lest significant risk lend a false air of objectivity to subjectively determined risk assessments and lest regulators be "overwhelmed by the spurious certainty of numbers."[10]

The Ethics of Significant Risk

Critics of the significant risk paradigm have challenged the ethics of accepting the deaths of certain unspecified individuals, which will inevitably result from low-level unregulated risks. Significant risk accepts the sacrifice of a few lives for the benefit of society as a whole. Yet those few lives are of paramount importance to their family and friends.

These critics would observe that we do not license the murder of just a few humans, on the grounds that this murderer presents no significant risk. The willingness to accept certain low-level risks of cancer may simply be due to the inability to identify the victims of most environmental carcinogens. One leading environmental organization has thus complained:

Presumably a police department would respond with the same urgency to a tip that a dangerous person has threatened to shoot randomly into a Times Square crowd until he kills one person as it would to a tip that the same dangerous person intends to kill a specific individual. Why then should a public health agency such as EPA respond less to the "statistical" death than the identified, specific death?[11]

Moreover, this same police department presumably would not wait for a quantitative risk assessment to demonstrate a significant risk before acting against the threat to the public health.

Thus some environmentalists are troubled by the concept of accepting any statistical risk of death from carcinogens. The murder analogy is misleading, however. Murder has no compensating benefits, in the form of safety or otherwise. The production of carcinogens, however, may possess compelling societal benefits.

The ethical justification for accepting low-level risks to health and some concomitant level of death is a contractarian one. Individuals in society accept some level of risk in return for the benefits offered by technology. Thus a social contract authorizes the allowance of some risk. Should the people object to the terms of this social contract, our democracy permits them to redress their grievances against the responsible party.

However troubling the significant risk paradigm may appear in the abstract, the critics must offer some preferable alternative that accounts for their ethical objections. No such alternative has been demonstrated. The zero risk paradigm itself may impose suffering and death upon Americans, in excess of the lives it saves. Because some loss of life is unavoidable, defenders of the significant risk paradigm need only show that it optimizes the quantity and quality of life, not that it saves all lives.

Another serious ethical concern remains about the significant risk paradigm. The distribution effects of risk acceptance must be considered. Theoretically, significant risk could be employed to benefit a privileged subgroup of society, while imposing mortality upon an underprivileged, underrepresented subgroup of society. This consequence is unacceptable. Under the contractarian justification, those who reap the benefits must also bear the risks. Fortunately, for most environmental carcinogens some such coincidence exists. Virtually all Americans utilize electricity, and virtually all are exposed to some carcinogenic hazard from electric power production. Expecting the correlation to be precise is unreasonable; some general coincidence of benefits and risks ensures that democratic processes will provide a fair result. Particular concern might be given to occupational carcinogens, however, where the workers exclusively bear risks and some of the benefit inures to consumers.

A final ethical concern with the significant risk approach arises out of the fear that the paradigm will provide moral legitimacy to causing small risks. Reliance on significant risk might create a view that causing small risks is acceptable, even when the risks are avoidable. This view, in turn, might spill over into other areas of the law, such as medical treatment, and result in unnecessary loss of life.

While the concern for legitimizing small risks is reasonable, the criticism depends upon the expressed basis for reliance on the significant risk paradigm. If proponents of significant risk assert that small risks are inherently unworthy of any government or other societal attention, the criticism is a substantial one. Most proponents of significant risk, however, do not make this claim. Rather, most advocates of significant risk contend that regulation of small risks should simply be postponed until greater risks are addressed. This attitude does not in any sense legitimize small risks but holds that these small risks should be temporarily accepted, pending action against other, more substantial risks to public health.

Absence of Cost Considerations

The above objections to significant risk arose from the environmentalist community, which feared that the paradigm would underregulate carcinogens. Industry, too, may have concerns about exclusive reliance upon a significant risk approach. The leading objection from this perspective is the failure of significant risk even to consider the costs of carcinogen control or the benefits of the endangering activity.

Consider, for example, an activity that imposes a significant carcinogenic risk yet carries an even greater societal benefit. Medical X-rays frequently fall into this category. Logically we should not prevent even significant risks when doing so would sacrifice more than counterbalancing benefits. Alternatively, a carcinogenic activity might create a very small risk but have no benefits worth mentioning. Some cosmetic food additives might fall into this category. Why should we accept any risk, however small, from an activity or substance that provides no societal benefit?

Other commentators call for use of cost-effectiveness analysis. The most significant risk might be unamenable to regulatory control or controls might be extremely costly. Regulatory action might accomplish much more if it focused upon some smaller risk that could be prevented quickly and efficiently.

The case for considering the full effects of carcinogen control in some manner is a strong one. There are serious difficulties, however, in the kind of cost/benefit balancing, or even cost-effectiveness, contemplated by this alternative. These difficulties are discussed in the following section. Moreover, the desire for cost considerations is not a criticism of significant risk analysis *per se*. Rather, the significant risk paradigm could be supplemented by some form of cost considerations in certain appropriate cases.

Implementing the Significant Risk Paradigm

Unlike the relatively simple zero risk approach, utilization of the significant risk paradigm requires a series of difficult policy judgments. First, the policymaker must choose a currency of risk by which to measure significance. At least three such currencies are possible, including the total number of cancers caused by a substance, the average lifetime probabilistic risk of cancer within the broad exposed population, and the average lifetime probabilistic risk of cancer within some smaller group of the population exposed to the maximum risk. Most advocates of the significant risk paradigm focus on the average lifetime risk of cancer but recognize the relevance of the other two criteria in at least some cases.

Once the currency of risk is chosen, the policymaker must decide what risk levels are considered significant enough to regulate and what risk levels are so low that regulation is unnecessary. This may take the form of a simple cutoff line. That is, regulators might decide that all average lifetime risks in excess of 1 in 100,000 (1×10^{-5}) require regulation, while risks of less than this level may be ignored. Others have proposed a three-tier grouping of risks. Thus, policymakers might regulate all substances or activities causing average lifetime risks in excess of 1 in 10,000 (1×10^{-4}), ignore all risks under 1 in 1,000,000 (1×10^{-6}), and use other factors to determine whether to regulate substances or activities producing risks between 1×10^{-4} and 1×10^{-6}. These other factors might include the total number of cancers caused by a substance or the costs of controlling exposures.

Deciding what level of risk assumes regulatory significance is a difficult one. The level of significant regulatable risk must consider normative issues of fairness as well as more pragmatic issues of efficiency and effectiveness in regulation. Nevertheless, there is some rough agreement among experts regarding the level of risk that should be considered so significant that government controls are warranted. Exhibit 4-1 reviews some significant risk proposals and regulatory practices, as expressed in average lifetime risk from environmental hazards. This exhibit reveals some proximate agreement about risk levels that should be deemed significant. The displayed results are somewhat incomplete, however, as all the cited sources would adjust the significant risk level based on factors beyond average lifetime risk (including the size of the exposed population, and the higher risk to any maximally exposed subgroup of the exposed population).

Even these proponents of the significant risk paradigm have reached no uniform consensus regarding the levels of risk that should be considered significant or *de minimis*. Even if this significant risk level is settled, other complexities remain. For example, policymakers should have some concern for any small group of people exposed to very high risk, even if the overall average risk is low. Thus, maximum lifetime risk levels must be factored into the significant risk equation. These maximum risk levels must be set differently from average risk levels, however. For example, some have suggested a 1×10^{-6} cutoff level for significant risk to the average exposed population, but

[a] large proportion of goods and services could not be produced if the one-in-a-million standard considered acceptable for the entire society were also to be applied to those discrete and very small populations that are uniquely at risk. Were we not to exceed the level of exposures implied by this level of risk, to cite a few examples, cooks could not cook (benzo(a)pyrene and other "indoor" carcinogens), roads could not be paved (hot asphalt and products of incomplete combustion) , dentists could not X-ray (X-rays), anesthesiologists could not anesthetise (halothane), and stone masons (thorium), plumbers (lead, fumes), painters (solvents, epoxides), carpenters (wood dusts), and farmers (UV from sunlight) could not work.[12]

Some slightly higher level of risk must be accepted for these maximally exposed individuals. In most cases the risk faced by this subgroup is to some degree voluntary and could be avoided through personal protective actions.

The significant risk paradigm also must consider other factors influencing the regulatability of risks. Special circumstances may call for different

Exhibit 4-1
Proposed De Minimis Risk Levels

Source	Risk Level
Albert (environmental risks) (based on regulatory objectives)	1×10^{-5}
Office of Technology Assessment (based on consensus)	1×10^{-5}
Cross (environmental risks) (based on comparative risk)	1×10^{-5}
Cross (occupational risks) (based on comparative risk)	1×10^{-4}
Crouch & Wilson (based on pragmatic issues)	7×10^{-5}
Nuclear Regulatory Commission	2×10^{-4}
Food and Drug Administration	1×10^{-6}
Okrent & Whipple (essential technologies)	2×10^{-4}
Okrent & Whipple (beneficial technologies)	2×10^{-5}
Okrent & Whipple (peripheral technologies)	2×10^{-6}
Adler & Weinberg (radiation risk) (based on standard deviation)	1×10^{-4}
Kinchin (nuclear power risks) (in the United Kingdom)	3×10^{-5}

significant risk rules. For example, occupational risks tend to be somewhat higher than that for the general population, and these higher levels may be more acceptable in the occupational context. As I have previously indicated:

Choice of occupation has at least some voluntary component, unlike general environmental exposures. Second, comparative risk is important in determining acceptable risk, and the inherently dangerous nature of some jobs raises the average risk level appropriately addressed by regulators. Third, workers in relatively risky occupations may demand wage premiums to compensate at least partially for increased workplace risk levels.[13]

For these reasons, a higher threshold of significant risk may apply to occupational risks of cancer. Other circumstances may also be relevant. Even low average levels of risk from a substance may be unacceptable if the exposed population is very large and the total number of cancer deaths is relatively high.

In short, utilization of the significant risk paradigm for carcinogen regulation requires a series of judgments regarding risk acceptability. In large part, though, these or similar judgments must be made every time an agency evaluates a carcinogen for regulation. The significant risk paradigm has the benefit of making the judgments public and subject to review and debate.

Overview of Significant Risk

The significant risk paradigm offers some distinct advantages for carcinogen regulation. This approach acknowledges the impossibility of zero risk and honestly confronts the necessary choices regarding which risks to regulate. By focusing regulation on the most substantial carcinogenic hazards, the significant risk paradigm may also effect more public health protection than alternative approaches, including the zero risk paradigm.

Reliance on significant risk cutoff levels faces some serious problems, however. The significant risk paradigm demands precision from the unavoidably imprecise science of quantitative risk assessment. Even the best risk assessment procedures may yield results that vary by a factor of 1,000 or more. The significant risk paradigm largely ignores this uncertainty, however. Suppose an agency chooses not to regulate a substance because risk assessment places its risk at 1 in 1,000,000. If this risk assessment is off by a factor of 100, the true risk could be 1 in 10,000, which is clearly a significant risk worthy of regulation. This danger of underregulation may be overcome, of course, by using the most conservative risk assessment estimates. This conservative course undermines much of the benefit of significant risk, however, as agencies may focus on regulating activities that present very little actual risk.

The inherent uncertainty of quantitative risk assessment is compounded by uncertainties surrounding the proper level of risk significance, the proper currency for risk evaluation, and the other factors to be considered under the significant risk paradigm. The approach has undeniable merit, but sole dependence on the significant risk paradigm relies too heavily on uncertainty and unprovable assumptions.

COST/BENEFIT ANALYSIS

Few if any risk management approaches are more controversial than cost/benefit analysis. Supporters contend that cost/benefit analysis is the only sensible approach to regulation. Detractors consider cost/benefit analysis tantamount to selling human life.

Much of this dispute is definitional. A myriad of differing balancing approaches are included in the term cost/benefit analysis. At one end of the spectrum is a mechanistic procedure whereby all costs of regulation are monetized, all benefits are assigned specific monetary value, and the two are compared. This approach reduces decisions to an economic equation. At the other end of the spectrum is a loose approach in which all costs are considered and all benefits are listed but not necessarily monetized. Then the decisionmaker uses some policy judgment to decide whether the benefits of regulation justify the costs. Between these two extremes are procedures employing incremental degrees of economic monetization. Placing all costs and benefits in a single currency (usually dollars) facilitates cost/benefit decisionmaking. In this way there is no need to "compare apples and oranges." To some, however, translating all values into dollars in itself distorts the regulatory process and oversimplifies public health regulation. Apples and oranges can be compared for certain purposes.

Any of the above approaches could be called cost/benefit analysis. At minimum, cost/benefit analysis implies a consideration of the advantages of regulation (the "benefits"), a consideration of any disadvantages of regulation (the "costs"), and a comparison of both. The objective of the decisionmaker is to ensure that the advantages of regulation outweigh the disadvantages.

Some commentators have suggested that all decisions are grounded in cost/benefit analysis. Supreme Court Justice Byron White commented: "Whether or not you're going to play an extra rubber of bridge, you weigh the pleasure of playing an extra rubber of bridge with the loss of sleep that's going to be incurred. Every decision that's made is a cost-benefit decision, is it not? Every rational decision?"[14] Such a broad conception, however, destroys all meaning of the term cost/benefit analysis. The general understanding of cost/benefit policy analysis includes an identification of all costs and benefits and at least some attempt to quantify the costs and benefits in a common currency, for purposes of their comparison.

In use, cost/benefit analysis takes different forms, and commentators who analyze the procedure may assume different types of cost/benefit analysis. Nevertheless, some commonality may be found. Many of the fundamental ethical and practical issues surrounding cost/benefit analysis do not distinguish between varying approaches.

The Ethics of Cost/Benefit Analysis

Critics of cost/benefit analysis have focused much of their attack on the alleged immorality of the procedure. This attack subsumes and goes beyond the ethical critique of the significant risk paradigm. All the criticisms of significant-risk-based decisionmaking and its acceptance of some human death and suffering apply to cost/benefit analysis as well. In addition, cost/benefit analysis suggests that even more substantial death and suffering may be justified by counterbalancing costs of preventing such consequences.

The best-known attack on the ethics of cost/benefit analysis was presented by Steven Kelman of Harvard's Kennedy School of Government.[15] The attack begins by observing that cost/benefit analysis relies upon a utilitarian philosophical perspective, assuming that we should be guided solely by the practical consequences of our actions. Kelman then persuasively notes that utilitarianism is an incomplete moral philosophy, in that it fails to recognize certain *a priori* moral obligations of persons. Honesty, for example, may be a moral duty even when it fails a cost/benefit test in application.

Cost/benefit analysis does not claim to be a complete philosophy, however, but merely a tool for decisionmaking. Demonstrating the immorality of cost/benefit analysis requires some indication of how the procedure is likely to violate *a priori* moral obligations in actual practice. Kelman particularly objects to the need for cost/benefit analysis to place some monetary value on human life, thereby demeaning human life. In the circumstance of carcinogen regulation, the primary benefit of regulation is saving lives, and placing a monetary equivalent value on human life is unavoidable.

The concept of monetizing human life is intuitively troubling. Life has some sacred character that seems beyond valuation. Kelman further fears that the very effort of placing monetary values on life will ineluctably reduce the ultimate perceived value of life and devalue life itself. Some things, such as friendship or life, may be valuable precisely because they cannot be bought. The ultimate value of life may be affirmed by saying that it is "not for sale," or priceless. Putting a price upon life may therefore facilitate a justification for taking life in any number of circumstances.

This ethical attack on cost/benefit analysis is compelling in the abstract. Yet as for so many other appealing theories, the problematic facts of cancer and its causation disrupt the analysis. The zero risk paradigm is unacceptable and would likely increase overall human suffering. Thus, society *must* accept some level of environmentally caused cancer and loss of human life. The absolute devotion to the sanctity of human life could succeed in a world without trade-offs. Such a world does not exist, however. The contractarian analysis described in the preceding discussion of significant risk can explain the justification for making the unavoidable trade-off, if some justification is even required.

Proponents of cost/benefit analysis respond to Kelman that some implicit economic valuation of human life occurs every time government regulates. Once some level of risk and some mortality is accepted by government, life is *de facto* valued. Cost/benefit analysis is simply a tool for making explicit the valuation.

Kelman anticipates this rejoinder and draws a distinction between the reasoning processes used to reach a regulatory decision. In the implicit *de facto* valuation without cost/benefit analysis, the valuation is a consequence of regulation, but not necessarily an input driving regulatory results. Under cost/benefit analysis, the explicit valuation helps determine the regulatory results, thereby assuming greater prominence. It is this expanded role for life valuation that Kelman finds objectionable.

This extension of the ethical attack on cost/benefit analysis is unsupportable. Indeed, Kelman assumes a surprising degree of ignorance on the part of government regulators and the public. Surely these actors are aware that they are placing an implicit value on human life every time that they accept some level of mortality. These people must know that they are actively trading off the risk of death against economic consequences. They are just being secretive about it. What's more, there is a distinct risk that the *ad hoc* implicit valuation of life will be inconsistent and may undervalue life. The greater rigor demanded by cost/benefit analysis could easily lead to a higher valuation of life than that provided by *de facto* regulation. This benefit is empirically demonstrable:

Through the early 1980s the Federal Highway Administration (FHWA) and most of its state counterparts employed a figure of around $200,000 for the benefit of preventing a highway fatality.... A good deal of the credit for the FHWA's recent adoption of higher values goes to economists, who pointed out the findings of more recent human capital studies as well as the [willingness-to-pay] literature. In this case, explicit analytic focus on the value of death prevention led to higher values being used.[16]

Exposing the valuative process to the light of public and congressional scrutiny could be a useful method to ensure that co-opted regulators do not undervalue life. At minimum, the process becomes more honest as regulators admit that they must somehow value the risk of death.

This is not to absolve cost/benefit analysis of all ethical shortcomings. Use of the cost/benefit paradigm involves risks that distribution concerns, individual human rights, and other moral values may be overlooked. Theoretically, though, cost/benefit analysis can encompass these values and consider them. Alternatives to cost/benefit analysis may be more likely to overlook important values. James T. Campen, a progressive advocate of cost/benefit analysis, argued that "[w]hen decision problems are approached rationally and systematically, when attempts are made to identify all of the consequences of the alternatives under review and to quantify the value of these effects as much as can reasonably be done, it is much more likely that no important features of a problem will be overlooked."[17] The potential ethical problem with cost/benefit analysis is much more practical than abstract. Cost/benefit analysis is neither inherently ethical nor inherently unethical. Only after examining the operation of cost/benefit analysis in practice can its ethics and effectiveness be settled.

Uncertainty and Cost/Benefit Analysis

The uncertainty plaguing the significant risk paradigm applies with even greater force to cost/benefit analysis. All approaches to cost/benefit analysis require a comparison and weighting of the costs and benefits of regulation. This process in turn requires the prior measurement of the costs and benefits. Uncertain, inaccurate measurement can destroy the effective operation of cost/benefit analysis.

The benefits to carcinogen regulation will be predominantly in the form of reduced morbidity and mortality. Quantitative risk assessment is required to determine the extent of morbidity and mortality reduction accomplished by any proposed regulation. As shown above, considerable uncertainty infects quantitative risk assessment, and this uncertainty carries over into benefits measurement in the cost/benefit paradigm.

The uncertainty of cost/benefit analysis goes far beyond this inherent uncertainty in risk assessment, however. After health benefits have been estimated, the decisionmaker must then value those health benefits. If valuation assumes monetary terms, a decisionmaker must adopt some dollar value for deaths and disease avoided. There are several established economic methods for valuing such health benefits, but none is universally accepted, and all yield different results. For example, the value of a life has been measured by means of popular surveys, future earnings potential, and tests of risk-taking behavior. The choice among these measurement tools is debatable. Uncertain valuation of benefits adds a second level of uncertainty to cost/benefit analysis.

Measuring the cost side of the equation compounds the overall uncertainty of cost/benefit analysis. Measuring the costs of regulatory action is surely more precise than quantitative risk assessment but is nevertheless somewhat uncertain. Current estimates of the overall cost of past environmental and occupational safety regulation range from virtually zero to upwards of $100 billion. Estimating the cost of future proposed carcinogen control regulations will be no more certain. Furthermore, such regulation may be "technology forcing," requiring the development of new control technologies to achieve emissions limitations. Assessing the costs of any such future technology is unavoidably speculative. Economic tools also have difficulty estimating the significance of indirect secondary costs of regulation, such as reduced innovation and productivity.

The substantial uncertainty attendant to cost/benefit analysis undermines much of the procedure's potential value. Ideally, a cost/benefit analysis will inform regulators of the net advantages or disadvantages of a proposed regulatory action. With the benefit of such analysis, a policymaker may confine his or her regulatory actions to those found to produce net advantages. Yet both sides of the cost/benefit equation are subject to great uncertainty, and the true value of each factor may vary several-fold from that estimated in the analysis. Obviously, the net results of the analysis will be correspondingly skewed, and beneficial programs may appear disadvantageous, or vice versa. If the costs or benefits of an analyzed action are grossly disproportionate to each other, the technique may provide reliable guidance. Otherwise, the perceived net advantages or disadvantages of proposed carcinogen regulation may simply be artifacts of imprecise measurement. Given current uncertainty, any results of cost/benefit analysis are necessarily somewhat arbitrary.

Complete cost/benefit analysis is even more complex. Rather than simply analyzing the overall net benefits of a given proposal, regulators ideally should evaluate the marginal net benefits as compared with incremental changes in the proposal or entirely different proposals. This marginal analysis requires additional uncertain data and further complicates optimal use of the cost/benefit paradigm.

The seeming arbitrariness of cost/benefit analysis, however, may simply reflect the inherently arbitrary process of valuation. A critic of overreliance on cost/benefit analysis has thus noted that "[d]espite its conceptual and practical frailties, cost-benefit analysis begins to look better when compared to the obvious alternatives."[18] The cost/benefit paradigm may simply expose hidden arbitrariness, not increase it. As expressed by Dr. Aaron Wildavsky of California, "better a flawed economics than a bogus politics."[19]

Economic Benefits Valuation

Attempts to quantify the economic value of such benefits as human life and environmental protection are inherently uncertain and arguably unethical, as discussed in the preceding sections. Some critics of cost/benefit analysis would go further and contend that meaningful economic valuation of these benefits is impossible. If true, this criticism would render any cost/benefit analysis of carcinogen regulation largely meaningless. In practice, a survey of fifteen major Environmental Protection Agency cost/benefit analyses in the 1980s revealed that benefits could be monetized in only six instances.[20]

The primary benefit of carcinogen regulation is reduced mortality, requiring monetary valuation of life savings for cost/benefit analysis. Economists suggest various approaches to valuation of life-saving actions. One traditional approach used discounted future earnings, the future wages lost by mortality. In this application, benefit valuation adopts questionable ethical principles by reducing human value to a person's work product, as measured by a capitalist system. This measure would consider a chief executive officer far more "valuable" than a custodian. Retired persons would be functionally valueless. Our basic philosophical understanding of human value, however, directs that persons have some worth beyond their work.

Recently, greater emphasis has been placed upon a "willingness-to-pay" measure of life valuation. This procedure observes human behavior and its willingness to assume risks to life in exchange for monetary compensation. For example, workers accept relatively high-risk occupations in exchange for higher wages. Using this approach yields an approximate average value of $1 million per life, although some estimates range as high as $10 million per life. Exhibit 4-2 lists some proposed valuations for loss of human life, both from economic studies and in regulatory practice.

Willingness-to-pay valuation and surveys described in exhibit 4-2 are certainly more acceptable than discounted future earnings, but these approaches still have their critics. Different people clearly place widely disparate values on life, and the avoidance of differing types of death may be valued differently. Many critics argue that a private, individual valuation, as measured by risk taking, is a poor proxy for universal public valuation of life saving. A person may be cavalier with his or her own life, yet support more cautious societal action. Individuals are clearly more comfortable with voluntary risks, and altruism may cause persons to value others' lives more than their own. Environmental protection legislation itself obviously reflects public values that are distinct from private preferences expressed in the marketplace. Economic models are still struggling to come to grips with these psychological attitudes, and one recent survey found that altruistic valuation could be quite substantial.[21]

Economic benefits valuation of human life may thus rest upon inadequate tools and inaccurate assumptions. Even acknowledging this point, attempts at valuation may be superior to any alternatives. As previously suggested, some implicit valuation of life by regulators is inevitable. As long as the valuation remains implicit and largely unanalyzed, however, life may be effectively undervalued. Empirical analysis confirms the inconsistency of implicit valuation. The Federal Aviation Administration and the

Exhibit 4-2
Valuation of Loss of Human Life

Source	Value
Blomquist (based on consumer studies)	$600,000
Viscusi (based on worker studies)	$3,500,000
Dillingham (based on worker studies)	$2,200,000
Gegax (based on worker studies)	$1,600,000
Jones-Lee (based on questionnaires)	$3,100,000
OSHA construction safety standard	$3,500,000
Office of Management and Budget	$1,000,000
CPSC flammability study	$1,000,000
Department of Transportation guidelines	$360,000
EPA benzene air emissions standard	$7,600,000

National Highway Traffic Safety Administration, for example, have implicitly valued life savings at $500,000, or even less. Within these agencies, more explicit economic benefits valuation would produce regulation that was more protective of human life. In any event, explicit valuation makes regulatory action more accountable to democratically expressed public preferences.

Even if human life valuation is well conducted, other benefits may be difficult to identify, much less value monetarily. Nicholas Ashford of MIT fears cost/benefit analysis will never be able to consider indirect benefits "derived from the pressure of regulation to induce industry to deal preventively with unregulated hazards, to innovate, and to find ways to meet the public's need for a cleaner, healthier environment while maintaining industrial capacity."[22] In truth, valuation of this form of derived benefit currently seems impossible, which may destroy the rigor offered by cost/benefit analysis.

Potential Abuse

Much criticism of cost/benefit analysis ultimately rests upon the apprehension that the process will be abused by empowered interests to avoid regulation through data manipulation. Even a vigorous defender of cost/benefit analysis has conceded that the procedure "is one of the techniques most prone to misunderstanding and misapplication in the hands of the uninitiated (not to mention the unscrupulous!)"[23] In practice, cost/benefit analysis has been required for approval of water supply construction projects, and analysis has frequently been manipulated to justify unnecessary projects. Similarly, reviewing courts have suggested that the National Highway Traffic Safety Administration "doctored" its cost/benefit analysis of installing air bags in automobiles, in order to avoid imposing costs on the automobile industry.

To many environmentalists, the cost/benefit paradigm is simply a ruse to avoid regulation. Arguably, "cost-benefit analysis is [merely] a 'numbers game' used to oppose regulations."[24] In view of the unavoidable uncertainty involved in cost and benefit measurement, regulatory critics can find it quite simple to dejustify virtually any proposed government action through the use of various different but plausible assumptions.

Even conscientious regulators may have difficulty conducting an unbiased cost/benefit analysis. Agencies occasionally have conceded that the industry to be regulated may have a virtual monopoly of information about pollution control technologies suitable to its facilities. This industry has an apparent self-interest in overstating costs and understating reliability and benefits of these controls. Experience has shown that pollution control costs may turn out to be much less than industrial sources had predicted. An Environmental Protection Agency study of predicted and actual compliance costs found that government cost estimates were invariably lower than industry cost estimates, but that government estimates have overstated actual compliance costs by 20 to 156 percent.[25] Available compliance cost assessment procedures thus may contain an inherent bias toward overestimation of these costs.

Indeed, the very act of conducting a cost/benefit analysis may forestall necessary regulations. In-depth analysis requires considerable study and time. Even after such analysis is complete, opponents may criticize various assumptions and demand that the cost/benefit analysis be redone. This procedure soon leads to "paralysis by analysis." William Rodgers, a professor of law at the University of Washington, argued that the "insatiable pursuit of data also facilitates delay and the avoidance of controversy; any decision dependent upon extensive data-gathering promises to be long in incubation and short on results and controversy."[26] Reliance on a cost/benefit analysis may thus contribute to a delaying strategy by industry or other opponents of carcinogen regulation.

Cost/benefit analysis may also be misused by pro-regulatory forces. Valuation of nonmonetary benefits inevitably contains a large potential "fudge factor." Dr. Aaron Wildavsky has observed that in some past analyses "intangibles like recreation values were credited with increasingly large shares of the benefits, thus representing a 'finagle' factor that could be enlarged almost at will to provide justification" for pro-environmental action.[27]

Cost/benefit analysis undoubtedly has been abused and distorted. Yet this criticism is hardly unique to the cost/benefit paradigm. Virtually any method for managing risk is subject to abuse, but this potential cannot justify rejection of the method itself. Judicial review of regulation and the threat of court action is almost certainly the greatest source of delayed or frustrated carcinogen regulation, and few would suggest the elimination of court review on these grounds. Ideally, regulators would choose the optimal risk management method and then strive to purge that method of potential for abuse, insofar as possible.

Overview of Cost/Benefit Analysis

Reliance on cost/benefit analysis has serious shortcomings, particularly resulting from the uncertainty of measurement of costs and benefits, which may lead to abuse or inaccurate calculations of societal interest in regulation. The cost/benefit paradigm nevertheless has some value in regulation. Only this approach recognizes the full range of implications that may result from government control of carcinogens. And regardless of whether cost considerations should drive policy decisions, most citizens would consider costs or other disadvantages to regulation to be a relevant concern of government.

Like risk assessment, the real issue concerning cost/benefit analysis involves the use to which the procedure is put. Proponents might argue that cost/benefit analysis should be outcome-determinative, directing regulatory decisionmaking. The process remains too uncertain, however, to produce such conclusive results. Cost/benefit analysis may yet have some benefit, though, as an information resource. Even fervent critics of cost/benefit analysis may concede that the procedure "may play a useful role in supplementing or informing political decision making."[28] Cost/benefit analysis may, for example, reveal less costly methods for achieving the same benefits or may identify consequences of regulation that might otherwise be ignored. In this role, cost/benefit analysis may still be helpful in carcinogen regulation. This role has been propounded by the National Research Council of the National Academy of Sciences, which concluded:

Benefit-cost analysis . . . is not a rule or formula which would make the decision or predetermine the choice for the decision maker. Rather, it refers to the systematic analysis and evaluation of alternative courses of action drawing upon the analytic tools and insights provided by economics and decision theory. It is a framework and a set of procedures to help organize the available information display trade-offs, and point out uncertainties.[29]

In this schema, cost/benefit analysis is simply a procedure to identify the consequences of regulation, and might more properly be called regulatory impact analysis. The General Accounting Office concluded that cost/benefit analysis can "be useful in making the most out of limited information" and "reduce although not eliminate the guesswork in environmental rulemaking."[30] Ultimately, cost/benefit analysis must be tested in application.

FEASIBILITY ANALYSIS

A fourth approach to carcinogen risk management is feasibility analysis. This approach has the government mandate whatever technical controls are currently feasible. As defined by the Supreme Court, feasible means "capable of being done, executed, or effected."[31] The feasibility paradigm has government require the use of available, effective technology to reduce exposure to carcinogens as far as reasonably possible. When the government elects to regulate a particular substance, the regulators need only identify the best available control technology and require its use.

The concept of feasibility initially seems a simple one that only requires a review of technological control options. Unfortunately, defining feasibility is actually more complex than this superficial concept. The Harvard Scientific Conflict Mapping Project observed:

The operational meaning of [feasibility] for the practice of standard setting is not obvious. One view is that there never really is a lowest-feasible standard; there are only successively more stringent and expensive emission or exposure limits. What is feasible in the future is itself a function of how much manpower and resources are devoted to the R&D function. The concept of technical feasibility might reduce, in the final analysis, to the amount of resources invested to modify existing production processes or invent and deploy new ones. At some point, an infeasibility judgment may embody implicit assumptions about the incremental benefits and costs of more stringent chemical exposure limitations.[32]

The "feasible" level of carcinogen control thus only has meaning in terms of some defined amount of resources that may be devoted to such control. In application, however, feasibility analysis has not been so complex. If a technology has been demonstrated, it is feasible, according to the courts. Courts have found no need to engage in sweeping analyses of speculative future developments in carcinogen control.

The cost of controls, does, however, play a role in determining whether those controls may be considered feasible. What if a technologically feasible device exists to reduce emissions, but that device is so expensive that its use will bankrupt any company that installs it? Courts have interpreted feasibility to include economic feasibility. If regulations require otherwise technologically feasible controls that would bankrupt an entire industry, those rules may be considered economically infeasible. Costs do not play a central role under feasibility analysis, however. A court interpreting "feasible" under the Occupational Safety and Health Act thus ruled:

Standards may be economically feasible even though, from the standpoint of employers, they are financially burdensome and affect profit margins adversely. Nor does the concept of economic feasibility guarantee the continued existence of individual employers.[33]

Only when a proposed regulation imposes extraordinary costs that would close down an entire industry will that proposal violate the tenets of feasibility analysis.

Feasibility analysis has some comparative advantages over other risk management paradigms. Unlike the zero risk paradigm, feasibility analysis does not demand the impossible, nor does it compel the destruction of the United States economy. Feasibility analysis is also more certain than the significant risk or cost/benefit paradigms, because feasibility analysis avoids the uncertainty inherent in risk assessment or valuation. No risk assessment is necessary if government simply does everything possible to reduce risk. Indeed, the uncertainty surrounding these measurements is so great that regulators arguably should do everything possible to reduce the risk from carcinogens. Feasibility analysis also avoids the ethical concerns of significant risk or cost/benefit analysis, by neither accepting nor valuing the loss of human life, when such a consequence can be feasibly averted.

Irrationality

Particularly to academics, feasibility analysis may seem painfully irrational. The paradigm simply fails to incorporate essential considerations. For example, feasibility analysis avoids the uncertainty of risk assessment only by ignoring the magnitude of a risk. Yet the significance of a carcinogenic risk is central to public health protection. Critics question the rationality of a paradigm that ignores such a central concern.

Imagine, for example, the existence of a substance that presents a severe risk of cancer to the American population. Further imagine that this substance is of very little benefit to the nation. Rational decisionmakers might choose to ban the production and use of this substance altogether. Yet feasibility analysis automatically rejects the prohibition option. The feasibility paradigm could only require the installation of the best available controls to prevent exposure to the substance. If a significant residual risk remained, even after application of such controls, feasibility analysis would permit no more public health protection.

Feasibility analysis also fails to consider the cost of controlling exposure to carcinogens, except in the extreme and unusual case of economic infeasibility. The failure to consider costs may also breed irrational policy decisions. Feasibility analysis could impose very high costs in the form of mandated new technology to control a substance that presents very little hazard to the public health. By diverting costs from other, more beneficial control programs, this feature of feasibility analysis may also undermine maximum protection of public health from carcinogens in the environment.

The economic irrationality of complete reliance upon a feasibility paradigm was recently highlighted by Daniel Byrd and Lester Lave, who commented:

> The standard of economic *feasibility* for OSHA that was upheld by the Supreme Court in the cotton dust case is that an entire industry cannot be eliminated, but a few participants can be put out of business. The first standard would bankrupt the weakest firms, the second the next weakest firms, and so on, until enough standards had been promulgated to eliminate most firms. Clearly, any single-minded pursuit of the notion that risks are to be lowered to the extent economically feasible would impoverish the nation, with each industry pushed to the edge of bankruptcy (assuming an agency did its economic feasibility analysis accurately). More important, a well-informed OSHA would remove any "surplus profit" in its first few regulations and leave the firms with no resources to tackle later, possibly more difficult, problems as they were discovered.[34]

Carcinogen regulation is not so pervasive as to create such a scenario at the present time. Nevertheless, the illustration demonstrates that complete reliance on feasibility analysis is logically unsound. The failure to even consider relative risks and costs intuitively makes little sense in carcinogen regulation.

The limited role played by cost considerations in feasibility analysis may itself be questioned. Under current standards of economic feasibility, the degree of carcinogen control may depend on the profitability of the industry being regulated. If government is regulating a marginally profitable industry, few actions may be economically feasible and "few emissions will be abated."[35] Ultimately, feasibility analysis holds public health protection hostage to industrial profitability.

OVERVIEW OF RISK MANAGEMENT

No single risk management approach is clearly preferable for carcinogen regulation. The four approaches discussed above rely on different value systems that would probably stymie any consensus in any public health program. The risk management problem is complicated, however, by the special features of carcinogens. The lack of any demonstrable safe threshold for carcinogens and the economically essential role played by many carcinogens make trade-offs inevitable. Trade-offs require compromise, however, and interested parties have often been reluctant to compromise their objectives in furtherance of a mutually acceptable carcinogen control policy.

The carcinogen risk management dilemma is not one that can be settled scientifically, or even logically. Logic, however, can contribute to a decision. The zero risk paradigm, for example, requires such radical action that its noble effort to avoid all risk could be counterproductive and undermine human health and welfare. Zero risk may be accepted as an ultimate utopian goal of regulation but must be rejected as a practical risk management tool in the near term.

The remaining paradigms (significant risk, cost/benefit, and feasibility analysis) each have their advantages and each have their advocates. Each paradigm has found its way into different carcinogen control statutes. Yet each paradigm seems insufficient by itself. Significant risk and cost/benefit analysis are too dependent upon an uncertain foundation of data. Significant risk and feasibility analysis seem incomplete, because they take no cognizance of control costs. It is precisely this cost consideration, however, that creates opposition to cost/benefit analysis, which seems to rely too heavily on control costs.

The difficulty in selecting a risk management paradigm is largely due to a tendency to view the different approaches in isolation and to consider each in an abstract, philosophical manner. The best answer for carcinogen risk management may involve some combination of paradigms. And finding this best answer is more empirical than abstract. The more abstract ethical concerns are surely appropriate for government consideration, but these concerns should not be permitted to subvert effective carcinogen regulation, which is itself a primary ethical objective. The following chapter on regulatory practice provides some empirical information on the various systems of risk management for carcinogens.

NOTES

1. E.A. Crouch, J. Feller, M. Fiering, E. Hakanoglu, R. Wilson, and L. Zeise, Energy and Environmental Policy Center. Harvard University. Prepared for the U.S. Dept. of Energy.

2. Aaron Wildavsky, *Searching for Safety* (London: Transaction Books, 1988): 48–50.

3. Richard Schwing, "Trade-Offs." In *Societal Risk Assessment*, ed. R. Schwing and W. Albers (New York: Plenum, 1980), 140.

4. Industrial Union Department, AFL-CIO v. American Petroleum Institute, 448 U.S. 607, 664 (Burger, J., concurring).

5. Bruce Ames, *Cancer Scares Over Trivia: Natural Carcinogens in Food Outweigh Traces in Our Water.* Quoted in Wildavsky, *Searching for Safety,* 50.

6. R. Albert, "Federal Regulatory Agency Approaches to the Assessment and Control of Risk from Carcinogens." In *Perceptions of Risk: Proceedings of the Fifteenth Annual Meeting of the National Council on Radiation Protection* (1979), 12.

7. 448 U.S. 607 (1980).

8. Id., 644.

9. Id., 688.

10. Frank Grad, *Risk Assessment and the Tyranny of Numbers: A Brief Comment,* 1 ENVTL. LAW AND LITIG. 1, 10 (1986).

11. Natural Resources Defense Council. *Comments on the Proposed Withdrawal of Proposed Standards for Benzene Emissions* (April 13, 1984), 13.

12. Paul Milvy, "A General Guideline for Management of Risk from Carcinogens," *Risk Analysis* 6 (1986): 70.

13. Frank Cross, *Beyond Benzene: Establishing Principles for a Significance Threshold on Regulatable Risks of Cancer,* 35 EMORY L. J. 1, 48–49 (1986).

14. Quoted in Marguerite Connerton and Mark MacCarthy, *Cost-Benefit Analysis and Regulation: Expressway to Reform or Blind Alley?,* National Policy Paper No. 4 (October 1982), 9.

15. Steven Kelman, "Cost Benefit Analysis: An Ethical Critique," *Regulation,* (January–February 1981): 33.

16. John Mendeloff, *The Dilemma of Toxic Substance Regulation* (Cambridge, Mass.: MIT PRess, 1988), 42.

17. James T. Campen, *Benefit, Cost, and Beyond* (Cambridge, Mass.: Ballinger, 1986), 81.

18. William Rodgers, *Benefits, Costs, and Risks: Oversight of Health and Environmental Decisionmaking,* 4 HARVARD ENV. L. REV. 191, 199 (1980).

19. Aaron Wildavsky, *Speaking Truth to Power: The Art and Craft of Policy Making* (London: Transaction Books, 1979), 156.

20. U.S. Environmental Protection Agency, *EPA'S Use of Benefit-Cost Analysis: 1981–1986* (August 1987), 4.

21. W. Kip Viscusi, Wesley Magat and Anne Forrest, "Altruistic and Private Valuations of Risk Reduction," *Journal of Policy Analysis & Management* 7 (1988): 227.

22. Nicholas Ashford, "Alternatives to Cost-Benefit Analysis in Regulatory Decisions," *Annals of N.Y. Academy of Sciences* 363 (1981): 129, 131–132.

23. Alan Williams, "Cost-Benefit Analysis: Bastard Science and/or Insidious Poison in the Body Politick?," *J. Pub. Econ.* 1 (August 1972): 199, 200.

24. Michael Baram, "The Use of Cost-Benefit Analysis in Regulatory Decision-Making is Proving Harmful to Public Health," *Annals of N.Y. Academy of Sciences* 363 (1981): 123.

25. Marguerite Connerton and Mark MacCarthy, 20.

26. Wm. Rodgers, 200.

27. Aaron Wildavsky, "Aesthetic Power or the Triumph of the Sensitive Minority Over the Vulgar Mass: A Political Analysis of the New Economics," *Daedalus* 96 (1967): 1115, 1116.

28. Mark Sagoff, *Economic Theory and Environmental Law*, 79 MICH. L. REV. 1393, 1409 (1981).

29. National Research Council, National Academy of Sciences, *Decision Making for Regulating Chemicals in the Environment* (1975), 39.

30. General Accounting Office, *Cost-Benefit Analysis Can Be Useful In Assessing Environmental Regulations, Despite Limitations* (April 6, 1984), 7.

31. American Textile Manufacturers Institute v. Donovan, 452 U.S. 490, 508–509 (1981).

32. John D. Graham, Laura Green and Mark J. Roberts, *Seeking Safety: Science, Public Policy and Cancer Risk* (to be published by Harvard Univ. Press).

33. Industrial Union Dep't, AFL-CIO v. Hodgson, 499 F.2d 467, 478 (D.C. Cir. 1974).

34. Daniel Byrd and Lester Lave, "Significant Risk Is Not the Antonym of De Minimis Risk." In *De Minimis Risk* (1987), 41–42.

35. Lester Lave, *The Strategy of Social Regulation* (Washington: Brookings Institution, 1981), 15.

5

FEDERAL EXPERIENCE IN CARCINOGEN REGULATION

Authority to regulate environmental carcinogens is spread widely throughout the federal government. Statutes have created regulatory authority correlative to different sources of exposure: the Occupational Safety and Health Administration regulates occupational exposures; the Food and Drug Administration regulates dietary exposures; the Environmental Protection Agency regulates most ambient environmental exposures; and so on.

Not only has the legislature provided separate agencies to regulate carcinogens, Congress also has established different standards for the differing agencies to utilize. Even a single agency, such as the EPA, may use very different standards to regulate different sources of environmental exposures to carcinogens. Given this background, it is unsurprising that the agencies have proceeded independently, with relatively little regard to the practice of other agencies that regulate carcinogens. Consequently federal agency policies have often been inconsistent, or even contradictory. This lack of integration in carcinogen regulation may have caused overall public health protection to suffer, but the history of contrasting approaches offers the opportunity to evaluate different standards empirically. Agency practice to date can be considered a broad experiment in conducting the undeniably difficult task of carcinogen regulation. This chapter briefly reviews the regulatory practice of the major federal agencies with authority to control carcinogens, as well as attempts to coordinate this practice among the various agencies.

OCCUPATIONAL SAFETY AND HEALTH ADMINISTRATION

OSHA has general authority to protect workers from threats to health, including carcinogens. The primary source of this authority is found in section 6(b) of the Occupational Safety and Health Act, which directs the agency to "set the standard which most adequately assures, to the extent feasible, on the basis of the best available evidence, that no employee will suffer material impairment of health or functional capacity even if such employee has regular exposure to the hazard dealt with by such standard for the period of his working life."[1] In addition, section 3(8) of the Act provides that a health standard is one that imposes requirements that are "reasonably necessary or appropriate to provide safe or healthful employment and places of employment."[2]

Congress created OSHA in 1968, and the agency initially focused upon accidents and other threats to worker safety, rather than worker health. While OSHA adopted existing industry consensus standards for 400 substances under expedited procedures, the agency's first attempt to regulate a substance as a carcinogen occurred in 1972, when it issued a standard for workplace exposures to asbestos. Even at that time, asbestos was widely acknowledged to be a carcinogen that presented a substantial hazard at some prevailing levels. OSHA conducted no quantitative risk assessment for asbestos and adopted a standard that allowed a maximum of five fibers per milliliter of air, averaged over an eight-hour workday.[3] The rule was accompanied by very little explanation, but presumably the standard was the lowest level to which asbestos could be feasibly controlled at that time. Industry unsuccessfully contested the lawfulness of the new asbestos rule.[4] The process of setting this standard consumed approximately twenty-nine months.

OSHA's carcinogen control efforts are supported by the National Institute for Occupational Safety and Health (NIOSH), a research agency that supports epidemiologic and toxicologic research and that recommends action to OSHA. Based on NIOSH data, the agency enacted an emergency temporary standard for fourteen carcinogens in May 1973.[5] Of these, three were identified as carcinogens based on epidemiologic evidence in exposed workers, and eleven were identified based on extensive testing in animals. The emergency standard was contested in court and overturned.[6] The court ruled that emergency standards should be reserved for exceptional hazards and emphasized that the government had relied almost exclusively on animal data without evidence of human carcinogenicity. OSHA then acted relatively quickly and promulgated permanent standards for the fourteen substances in January 1974.[7] The permanent standard was challenged by both industry and labor organizations in two separate actions and ultimately upheld in 1975.[8] Once again, the agency conducted no quantitative risk assessment and failed to explain the basis for its control standards. Completion of the fourteen carcinogens standard, including judicial review, consumed forty months.

Also in 1974, a B. F. Goodrich plant in Kentucky announced that four of its workers had recently died of liver cancer, which is relatively rare. This plant produced products from vinyl chloride, a common constituent in construction and packaging materials. OSHA responded with an emergency temporary standard in April allowing a maximum of 50 parts per million and a final permanent standard in October 1974 allowing only one part per million. The lower permanent standard was set at the lowest level that industry could feasibly meet. No quantitative risk assessment was done, but animal studies had found statistically significant increases in liver cancer even at 50 parts per million. Industry challenged the vinyl chloride standard as infeasible, and labor unions challenged the standard as too lenient, but the reviewing court upheld OSHA.[10] The entire process of vinyl chloride regulation took only fifteen months.

OSHA's next carcinogen standard addressed emissions from coke ovens, based on both human and animal studies. Hearings on coke ovens were first held in 1974, a proposed rule was published in 1975, and the final standard was promulgated in October 1976. OSHA also broke with precedent and for the first time conducted a quantitative risk assessment to justify the rule. The risk assessment revealed an average cancer risk of nearly 1 in 100 (1×10^{-2}).[11] This rule also survived a court challenge by industry and labor organizations.[12] The coke ovens standard took twenty-six months at OSHA and eighteen more months in judicial review.

OSHA had also published an advance notice of proposed rulemaking to control occupational exposures to carcinogenic inorganic arsenic in 1974.[13] OSHA published a proposed standard for inorganic arsenic exposures in 1975,[14] but regulatory consideration dragged through the end of the Ford Administration. A final standard was not promulgated until May 1978,[15] nearly four years after the first announcement, not even counting judicial review time.

No further occupational standards for carcinogens were set by 1977, which saw the inauguration of President Jimmy Carter. President Carter was highly committed to occupational safety and health, and he appointed Eula Bingham as OSHA administrator. Ms. Bingham determined to redirect OSHA toward more emphasis on health standards in general and carcinogen control in particular. Bingham was responding to criticism of OSHA under Presidents Nixon and Ford for "its slow pace of rule making on major health hazards, especially occupational carcinogens."[16] NIOSH had identified dozens of occupational carcinogens against which the agency had taken no action.

OSHA under the Carter administration adopted a new strategy for regulating occupational carcinogens. The agency proposed a generic policy for all future carcinogen regulation. The expressed reason for the policy was to enable OSHA to identify and regulate carcinogens "in a relatively short period of time."[17] In form, OSHA's proposed generic cancer policy consisted of a series of scientific presumptions that OSHA adopted as "policy decisions." In operation, OSHA intended that positive results from NIOSH studies would be used to classify substances as "Category I" carcinogens, which in turn would prompt automatic regulation under a model standard contained in the cancer policy. The proposal eschewed any reliance on quantitative risk assessment and was based on the assumption that all carcinogens should be regulated to the limits of feasibility. The policy purposely left little room for scientific dispute or judgment and promised a quick, almost mechanistic procedure for regulation.

OSHA's proposed generic cancer policy became quite controversial. Virtually every interested party supported the concept of a generic policy, but industry in particular objected vigorously to the specific terms of the proposal. In particular, industry objected to the scientific presumptions that effectively prevented companies from introducing certain evidence of non-carcinogenicity. Industry also objected to the lack of any quantitative risk assessment provision in OSHA's cancer policy.

In an effort to make the policy binding on all future decisions, OSHA published the policy as a proposed rule in the *Federal Register* and conducted extensive public hearings on the proposal. These hearings took three years and consumed a vast amount of agency resources. This expenditure was justified in order that future rulemakings might be conducted "without rediscussing or relitigating, time and time again, the same issues and without unnecessarily draining limited industry, union, public interest, scientific and government resources."[18] OSHA's generic carcinogen policy was finally officially adopted in 1980, with very little change from the original proposal. Industry promptly challenged the terms of the policy in court.

In 1978, while OSHA's proposed cancer policy was undergoing hearings, the agency proposed and published a final standard for occupational exposures to benzene, which was shown to cause leukemia in humans.[19] Benzene was first identified as a carcinogen by NIOSH in 1974. The benzene standard was grounded largely in the policy decisions of the proposed cancer policy and was widely viewed as a test case of the policy. OSHA had the benefit of quantitative risk assessment for benzene but expressly declined to rely on this data in standard-setting. OSHA first issued an emergency temporary standard of one part per million, down from the prior national consensus standard of ten parts per million, but the emergency standard was vacated by a reviewing court. OSHA then promulgated a 1 ppm permanent standard. The benzene standard was adopted after roughly three years of inaction and one additional year of incubation in OSHA and was once again challenged by the regulated industry. The reviewing court vacated the benzene standard in 1978, primarily because OSHA had not conducted any form of cost/benefit analysis to justify the standard.[20]

OSHA promptly appealed the decision vacating its benzene standard to the Supreme Court, which accepted the case. The Court affirmed the decision vacating the benzene standard in 1980, but for a different reason than that given by the circuit court of appeals. The Supreme Court vacated the standard because OSHA did not prove that benzene represented a "significant health risk" to workers.[21] The Court held that OSHA could not regulate to create an "absolutely risk-free work place" but instead had to recognize that some risks were so insignificant that they did not warrant regulation under the Occupational Safety and Health Act.[22]

The Occupational Safety and Health Act clearly required feasibility analysis prior to imposing controls on workplace carcinogens. The Supreme Court's benzene decision also required that OSHA demonstrate a significant risk before commencing regulation. Now OSHA must fulfill both paradigms before acting against carcinogens.

Not only did the Supreme Court decision vacate OSHA's benzene standard, the Court also virtually required reliance on quantitative risk assessment and directly criticized OSHA's generic cancer policy. Key provisions of the policy were deleted by OSHA and the entire policy ultimately was suspended for reevaluation. OSHA's standard for inorganic arsenic, set in 1978, was also remanded back to the agency for reconsideration in light of the Supreme Court's decision.[23]

The only other occupational carcinogen standard set during the tenure of President Carter's administration was for acrylonitrile. In June 1977, OSHA first requested comments on acrylonitrile regulation based largely on epidemiologic data voluntarily submitted by industry, and the agency published an emergency temporary standard in January 1978.[24] Industry challenged the emergency standard, which was temporarily stayed by the reviewing court. After one month, new information from animal bioassays became available and supported OSHA's standard. The court lifted the stay, and industry did not pursue its challenge. A final permanent standard for acrylonitrile was published in October 1978,[25] and this rule was not challenged by industry.

Shortly after the Supreme Court's decision vacating the benzene standard, President Carter lost his bid for reelection. Although Carter's OSHA appointees came into office dedicated to protecting occupational health, they accomplished little. Eula Bingham's pro-worker approach was considered antagonistic by industry. Industry fought most of OSHA's efforts and was largely victorious. OSHA took final action on only three substances, and their action was largely ineffective for two of these substances (benzene and arsenic). The attempt to promulgate a generic carcinogen policy consumed much of OSHA's regulatory resources. The resultant policy was perceived as extreme by industry and the courts and these resources were functionally wasted. The Carter era at OSHA testifies for the proposition that even the best of intentions are insufficient to build an effective regulatory program for carcinogens.

President Carter was succeeded by President Reagan, who was publicly critical of much federal regulation, including that promulgated by OSHA. President Reagan espoused deregulation, and his appointees did not share the Carter administration's commitment to occupational carcinogen regulation. President Reagan appointed an industry official, Thorne Auchter, to head OSHA. Efforts to reinvigorate and repromulgate OSHA's generic carcinogen policy lay dormant. Lethargy appeared to characterize regulatory efforts. OSHA issued an advance notice of proposed rulemaking for occupational exposures to ethylene dibromide in 1981,[26] but no final rule has been issued for over six years.

Even under the Reagan administration, OSHA took some action against carcinogens. Initially, the agency was forced to repromulgate the standard for inorganic arsenic in a manner consistent with the Supreme Court's benzene decision. OSHA used quantitative risk assessment based upon conservative assumptions and concluded that the lifetime average risk for workers was 40 percent (4×10^{-1}).[27] This remarkably high level obviously presented a significant risk under the Supreme Court's standards. OSHA explained further that any risk that exceeded the average risk of death from other occupational sources should be considered significant enough for regulation. Consequently, the agency repromulgated its same standard for inorganic arsenic in 1983. Industry challenged the final rule for arsenic, but the court upheld OSHA in a decision issued in September 1984. This first effort to comply with the dictates of the Supreme Court benzene ruling required years to complete.

In 1975, OSHA had issued a proposed rule to lower the allowable workplace exposure to asbestos.[28] This proposal lay dormant until OSHA enacted an emergency temporary standard for asbestos in November 1983.[29] This standard was based on a quantitative risk assessment that showed that exposures at the then-existing standard would cause a 6×10^{-3} risk of cancer. The emergency standard was promptly vacated, however, in judicial review, for failure to establish a grave danger at the levels actually prevailing in workplaces. OSHA then initiated proceedings to establish a new permanent lower standard for occupational asbestos exposures. The final standard was adopted in July 1986.[30] Industry organizations attacked the rule largely on feasibility grounds, and unions sought a stricter rule, but a reviewing court upheld the primary requirements of the new standard.[31]

Evidence of the carcinogenicity of formaldehyde became well known in 1981, and unions pressured OSHA to initiate rulemaking to control exposures. Auchter largely disavowed OSHA's generic carcinogen policy and rejected any regulation of formaldehyde in 1982, but in 1984 a federal court ordered reconsideration of this decision. By this time, Robert Rowland was the new OSHA director, and he rejected an emergency temporary standard but initiated a rulemaking for a permanent standard in April 1985. Quantitative risk assessment indicated a risk of 7×10^{-4} at the then-prevailing national consensus standard. A final rule was promulgated in November 1987 and is currently being challenged in federal court. OSHA consideration of formaldehyde took more than five years, and the rulemaking itself consumed thirty-one months.

Also in 1983, public health organizations frustrated by OSHA inaction sued the agency to compel regulation of ethylene oxide. A federal district court directed OSHA to prepare rules for this substance, based upon a risk assessment showing a lifetime risk as high as 5×10^{-1}.[32] OSHA proposed a rule later that year, and in June 1984 OSHA enacted the final ethylene oxide standard, which set long-term maximum average exposure levels. By now, OSHA had largely forsaken the generic carcinogen policy, although the ethylene oxide regulation was based upon some of the same policy decisions about scientific evidence contained in the generic policy. This rule was adopted within fourteen months of the proposal, although evidence of carcinogenicity had been available for roughly five years before OSHA acted. After the rule's adoption, public health and industry representatives challenged the rule. The court upheld the OSHA requirements, and ordered the agency to go further and develop maximum short-term exposure limits as well.

In 1983, labor unions and public health groups petitioned OSHA to issue a new standard for workplace benzene exposures based on new epidemiologic evidence. OSHA stalled, and in December 1984 the steelworkers union asked a federal court to compel regulatory action. While the court was considering this request, OSHA initiated a new standard and in December 1985 proposed to reinstitute the one part per million exposure level from the original occupational benzene standard. This standard was promulgated as a final rule in September 1987.[33] The rule was based on quantitative risk assessments suggesting an average lifetime risk of approximately 1×10^{-3} at the 10 ppm standard then in effect. Promulgation of this standard took approximately fifty months from the time of the original union petition and twenty months from the date of the proposed rulemaking. Court review of this standard is still pending.

In June 1988, OSHA proposed a sweeping standard for "air contaminants," which set health standards for over 400 substances.[34] These standards were based on a wide range of adverse health effects, but seventeen substances were proposed for regulation because of their carcinogenicity. OSHA relied substantially upon quantitative risk assessment which revealed occupational lifetime risks in excess of 10^{-4} and much higher for some substances. Although the agency did not uniformly apply conservative assumptions in risk assessment, OSHA estimated that the proposed standard for only four of these substances would prevent over 5,000 cancer deaths.[35] While this recently proposed standard has not been finalized, much less survived court review, OSHA's approach here is especially promising for future carcinogen control.

Ironically, the Reagan administration was more effective in regulating more carcinogens than was the Carter administration. Concededly, Reagan's OSHA typically acted only after extensive prodding by unions and the courts. The Carter administration regulations also tended to be relatively stricter than those developed under Reagan. Nevertheless, OSHA has acted more often and has been less likely to have its rules overturned under judicial scrutiny. Nor has the demise of the generic cancer policy hampered regulation seriously. Rulemaking still takes years in most cases, but quantitative risk assessment has not delayed the process. Furthermore, risk assessment appears to have made OSHA's rules more defensible under review.

In sum, OSHA's carcinogen control policy has evolved over the years and through different political administrations. The Supreme Court benzene decision and the ill-fated effort to develop a generic carcinogen policy stalled regulation for years, but OSHA has adapted and developed a more effective carcinogen assessment and risk management program. Notwithstanding these advances, however, dozens of occupational carcinogens remain unregulated, and a large number of annual cancer deaths are still attributable to workplace exposures to hazardous chemicals. Much may rest on the fate of OSHA's proposed air contaminants standard.

ENVIRONMENTAL PROTECTION AGENCY

The Environmental Protection Agency administers a series of statutes that govern environmental hazards from carcinogens. Many of these statutes employ different standards for regulation and are administered by different divisions of EPA. Practice under the different sources of authority is now summarized.

Clean Air Act

Carcinogen regulation under the Clean Air Act takes place under section 112, governing hazardous air pollutants. Under this section, the administrator must first "list" a substance as a hazardous air pollutant. Then, within a year, the administrator is directed to prepare a National Emission Standard for Hazardous Air Pollutants (NESHAP). The administrator is to set the section 112 NESHAP "at the level which in his judgment provides an ample margin of safety to protect the public health."[36] The margin of safety language suggests a zero risk approach. EPA has struggled to apply this mandate to the unique circumstances of environmental carcinogens.

EPA's first NESHAP for a carcinogenic air pollutant was set in 1973 and controlled emissions of asbestos.[37] At this time, EPA declared it impossible to prepare a quantitative risk assessment for airborne asbestos exposures. The agency defined five major sources of asbestos that required control, but rejected a proposed ban on asbestos primarily for economic reasons. EPA gave no basis for its use of cost considerations under section 112, nor did the agency explain how continued emissions of carcinogenic asbestos could be squared with the mandate to provide a margin of safety.

The EPA adopted a similar approach in its next NESHAP, for vinyl chloride in 1975.[38] The administrator listed vinyl chloride based solely on a finding of carcinogenicity, without consideration of potency, exposure, or quantitative risk assessment. The listing was delayed for over a year, however, as the agency feared the adverse economic consequences of a NESHAP. After listing, EPA issued its NESHAP in October 1976, requiring certain emission control equipment and operations. David Doniger of the Natural Resources Defense Council noted that the "agency explicitly based the standard on a consideration of economic costs as well as health risks: EPA was determined to interpret section 112 to allow this result, apparently preferring a strained reading of the section to the imposition of a standard with what it viewed as unacceptably severe economic consequences."[39] The vinyl chloride standard is functionally based upon feasibility analysis, notwithstanding the language of section 112.

Shortly after the vinyl chloride NESHAP was promulgated, the Environmental Defense Fund (EDF) sued EPA, alleging that the standard improperly considered costs and was insufficiently protective of public health. Significantly, EDF did not insist upon the zero risk interpretation suggested by the language of section 112. In February 1977, EDF and EPA settled the lawsuit, and EPA pledged to phase out remaining vinyl chloride emissions with future stricter standards. EPA's vinyl chloride NESHAP took two years to come to fruition, but court review was settled promptly and amicably.

The difficulties in regulating asbestos and vinyl chloride within the strictures of section 112 led EPA to seek out a generic carcinogen policy to facilitate future regulations. The agency prepared risk assessment guidelines in 1976 to promote greater use of quantitative risk assessment in all agency carcinogen regulation. David Hawkins, formerly of the Natural Resources Defense Council, was appointed assistant administrator of EPA in charge of air and water pollution regulation under the Carter administration. As in the case of OSHA, President Carter had EPA administrators committed to full and effective enforcement of the Clean Air Act. One of the first, ambitious acts of the Carter EPA was to list forty-three priority candidates for regulation under section 112.

In 1977, EPA reexamined its vinyl chloride standard pursuant to its settlement with EDF and proposed new emission control requirements. In 1978, the agency conducted a quantitative risk assessment and concluded that the prevailing average lifetime risk under the existing NESHAP was 1×10^{-5}. Based on this finding, EPA's Carcinogen Assessment Group recommended against tightening the standard and argued that an extremely low probability of cancer could be consistent with the adequate margin of safety language found in section 112.[40] Economic costs were not explicitly considered at this time, and EPA seemed to shift from feasibility or cost/benefit analysis to a significant risk paradigm under section 112. Zero risk was once again rejected as an impractical policy for carcinogens. The 1977 proposal languished without agency final action.

EPA's shift to significant risk consideration was manifest in its next section 112 action—the listing of radioactive particles known as radionuclides as a hazardous air pollutant in 1979. The listing decision itself imposed no risk management action, but EPA carefully quantified the risk from various radionuclide sources and expressly focused only on "significant public exposure" to these carcinogens.[41]

After listing radionuclides, EPA's regulatory process stalled. Agency officials were openly concerned that their significant risk interpretation of section 112 would not stand up in court and were fearful of acting, lest they cause severe economic consequences. Inauguration of the Reagan administration in 1981 did nothing to speed up the process, until in 1982 a federal district court ordered EPA to prepare a NESHAP.[42] In 1983, EPA proposed emission standards for radionuclides based explicitly on the significant risk paradigm, limiting emissions from sources that presented serious risks.[43]

EPA's implementation of the significant risk paradigm for radionuclides was poor, however, and the NESHAP permitted a residual risk as high as 2×10^{-3} in the case of exposures from underground uranium mines, while regulating much smaller risks from other sources. EPA was bombarded with criticism for this proposed NESHAP, and in 1984 the agency withdrew the proposal and categorized the risk from radionuclides in general as "relatively trivial."[44] Environmental organizations challenged this withdrawal in federal court.

In 1980, the Carter EPA listed inorganic arsenic as a hazardous air pollutant. In 1983, Reagan's EPA prepared a proposed NESHAP for arsenic, which was based upon quantitative risk assessment and significant risk principles.[45] In August 1986, EPA published final emission control standards for four major sources of inorganic arsenic.[46] The Natural Resources Defense Council was unhappy with some aspects of the new arsenic rules, but these standards were not challenged in court. While the inorganic arsenic rulemaking took more than six years, it represents the most successful recent regulatory effort under section 112 of the Clean Air Act.

In response to a 1977 petition from the Environmental Defense Fund, EPA listed benzene as a hazardous air pollutant based on carcinogenicity without any quantitative risk assessment.[47] Once again, EPA had difficulty preparing a NESHAP, but in the waning days of the Carter administration in December 1980 the agency proposed emissions controls for four categories of sources of airborne benzene. The agency conducted a detailed quantitative risk assessment and avoided some stringent regulatory requirements in "view of the relatively small health benefits that would be gained."[48]

The newly-appointed officials of the Reagan EPA took no final action on the four benzene NESHAP proposals. In 1984, EPA proposed to withdraw three of the four proposed standards, because the maximum risk level from the source categories subject to these proposals had been reduced to 7×10^{-5} or less.[49] The administrator justified the withdrawal of these standards under a theory that section 112 was intended to protect only against significant risks from hazardous air pollutants. The Natural Resources Defense Council sued EPA over this attempted withdrawal of emission standards.

In January 1985, the Reagan EPA threw down a gauntlet to the environmental community by withdrawing the 1977 vinyl chloride proposal because the proposed NESHAP imposed some "unreasonable" costs and because no control technology "has been demonstrated" to meet the standard.[50] EPA apparently required both cost/benefit and feasibility tests for new regulations under section 112. The Natural Resources Defense Council promptly sued the agency, but the court's initial decision upheld EPA consideration of costs under section 112. After considerable criticism, the court reheard this case and modified its decision. The court held that cost and feasibility could not be considered in setting the level of the standard, which must be based exclusively on health considerations. The court further emphasized that a section 112 NESHAP need not eliminate all risk but could permit some residual "acceptable risk" to remain.[51] Only after this "safe" level was set could EPA consider cost and feasibility analysis in dictating emission controls. This decision became the first clear legal definition of section 112 regulatory standards, and the ongoing benzene and radionuclides cases were immediately remanded to EPA for reconsideration in light of the vinyl chloride decision.

EPA has had very little success regulating carcinogens under the Clean Air Act, regardless of the administration in power. The Carter administration succeeded in listing and proposing NESHAPs for several substances but issued *no* final emission regulations. The Reagan administration withdrew more standards than it promulgated but did succeed in regulating some sources of airborne benzene and inorganic arsenic. When NESHAPs were developed, the process took an average of nearly four years. The Carter administration's failure, at least, cannot be attributed to any lack of commitment to public health. Rather, much of the failure may be laid at the feet of the statutory standard, which implies a zero risk paradigm, which was too strict for even Carter administration environmentalists. Former EPA Administrator William Ruckelshaus testified that "[m]ost parties agree that the current statutory test is unworkable, if interpreted literally, and . . . this test can lead to a certain paralysis in decisionmaking."[52] Of the forty-three priority candidates for regulation established in 1976, emission standards have been adopted for only six. In the 1980's the EPA published notices of an intent to list ten additional substances, but no further action has been taken on any of these.

Clean Water Act

Clean Water Act regulations follow a somewhat more complex procedure than that of the Clean Air Act. Individual polluters must obtain permits under the National Pollution Discharge Elimination System (NPDES). These permits cover all pollutants, including carcinogens, and are based upon available state water quality standards or federally promulgated uniform effluent standards for sources or substances. Section 307 of the Act provides a specific mechanism for controlling effluents of "toxic" pollutants such as carcinogens.[53] Sections 301 and 304 of the Clean Water Act also authorize EPA to establish more general "technology based effluent limitations" known as "effluent limitations guidelines."[54] These two sources of effluent guidelines provide the primary federal regulatory tool for waterborne carcinogens.

From 1972 to 1976, EPA promulgated section 307 toxic effluent standards for six pollutants—the pesticides aldrin/dieldrin, DDT, endrin, toxaphene and the more generally used chemicals benzidine and PCB. While these substances have been identified as carcinogenic, EPA adopted control standards without much explanation. Quantitative risk assessments were conducted but were considered too imprecise for standard-setting. Section 307 standards are to be purely health-based, but EPA seemingly considered compliance costs and failed to explain why more stringent requirements were not imposed. These regulations were adopted promptly, averaging about six months between proposal and promulgation. Moreover, only the standards for PCBs and toxaphene were challenged in federal court.

Environmental groups, however, were frustrated by the slow pace of EPA's regulation of toxic water pollutants and sued EPA to compel the regulation of more substances. Several suits were consolidated and resulted in a victory for the environmental organizations. EPA settled with the plaintiff organizations and agreed to control sixty-five additional pollutants primarily discharged by twenty-one distinct industries.[55] In exchange for this promise, environmental groups agreed that future carcinogen regulation would take place under sections 301 and 304. Unlike section 307, sections 301 and 304 are feasibility-based standards and provide for regulation by industry category, rather than by individual pollutant.

EPA has failed to meet the court-imposed deadlines in the consent decree, but the agency has made significant progress in regulating toxic water pollutants. The consent decree subsequently has been modified to extend regulatory deadlines and to include twenty-eight industry categories, and EPA has developed effluent guidelines for twenty-six of these categories. While this represents considerable progress, the effluent guidelines do not cover all industrial sources of the designated pollutants.

One very recent and important set of effluent guidelines applies to the organic chemicals, plastics and synthetic fibers industrial category.[56] This rule originally was proposed in March 1983 and finally was promulgated in November 1987. EPA did not base this rule on risk levels, perhaps because agency action was compelled by court order. Nevertheless, the agency considered a quantitative risk assessment and noted that for thirty regulated pollutants the individual risk exceeded 10^{-6}. The rulemaking adopted a series of standards controlling the discharge of over 100 chemicals, based upon feasibility analysis.

In addition to the above-described federal water pollution control standards, the Clean Water Act also provides for EPA to develop nonbinding criteria documents for water pollutants, which are to be used in setting state effluent standards.[57] Section 311 of the Act also requires EPA to adopt regulations designating reportable quantities of hazardous substances released into the water.[58] Under these sections, EPA has dealt more directly with the health risks of carcinogens in the water.

In establishing regulations under the water criteria provision, EPA acknowledged that only zero exposure provided complete protection for public health but contended that this zero risk approach was infeasible. Consequently, in 1979 EPA estimated standards necessary to limit the risk to 10^{-5}, 10^{-6}, and 10^{-7}, with the *de minimis* acceptable level to be selected by the state setting control standards.[59] In 1980 EPA adopted a similar significant risk standard under section 311, establishing reportable levels for carcinogens at the emission capable of causing a 1×10^{-6} increase in cancer risk.[60]

Both these section 304 and section 311 regulations are informative for the significant risk paradigm, as EPA under the Carter administration either directly or indirectly set a series of acceptable risk levels for carcinogens. Neither of these sections directly controls effluents of carcinogens, however, nor do they impose expensive control requirements. Consequently, these regulations are not directly applicable to regulatory control requirements for carcinogens.

As compared with other sources of carcinogen control authority, EPA has had great success under the Clean Water Act. Prior to 1976, the agency regulated six substances. Even this moderate success surpasses the regulatory record under the Clean Air Act, the Occupational Safety and Health Act, and most other sources of carcinogen control authority. Since the consent decree, EPA has regulated dozens of carcinogens on an industry-by-industry basis, using feasibility-based standards. Court review has been avoided or has deferred to EPA's efforts to "formulate policy with respect to what risks are acceptable."[61]

Clean Water Act regulation of carcinogens is not an unmitigated success, however. EPA has taken longer than anticipated and has needed eight separate extensions of regulatory deadlines imposed by the court. EPA also missed its goal of regulating all the covered substances by January 1987. While the consent decree was issued in 1976, complete regulation of industry source-categories will not be complete until 1990. Nevertheless, when compared with other statutes, Clean Water act regulation of carcinogens has been far more extensive and also more prompt.

Toxic Substances Control Act

The 1976 Toxic Substances Control Act (TSCA) provides a variety of authorities for controlling exposure to carcinogens. Perhaps the best known provision is TSCA's requirement that new chemicals be tested before marketing. TSCA also contains authority for regulating carcinogenic risks from existing chemicals. Regulatory action under TSCA is triggered by a section 4(f) finding that a substance presents "a significant risk of serious or widespread harm to human beings."[62] Once the significant risk finding is made, section 6 of TSCA permits EPA to regulate or ban substances that present an "unreasonable risk of injury to health or the environment."[63] TSCA thus provides broad authority to regulate carcinogens whatever the source and whatever the route of human exposure.

EPA has done little to use its TSCA authority over existing carcinogens, however, and no section 4(f) significant risk findings were issued during the first six years of the act's existence. TSCA also authorized an Interagency Testing Committee to review existing chemicals and make recommendations to EPA for regulation. EPA is to respond to the recommendations within twelve months. For the first three years of TSCA, EPA took no regulatory action and uniformly failed even to respond within the statutorily designated one year deadline. In 1980, a federal court compelled EPA compliance with the response deadline, but the agency has still done little to regulate under TSCA.

The first section 4(f) decision under serious consideration created a tremendous controversy when EPA rejected such a finding for formaldehyde in 1982. EPA received evidence of formaldehyde's carcinogenicity in November 1979, and in 1980 EPA initiated consideration of a section 4(f) listing for formaldehyde. In 1982, under the Reagan EPA, Assistant EPA Administrator John Todhunter issued a memorandum explaining the decision not to declare formaldehyde a significant risk. This decision was based upon two sets of questionable premises. First, EPA conducted a quantitative risk assessment but departed from past practice in estimating risks. For example, the agency discounted positive data from animal bioassays based upon negative epidemiologic data, and the agency used quadratic, nonconservative dose/response extrapolation models. Second, Todhunter declared that the resulting estimates were not significant because "the various general agencies do not tend to regulate risks of one chance in one hundred thousand or lower and tend to be ambivalent about risks between one chance in one hundred thousand and one chance in ten thousand."[64] Assistant Administrator Todhunter thus suggested that risks of less than 1×10^{-4} were insignificant.

The Todhunter memorandum and consequent EPA decision not to list formaldehyde produced a firestorm of criticism in Congress and in the media. Commentators suggested that "Todhunter's analysis advanced theories that conflicted with prevalent scientific opinion in the field and that departed from prior cancer policies of EPA and other regulatory agencies."[65] In 1983, the Natural Resources Defense Council and the American Public Health Association filed suit to compel EPA reconsideration of its decision not to list formaldehyde under section 4(f). At roughly the same time, President Reagan appointed a new EPA administrator, William Ruckelshaus, who was widely regarded as more environmentally responsive than the prior administrator.

In 1984, EPA voluntarily reversed its position and applied section 4(f) to two formaldehyde exposure categories: manufacture of clothing from fabrics treated with formaldehyde resins and construction of mobile homes using formaldehyde resin.[66] This reversal was not based on new data, but EPA did place greater emphasis on conservative upper confidence limits in its new quantitative risk assessment. The agency found that large populations were subject to an upper risk estimate of approximately 1×10^{-4}.

The struggle to list formaldehyde under section 4(f) of TSCA took fifty-five months, and even this listing did not invoke regulation. EPA still has not imposed actual restrictions on exposure to formaldehyde under TSCA's authority.

EPA has had only slightly more success regulating other carcinogens under TSCA. Of forty-one existing chemicals that EPA has identified as carcinogens subject to TSCA, only four have been listed as significant risks under section 4(f). Of these four, EPA has yet to issue any TSCA regulations. The only final carcinogen regulations issued under section 6 of TSCA cover PCBs, which are the subject of a specific statutory mandate, and certain asbestos removal operations in schools. In 1986, EPA issued a section 6 proposal banning certain applications of asbestos, but no final action has yet been taken.

TSCA's statutory framework intuitively seems well suited to control of carcinogens. The coverage of the statute is quite broad, and regulation can be flexible, considering both significant risk and cost/benefit analysis. In practice, however, EPA has done virtually nothing to regulate carcinogens under TSCA authority.

Safe Drinking Water Act

The Safe Drinking Water Act (SDWA) of 1974 authorizes EPA to establish national drinking water quality standards for hazardous substances, including carcinogens. EPA first adopted interim primary regulations for twelve substances in 1975, which were based upon 1962 recommendations of the U.S. Public Health Service.[67] EDF challenged these standards as insufficiently extensive, but the court largely upheld EPA's interim standards.[68] Additional interim standards were established for radionuclides in 1976.[69] Having set interim standards, the SDWA directed EPA to establish recommended maximum contaminant levels (RMCLs), which are now known as maximum contaminant level goals (MCLGs). These goals are to be set at the level at which "no known or anticipated adverse effects on the health of persons occur and which allows an adequate margin of safety."[70] The MCLGs are merely nonenforceable, nonbinding objectives, however. Binding standards take the form of maximum contaminant levels (MCLs), which are to be set "as close to the [MCLGs] as is feasible" using the best control technology "generally available (taking cost into consideration)."[71]

The first significant MCL under the SDWA was established in 1979, for a group of compounds known as trihalomethanes[72]. These compounds are produced by the interaction of organic chemicals and chlorination of public drinking water supplies. EPA conducted a quantitative risk assessment of carcinogenic risk from trihalomethanes but chose not to rely on quantitation of risk in setting its standard. The trihalomethane standard was set exclusively through feasibility analysis and left a residual risk as high as 4×10^{-4}.

In 1978, EPA sought to depart from contaminant-by-contaminant regulation of drinking water contaminants and shift to establishing generic treatment regulations for drinking water systems that used surface waters. Cost and feasibility problems obstructed this new program, however. By the end of the year, EPA returned to regulating individual contaminants, with increased attention given to groundwater contamination.

EPA next addressed volatile organic compounds (VOCs) in drinking water, and issued an advance notice of proposed rulemaking in March 1982. The agency was unable to issue proposed MCLs, however, until November 1985.[73] Final regulations were not adopted until June 1987, sixty-three months after the rulemaking process commenced.[74] This process was undeniably delayed by efforts to establish nonbinding RMCLs for the VOCs, a process that consumed at least thirty months, only to conclude that RMCLs for carcinogens must be set at zero. At least this final VOC rule successfully placed exposure limits on eight independent volatile organic compounds. These standards were based primarily on feasibility analysis and reduced even upper-bound cancer risk to approximately 10^{-5} and below.

The mid-1980s saw a small burst of activity toward promulgating SDWA standards. EPA issued a notice of proposed rulemaking to establish RMCLs for twenty-one substances in November 1985. In 1983, the agency announced an advance notice of rulemaking for revising the radionuclide standard. None of these actions has even reached the stage of a proposed MCL, however. In 1986, EPA once again announced an advance notice of proposed rulemaking for radionuclides. Congress grew impatient with EPA's failure to establish drinking water standards for carcinogens and in 1986 required EPA to regulate eighty-three chemicals under SDWA, with a 1989 deadline for completion. Congress also modified the two-step regulatory procedure and required that MCLs be established simultaneously with the RMCLs, now renamed MCLGs. While this congressional action has motivated renewed EPA effort under the SDWA, the agency shows little evidence of ability to meet the new statutory deadline.

Federal Insecticide, Fungicide, and Rodenticide Act

The Federal Insecticide, Fungicide, and Rodenticide Act predates most environmental legislation and employs a slightly different regulatory program. Pesticides may not be produced and sold for domestic use unless they are lawfully registered. EPA may register a new pesticide if when "used in accordance with widespread and commonly recognized practice it will not generally cause unreasonable adverse effects on the environment,"[75] which includes "any unreasonable risk to man or the environment, taking into account the economic, social and environmental costs and benefits of [its] use."[76] For existing pesticides, registration may be cancelled, suspended, or conditioned on safety precautions under a similar "unreasonable risk" test. FIFRA's structures differs from many other regulatory statutes in that pesticide regulatory decisions are typically made in adjudications on individual products rather than in the form of broad notice-and-comment rulemaking.

The adjudicatory format of FIFRA decisions makes it more difficult to identify the basis for decisions and generalize regarding agency practice. Some conclusions are possible, however. EPA has issued notices of intent to suspend or cancel registration for seventeen pesticides, based on carcinogenicity. With or without this notice of intent, manufacturers have voluntarily cancelled at least some uses for twenty allegedly carcinogenic pesticides. EPA has taken final regulatory action for twelve other pesticides, in the form of cancellation, suspension, establishment of maximum tolerance levels for carcinogens, or labeling requirements. Although a number of these decisions have been challenged in court, EPA has been largely successful in justifying its decisions.

EPA's regulatory decisions under FIFRA are to be considered under a cost/benefit test. In practice, the agency has considered the risks of continued use of a carcinogen and considered the agricultural benefits of a pesticide, but EPA has used little rigor in assessing the full costs and benefits of regulatory action and in comparing these terms. On a number of occasions, EPA has used little cost/benefit analysis but has employed significant risk principles under FIFRA. In 1980, EPA adopted a general policy decision that a carcinogenic risk of 1×10^{-6} was "acceptable."[77] Under the Reagan administration, the acceptable risk level was tacitly changed and numerous pesticides were registered despite presenting risks in excess of 1×10^{-5} or even 10^{-3}.

Ethylene dibromide (EDB) control illustrates EPA difficulties in regulation under FIFRA. In 1977, animal bioassays first demonstrated that EDB might be a potent carcinogen. Consumer exposure to EDB residues in fruit and grain products was relatively high. EPA spent four years, however, debating proper risk assessment for EDB. By 1983, the agency accumulated evidence of extensive EDB contamination of groundwater, and EPA abruptly ordered an emergency suspension of ground fumigation uses of the chemical. EPA further announced its intent to cancel other uses of the pesticide to protect consumers from food residues. Some uses of EDB on grain were then suspended in early 1984. While EPA eventually regulated the carcinogenic hazard from EDB, agency action was unnecessarily slow and the ultimate EPA restrictions may have been unnecessarily stringent.

In some respects, FIFRA regulation of carcinogenic pesticides seems particularly successful. Certainly, EPA has regulated more carcinogens under FIFRA than under its broader regulatory authorities. FIFRA's experience with carcinogen regulation is far from uniformly positive, however. EPA has identified twenty-nine carcinogenic pesticides for which no action has been taken. Agency action on pesticides has also been slow. For example, EPA initiated review of the carcinogenic pesticide DBCP in September 1977 but did not take final regulatory action until January 1985. A survey of FIFRA actions concluded that the average time of agency review for subsequently restricted pesticides was forty-four months, with recent actions taking even longer.[79]

Indoor Air Pollution

Although indoor air pollution is currently the largest man-made, involuntary source of carcinogenic hazard in the United States, no major federal statute specifically addresses the indoor problem. Where the indoor air problem arises from consumer products, the Consumer Product Safety Commission has authority to respond. In other cases, the broad authority of the Toxic Substances Control Act might be used. EPA has interpreted the Clean Air Act, however, as applying only to "outdoor" pollutants.[80]

In the absence of explicit statutory authority, EPA and other federal agencies have been reluctant to act against indoor air pollution. In November 1985, EPA initiated a program to implement a strategy against indoor radon exposures. This strategy consists primarily of surveys to identify radon problems, guidelines regarding hazardous exposure levels, publications about the potential hazard, and other nonregulatory assistance to states and individual citizens. Indoor radon control regulations have not been proposed, and the federal response to indoor radon has been minimal.[81] Federal regulatory agencies have given even less attention to many other indoor carcinogens, such as combustion products.

The only significant risk management for indoor carcinogens involves asbestos. In 1986, Congress passed the Asbestos Hazard Emergency Response Act (AHERA) to control asbestos exposures in the nation's schools.[82] In 1987, EPA adopted a final rule requiring local school systems to inspect facilities for asbestos and "select and implement in a timely manner the appropriate response actions."[83] In adopting this regulation, EPA essentially ignored quantitative risk assessment and deflected judgments about asbestos containment and removal to local school districts. EPA's rules on asbestos in schools were upheld on judicial review.[84]

The Consumer Product Safety Commission's decision to ban formaldehyde-based insulation, discussed below, represents the lone important indoor air pollution regulation of carcinogens. EPA seems fearful of action, despite recent congressional prodding. Even when given explicit authorization in AHERA, EPA avoided difficult regulatory decisions. Controlling carcinogens in indoor air remains a low priority, notwithstanding the public health threat from these substances.

FOOD AND DRUG ADMINISTRATION

The federal Food and Drug Administration (FDA) is charged with the protection of the food supply from hazardous substances, including carcinogens. Unlike most statutes, the enabling authority of the FDA specifically refers to regulating carcinogens. The now infamous Delaney Clause provides that the FDA shall prohibit the use of intentional food additives whenever such a substance has been "found . . . to induce cancer in man or animal."[85] FDA thus must prohibit any intentional food additive that is carcinogenic, a statutory requirement that seems to invoke the zero risk paradigm.

The Delaney Clause does not prohibit all carcinogens in food, however. The clause covers only substances "added" to food and does not address natural carcinogens. Additionally, carcinogenic residues of pesticides are outside the scope of the Delaney Clause. Animal drugs are also excluded if the drug leaves no residue in meat. FDA has also declined to apply the Delaney Clause to unintentional contaminants found in intentional food additives. Thus, the Delaney Clause is reserved for instances when a substance such as an artificial coloring agent is added to food products. When such a substance is carcinogenic, the Delaney Clause prohibits its use.

Other more general authority in the Food, Drug and Cosmetic Act permits action against other types or sources of carcinogens in food. Sections 402 and 406 of the Act cover any added poisonous or deleterious substances found in food. When some contamination from such a substance cannot be avoided, the statute directs FDA to "promulgate regulations . . . to such extent as [it] finds necessary for the protection of public health."[86] This section has been used to limit human exposure to chemical contaminants in fish, and aflatoxin in peanut products. Section 402 of the Act also permits FDA to control naturally occurring poisonous or deleterious substances found in food.[87] FDA has greater flexibility than most regulatory agencies, as it may proceed through rulemakings or through more informal "action levels," which set a maximum permissible level of a substance and which do not require full rulemaking procedures.

FDA has a longer history of and greater expertise in carcinogen regulation than do other federal agencies. In 1950, prior to the adoption of the Delaney Clause, the FDA prohibited the use of two carcinogens as food additives. In 1968, the FDA prohibited oil of calamus, a carcinogenic flavoring agent, but eschewed reliance upon the Delaney Clause. In more recent years FDA has struggled to cope with the Delaney Clause and regulate carcinogens in food, drugs, and cosmetics.

An early controversy involved use of the carcinogen acrylonitrile in beverage containers.[88] Recognizing that some amount of acrylonitrile in containers may migrate into the consumable beverage itself, FDA in 1975 established a rule setting maximum allowable acrylonitrile levels in such containers.[88] In 1977, the FDA Commissioner proposed to prohibit all acrylonitrile in beverage containers because the substance was a carcinogenic food additive.[89] After administrative proceedings and issuance of a final order, acrylonitrile manufacturers sued the FDA, contending that the diffusion of the substance into food or drink was negligible. The reviewing federal court characterized the FDA action as unduly precipitate and remanded for further agency consideration. The court ruled the FDA need not take a "strictly literal" interpretation of its enabling statute but rather "there is latitude inherent in the statutory scheme to avoid literal definition of 'food additive' in those *de minimis* situations that, in the informed judgment of the Commissioner, clearly present no public health or safety concerns."[90]

A particularly intractable Delaney Clause problem arose over selenium in animal feeds. High levels of selenium were shown to induce liver cancer in experimental animals. Yet at lower levels selenium is an essential nutrient and may prevent cancer. FDA elected to permit continued use of selenium in animal feeds, because the Commissioner found that the carcinogenic effects of selenium resulted only indirectly from the substance's toxic effects at high levels and that these toxic effects had a safe threshold.[91]

FDA's most significant carcinogen regulations have employed section 406, not the more famous Delaney Clause. One important action was taken against aflatoxins, a carcinogenic mold contaminating some foods, such as corn and peanuts. In 1965, FDA set an informal action level of 30 parts per billion of aflatoxin in certain food commodities. In 1969, the agency reduced this action level to 20 ppb. In 1974, FDA used new data to propose a formal rule reducing the aflatoxin tolerance level to 15 ppb in some peanut products.[92] FDA considered lower 5 and 10 ppb standards but rejected them, primarily because they "could result in significant losses to producers, manufacturers, and consumers alike."[93] The agency apparently employed the cost/benefit paradigm in proposing its standard but conducted little actual analysis to support its conclusion.

The proposed 15 ppb rule for aflatoxins languished for nearly four years without action until the FDA sought more public comments in 1978, in response to another study and a relatively sophisticated quantitative risk assessment.[94] In this new proceeding, FDA seems to have shifted in part to a significant risk standard. FDA staff continued to support the 15 ppb proposed standard, because it left a maximum residual risk of only 2×10^{-5}, which the agency characterized as minor.[95] A later notice suggested that the FDA employed feasibility analysis in its aflatoxin standard, stating that "FDA's regulatory policy has been aimed at limiting aflatoxins in the food supply to the lowest extent possible."[96] Whatever the paradigm used, FDA has never adopted the proposed 15 ppb aflatoxin standard, even after fourteen years of intermittent consideration.

In February 1974, FDA reacted to a petition from the Health Research Group and proposed a ban on drug and cosmetic uses of vinyl chloride, based on evidence of carcinogenicity. In August 1974, FDA issued a final rule preventing these uses of vinyl chloride.[97] This successful regulation did not employ the Delaney Clause but relied upon the more general safety authority of the FDA.

In 1975, published studies indicated that PCBs, an industrial chemical now dispersed throughout the environment, could cause cancer. FDA already had established a maximum PCB tolerance in food under section 406, based on acute toxic effects, and the NRDC and EDF petitioned FDA to set a zero tolerance for PCBs in food. In 1977, the agency proposed reducing its tolerance for PCBs.[98] The proposal rejected zero tolerance as impractical and focused on fish as the source of most human exposure to PCBs in food. FDA's PCB proposal relied centrally upon cost/benefit balancing. A 1 ppm tolerance was rejected as having a cost of $127 million, which was deemed "excessive."[99] The agency then proposed a 2 ppm tolerance, which had a cost of $65 million. No quantitative risk assessment was discussed in connection with setting the level of PCB tolerance.

In 1979, FDA promulgated its PCB standard at 2 ppm.[100] In so doing, the agency emphasized the excessive cost and loss of food from a lower 1 ppm standard. The agency also utilized quantitative risk assessment and stressed that under conservative assumptions, the 2 ppm standard left a residual cancer risk of only 7×10^{-5} for heavy consumers of fish. Promulgation of this standard took approximately forty-five months.

The FDA did relatively little during the 1970s to control carcinogens in food. In addition to the above proceedings, the agency banned ten relatively minor food additives as carcinogenic. One additional interesting development concerned cyclamates, a category of artificial sweeteners. First in 1976, and again in 1980, the FDA refused to approve cyclamates as additives. While some studies had shown carcinogenicity of cyclamates, and the substance seemed a likely candidate for application of the Delaney Clause, the FDA declined to use the Delaney Clause "because the evidence submitted does not conclusively establish that cyclamate is a carcinogen."[101] The cyclamates decision illustrates the agency's fear of reliance on the absolutist Delaney Clause, *even when* the agency intended to ban a substance. In another 1980 decision, the FDA strained to avoid applying the Delaney Clause to lead acetate and permitted this color additive in cosmetics because its cancer risk of less than 1×10^{-6} was " 'acceptable' and thus safe" by the standard of reasonableness established by Congress.[102]

In 1977, years after scientific evidence was first available, the FDA officially determined that saccharin was carcinogenic in animal bioassays and proposed banning the artificial sweetener.[103] FDA estimated that consumption of one saccharin-containing diet beverage per day could yield a bladder cancer risk as high as 4×10^{-4} and that more than 1,000 such cancer cases could be caused annually. Once again, FDA's Commissioner avoided reliance on the Delaney Clause and proposed banning saccharin under his general safety authority. The proposed saccharin ban produced massive public opposition, Congress suspended the proposal in response to public pressure, and FDA withdrew the proposal in response to congressional and public pressure.

The Carter FDA moved farther from the zero risk Delaney Clause in a generic rulemaking for chemical compounds used in food-producing animals. Historically, the agency had allowed use of carcinogens in animal feed, if no residue of the carcinogen remained in the animal as food product. Advancing technology, however, permitted the detection of miniscule amounts of a substance in food. To avoid banning animal growth stimulants because of miniscule residues, FDA proposed in 1979 and adopted in 1980 a significant risk rule governing these chemicals fed to animals.[104] Under this rule, carcinogenic residues would be allowed if they presented a risk of 1×10^{-6} or less, a risk level that FDA considered "safe." Whatever the public prominence of the Delaney Clause, it was largely a dead letter even under the Carter administration. The Delaney Clause was used only twice, for very minor indirect food additives.

President Reagan's inauguration in 1981 ushered in a period of deregulation throughout government, including the FDA. In 1982, the FDA addressed the Delaney Clause head on and issued an advance notice of proposed rulemaking that would permit any food or color additives that presented only a *de minimis* risk.[105] While the Delaney Clause had always been the paradigmatic example of a congressionally imposed zero risk standard, the government now sought to convert even this language to a significant risk standard.

Throughout the 1980s, FDA began applying its *de minimis* risk principle to additives containing carcinogenic contaminants. Certain color additives were approved in 1982, for example, because the risk from their carcinogenic contaminants or impurities was no greater than 1×10^{-7}.[106] This decision to allow some level of carcinogenic impurities in food additives was upheld in court.[107] In 1986, FDA for the first time approved color additives which were themselves carcinogenic, using its *de minimis* principles to permit additives that presented a carcinogenic risk of less than 1×10^{-6}.[108] Such blatant disregard for the express terms of the Delaney Clause went too far for public interest groups, which sued FDA.

In 1987, a federal court of appeals struck down the FDA's decision to allow small risks from the direct and intentional addition of carcinogens in food.[109] The court was obviously reluctant to overturn FDA's *de minimis* policy for such minor cancer risks but held that the plain language of the Delaney Clause compelled an "extraordinarily rigid" zero risk policy for direct additives.[110]

The FDA's carcinogen control policy must be considered a failure. The Reagan administration has done very little to control carcinogens in food, save a few minor restrictions and action levels. The Carter administration had done little more. Review of the record reveals considerable administrative effort to evade the strictures of the Delaney Clause's rigid prohibition of carcinogenic additives. This effort was largely successful for animal growth stimulants and impurities in additives. Because additives appear to pose very little carcinogenic risk, the agency's inaction in this field is somewhat understandable. More seriously, FDA has taken little action to regulate significant carcinogenic risks in food products, such as those from natural carcinogens. The significant regulations of aflatoxin and PCBs took years, while FDA stumbled about, unable even to choose a consistent risk management paradigm. The extensive effort devoted to additives inevitably detracted from FDA's ability to attend to more serious carcinogenic risks in food products.

CONSUMER PRODUCT SAFETY COMMISSION

The Consumer Product Safety Commission (CPSC) was established in 1972 and authorized to control hazards from consumer products, including risks of cancer. The primary regulatory authority possessed by the Commission is found in the Consumer Product Safety Act, which enables the Commission to promulgate product safety standards or to ban products that are "reasonably necessary to prevent an unreasonable risk."[111] The Commission possesses similar authority under the Federal Hazardous Substances Act.[112] Under this standard, CPSC must take a "hard look" at the costs, benefits, and feasibility of any proposed standard.[113] The CPSC also differs from other agencies that regulate carcinogens by being an independent regulatory agency, outside the direct control of the President, and at least theoretically free from political changes of administrations.

The Consumer Product Safety Commission historically has focused on product-caused injuries but has remained aware of potential cancer risks from consumer products. In 1974, the commission responded to a public petition and proposed to ban all household products containing vinyl chloride, based largely on OSHA and EPA findings of vinyl chloride's carcinogenicity.[114] Within months, CPSC promulgated this ban as a final rule.[115] The ban was based upon a somewhat casual risk assessment, in which CPSC concluded that product-related exposures could exceed the occupational exposure levels and the levels at which increased cancer had been demonstrated in laboratory animals (with a resultant product risk as high as 1×10^{-3}).

Manufacturers objected to CPSC's proposed ban, alleging that the hazard was too small to justify product prohibition costs. The manufacturers requested a hearing on the scientific evidence, but CPSC rejected their request. These manufacturers sued, and the reviewing federal court held that CPSC had violated the law in denying manufacturers a hearing, thus vacating the standard.[116] By the time of the 1977 decision, all known manufacturers had already voluntarily phased out the use of vinyl chloride in consumer products. Nevertheless, the CPSC repromulgated its ban on vinyl chloride in consumer products in 1978.[117] The CPSC's effort to ban vinyl chloride in products required only five months, a remarkably prompt promulgation of a carcinogen control standard. In its haste, however, the Commission violated statutory procedural requirements, and the rule was not legally adopted until four years after its initial proposal.

CPSC more successfully regulated asbestos exposures from certain consumer products, primarily patching compounds and artificial fireplace logs. In July 1976, the NRDC and Consumers Union petitioned for control of these exposures, and in July 1977, CPSC proposed a ban on asbestos products in these consumer products. The proposed ban was based upon a careful quantitative risk assessment that revealed carcinogenic risk to consumers as high as 1×10^{-3}. CPSC found this risk unacceptable in light of the limited benefits of the asbestos-containing products and banned further production of these products in December 1977.[118] The final prohibition on patching compounds was not immediate but phased, in order to minimize the economic costs to manufacturers. Industry did not bring a court challenge against the terms of this ban on certain asbestos-containing products.

Also in 1977, the CPSC adopted a ban on children's garments containing TRIS, a chemical fire retardant. In 1975, short term tests had found TRIS to be mutagenic. By early 1976, the Environmental Defense Fund petitioned CPSC for a standard regulating consumer exposures to TRIS. By February 1977, animal bioassays evaluating TRIS had produced positive results, and EDF promptly sued CPSC to compel a standard. The Commission adopted a ban under the rubric of an "interpretation" in April 1977.[119] CPSC prohibited all new TRIS-containing products, based upon a quantitative risk assessment showing an average lifetime cancer risk ranging from 2.5×10^{-5} to nearly 2×10^{-3}, depending upon exposure assumptions. The Commission declined to order the repurchase of existing stocks of TRIS-treated garments, which presented an outstanding cancer risk of 1×10^{-6} to 8×10^{-4}.

CPSC's abrupt promulgation of a ban on TRIS-containing products, without issuance of a preliminary proposal, led to court challenge. Upon such review, a federal district court held that the Commission acted illegally in publishing no proposal and allowing no opportunity for public comment on its product ban.[120] CPSC has not repromulgated its ban, but the agency may legally proceed against individual producers in case-by-case enforcement proceedings. After CPSC initiated such actions, manufacturers have voluntarily ceased the use of TRIS in treating children's garments.

In May 1977, the Health Research Group petitioned CPSC to ban benzene in consumer products. By 1978, CPSC proposed a rule to ban benzene as an intentional ingredient in most chemicals and set standards for unintentional benzene contamination of consumer products.[121] In proposing its benzene rule, the Commission disclaimed any reliance upon quantitative risk assessment and argued that few products would be affected by this action. The proposed CPSC benzene rule languished for three years, during which time intentional use of benzene in consumer products was halted voluntarily. This fact, along with the Supreme Court decision invalidating the OSHA benzene standard, led CPSC to reconsider and withdraw its proposed benzene regulation in 1981.[122] The withdrawal was based upon quantitative risk assessment which demonstrated that benzene in consumer products no longer presented a significant risk to health.

To facilitate carcinogen regulation, the CPSC in 1978 adopted its own generic policy for regulating carcinogens, much like OSHA's generic cancer policy. Unlike OSHA, the Commission abruptly published its policy as a "statement of policy," without accepting public comments on its terms.[123] This policy called for automatic regulation of any substance with positive results from well-conducted animal bioassays or human epidemiology. Dow Chemical Company and other manufacturers sued to enjoin use of this policy, because it was adopted without public comment rulemaking procedures. The court held that CPSC's cancer policy had been adopted unlawfully and could not be used in regulation.[124] After some slight resistance, the Commission withdrew its cancer policy.[125]

By 1981, CPSC truly had a strange history of regulating carcinogens. The Commission actively struggled to speed up the regulatory process, forgoing procedural requirements and causing its rules to be overturned in court. While few final rules were promulgated, the CPSC's procedurally unlawful rules succeeded in pressuring industry to comply voluntarily. This extralegal pressure represents a questionable regulatory practice, however, and succeeded only because the Commission acted on minor, economically unimportant carcinogens in consumer products. Nor had the Commission defined any consistent role for quantitative risk assessment or risk management standards. While the CPSC's "unreasonable risk" standard suggests the propriety of cost/benefit analysis, the Commission's risk management decisions have been haphazard, with little analysis of costs or benefits. An extensive review of CPSC regulation concluded that the Commission was "slow in determining its proper role in the regulation of chronic hazards and clumsy in implementing actions."[126]

Since 1980, the CPSC has undertaken one major rulemaking to control carcinogens, in the form of a ban on urea-formaldehyde foam insulation. Formaldehyde exposure from such insulation historically had been linked to complaints of respiratory problems, and animal studies suggested the carcinogenicity of formaldehyde in 1979. CPSC initiated its investigation in June 1980 and proposed its ban in February 1981.[127] The Commission's quantitative risk assessment suggested a risk level of nearly 1×10^{-4}, and twenty-three annual deaths ascribable to formaldehyde exposures from insulation, estimates that were based upon certain limited exposure data. In electing a ban, CPSC balanced the costs and benefits of its action but declined to quantify all such costs and benefits. An industry group known as the Formaldehyde Institute vigorously attacked the Commission's proposal, seeking a safety standard rather than an absolute prohibition.

In February 1982, the Commission voted 4-1 to promulgate its ban on urea-formaldehyde insulation.[128] The Formaldehyde Institute quickly filed suit against the Commission, and in April 1983 a federal appellate court unanimously vacated the CPSC action.[129] The court identified some procedural problems but focused primarily on the Commission's lack of substantive evidence for its action. In the mind of the court, CPSC's exposure data was too limited and the Commission relied too heavily on animal bioassays and placed insufficient reliance on epidemiologic data on formaldehyde's carcinogenicity.

By the time of the court decision invalidating CPSC's formaldehyde ban, the formaldehyde-based insulation industry was virtually dead, due to adverse publicity and other economic circumstances. CPSC did not attempt to repromulgate its ban but simply sought voluntary cooperation from the pressed wood industry to limit formaldehyde emissions from the few remaining installations of urea-formaldehyde foam insulation.

INTER-AGENCY ACTION

While the various federal agencies and divisions of agencies have struggled independently to cope with environmental carcinogens, some interagency effort has developed to lend information and consistency to agency decisions. President Carter initially proposed a government-wide approach to toxic substances in a 1977 address. Since 1977, this interagency coordinated action has contributed little to carcinogen regulation, but recent efforts may play a greater role in influencing the decisions of individual agencies.

The most effective integrated interagency coordination has occurred in the area of carcinogen identification. The National Toxicology Program (NTP) was established in 1978 to broaden the federal government's ability to test chemicals and other substances for carcinogenicity. While the NTP is officially located under the Department of Health and Human Services, all carcinogen regulatory agencies have worked with the NTP and made considerable use of its results. For example, the choice of chemicals for NTP testing and the type of tests to be undertaken is decided primarily by an Executive Committee, which includes representatives from all the major carcinogen regulatory agencies. The NTP conducts both short-term tests and animal bioassays, then evaluates the results and publishes conclusions regarding the strength of evidence of carcinogenicity. The NTP does not, however, perform quantitative risk assessments on subject chemicals.

While NTP coordination of carcinogen identification has been constructive, this step is the least controversial part of carcinogen control. Relatively less progress has been made in integrative risk assessment and management. Within the last ten years, however, some tentative progress has been made in interagency risk assessment policy.

The first significant development in interagency cooperation was the 1978 proposed cancer policy of the Interagency Regulatory Liaison Group (IRLG), which was published in the *Federal Register* for public comment.[130] This Group included representatives from OSHA, EPA, FDA and CPSC, and was headed by OSHA Administrator Eula Bingham. The 1978 report of the IRLG primarily set forth proposed "scientific bases" for identifying carcinogens and assessing carcinogenic risks quantitatively. Many of these scientific conclusions in fact represented policy judgments, and the IRLG report emphasized the use of conservative, risk-averse assumptions in quantitative risk assessment. Significantly, the IRLG emphasized and encouraged the conduct of quantitative risk assessment, at a time when OSHA and EPA were reluctant to incorporate such quantitation in their regulatory judgments. In addition, this report constituted the first evidence that all the federal regulatory agencies largely agreed on the policy assumptions involved in identifying carcinogens and assessing risks.

The IRLG policy brought together the various federal regulatory agencies but had no binding effect on subsequent regulatory decisions. IRLG's cancer policy was only hortatory. OSHA, for example, resisted reliance on quantitative risk assessment even after the date of the IRLG report. The conservative assumptions of the IRLG also led to some industry criticism. Industry groups typically stressed that scientific conclusions should be separated from policy judgments. For whatever reason, the IRLG issued no final cancer policy, nor did any agencies formally adopt the group's conclusions. Although it is occasionally referenced, the IRLG report had no demonstrable impact upon federal carcinogen regulation and the group has now been disbanded.

Parallel to the IRLG cancer policy, the federal Office of Science and Technology Policy (OSTP) began preparing its own policy on carcinogen identification and risk assessment under the Carter administration. OSTP's first report was issued almost simultaneously with IRLG's policy, but the OSTP report was less detailed and received far less attention. The Reagan administration shifted the interagency focus from the IRLG, a cooperative effort of the regulatory agencies, to the OSTP, a separate group accountable directly to the White House. The OSTP set to work preparing its own detailed cancer policy for use throughout the federal government and published its final cancer policy in 1985, in the form of a "notice of review of the science and associated principles" for carcinogen assessment.[131] OSTP ambitiously intended the report to "serve as the basis for consistent regulatory cancer guidelines that the Federal agencies can tailor to meet the requirements of the legislative acts they are charged to implement."[132] The OSTP report focuses on quantitative risk assessment but, unlike the earlier IRLG report, the OSTP strives to avoid "mixing of scientific knowledge with risk assessment science policy."[133] OSTP's cancer policy was more open to industry arguments, such as metabolic considerations allegedly justifying a sublinear risk assessment model. OSTP also inched away from the no-threshold assumption for epigenetic carcinogen promoters.

The OSTP report contains some valuable review of the scientific evidence regarding carcinogenesis, but its significance is still questionable. The OSTP policy does not legally bind federal regulatory agencies. Precisely because the OSTP stresses science rather than policy judgments, the Office's report gives limited guidance to regulatory agencies. These agencies are free to employ disparate policy judgments in quantitative risk assessment, as they occasionally have. Environmental groups have criticized the OSTP policy as too pro-industry, while some industry groups have complained that OSTP still mixes science with conservative policy judgments in quantitative risk assessment.

Given the difficulty in framing a consistent federal policy for quantitative risk assessment, it should be unsurprising that virtually nothing has been done to integrate risk management policies. Agencies suffer widely varying statutory mandates for risk management, which compel different agency practices. Some statutes require cost/benefit balancing while others reject any cost consideration whatsoever.

The Reagan administration attempted to bring some consistency and cost consideration into all federal regulation, including control of environmental carcinogens. Shortly after assuming office, President Reagan issued Executive Order 12291, which required all administrative agencies to analyze the benefits and costs of all proposed rules and to adopt only those rules found cost/beneficial.[134] The order could not override congressional statutes, however, and did not apply where a law precluded cost/benefit comparisons. Compliance with the executive order was monitored by the Office of Management and the Budget (OMB).

OMB is institutionally committed to limiting regulation of business and questioned a number of proposed carcinogen regulations. OMB urged greater cost consideration and reliance on the valuation of human life at $1 million in public health regulation. The Office bears responsibility for delaying or obstructing some significant carcinogen rules, such as EPA asbestos regulation under TSCA.

As presently structured, Executive Order 12291 and OMB can bring little consistency to federal carcinogen regulation. These sources have produced greater attention to regulatory costs in agency policy. Enabling statutes, however, are too diverse to be simply incorporated in OMB's cost/benefit scheme. Moreover, OMB's emphasis on cost considerations and relative lack of scientific expertise is so politically controversial that the Office is unlikely to provide any acceptable consensus for interagency carcinogen regulation.

Interagency coordination in risk assessment and other cancer policy principles has largely failed. One commentator observed:

The coordination or regulatory reform effort itself appeared uncoordinated. There were many committees and interagency groups doing virtually the same things. In addition, the agenda for cancer policy and regulatory reform was an extremely ambitious one and threatened to overload the capacity of the political system to address issues.[135]

The promise of interagency cooperation in carcinogen control is still unrealized.

OVERVIEW OF AGENCY PRACTICE

As described above, federal agencies now have over a decade of experience in regulating environmental exposures to carcinogens. Indeed, the above discussion omits a number of regulations and, in some cases, entire agencies (such as the Nuclear Regulatory Commission). Based on this experience, certain conclusions may be drawn. The federal regulatory program is widely regarded as a failure, and action to date has been slow, incomplete, and inconsistent.

Americans are regularly exposed to thousands of substances, of which hundreds may be carcinogenic. The 1985 Fourth Annual Report on Carcinogens of the Department of Health and Human Services lists 145 identified carcinogenic substances, and NTP studies reveal 144 substances with at least one positive study result. Federal agencies have regulated only a small fraction of this number of carcinogens. The National Toxicology Program lists sixty-one chemicals with positive results in three or more experiments, yet no federal agency has actually regulated more than seven of these chemicals. In fairness, some of these chemicals may present little actual risk to public health. Yet there are plainly some significant hazards that remain uncontrolled, particularly in occupational and other indoor settings. The federal agency record of action (and inaction) is illustrated in exhibit 5-1, taken from a chart prepared by the Office of Technology Assessment.

In addition to being incomplete, federal carcinogen regulation has been painfully slow and inefficient. OSHA's administrative procedures required more than four years to issue an arsenic standard, and revision of the benzene standard has taken over a decade, including court review. EPA control of airborne carcinogens has averaged nearly four years for issuance of final rules. Other agencies have taken nearly as long to complete carcinogen rulemakings. When final rules were issued, they frequently failed judicial review, necessitating lengthy additional proceedings for repromulgation.

When federal agencies have finally decided upon regulatory action for carcinogens, the actions have often been erratic and inconsistent. Formaldehyde regulation provides an obvious example of this inconsistency. In 1981, the CPSC proposed a ban on formaldehyde insulation, based on animal studies and a linear extrapolation model that produced a risk of about 10^{-4}. In the same year, OSHA declined to regulate formaldehyde exposures, perhaps because that agency employed sublinear quantitative assessment models that produced lower potency estimates. Ironically, the unregulated occupational formaldehyde exposure levels were higher than the indoor household exposures controlled by the CPSC. In 1982, EPA declared that environmental formaldehyde posed no significant risk, using sublinear extrapolation and concluding that risks of 10^{-4} were not particularly significant. Then, in 1984, EPA reversed itself and held that some formaldehyde exposure categories did present a significant risk. Shortly thereafter, OSHA also proposed a new formaldehyde regulation. These varying conclusions and policy reversals cannot be explained by any principled reassessment of the scientific evidence.

Formaldehyde is not an isolated instance of the regulatory incoherence that is rife throughout the history of federal carcinogen control. When reg-

Exhibit 5-1
Federal Regulation of Carcinogens

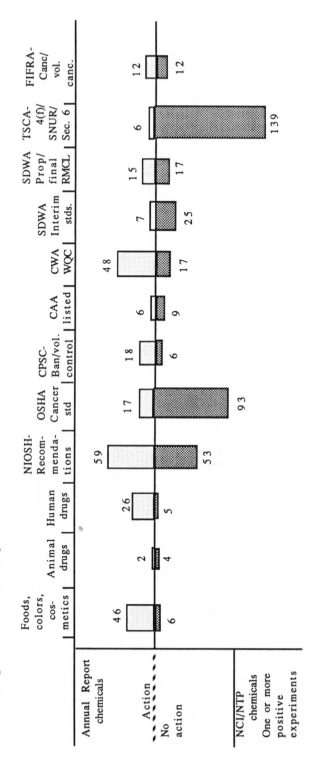

Exhibit 5-1 (Continued)

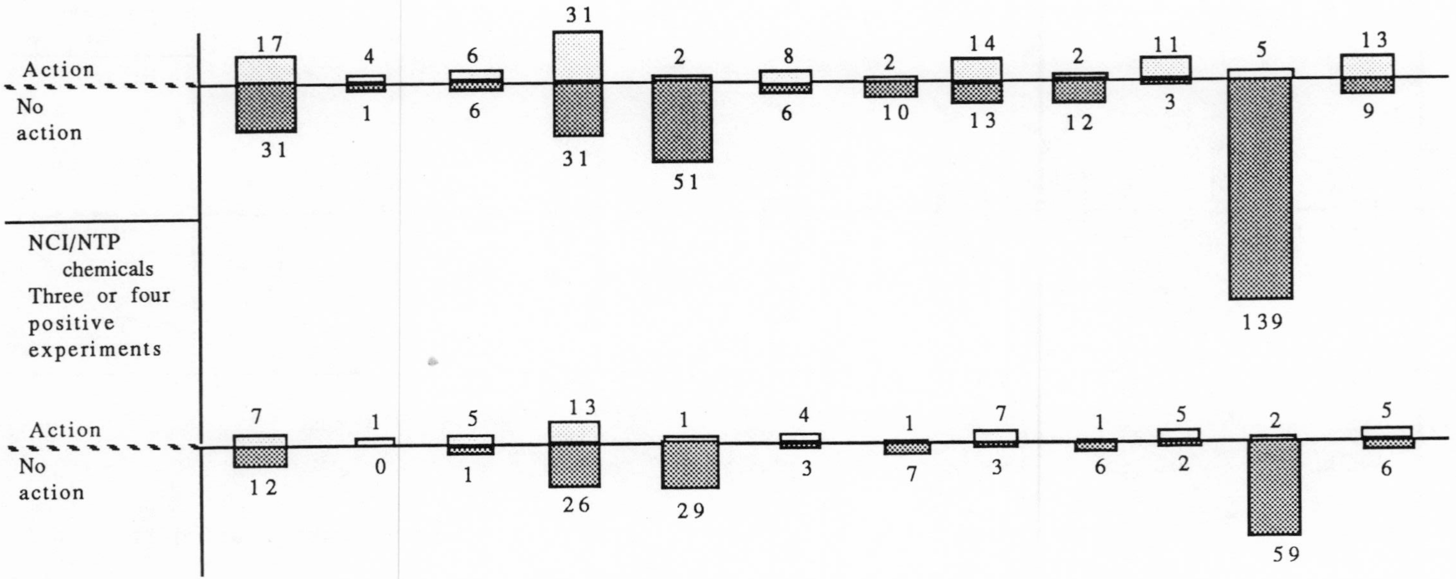

NCI/NTP
chemicals
Three or four
positive
experiments

Action
No action

Action
No action

17 31 · 4 1 · 6 6 · 31 31 · 2 51 · 8 6 · 2 10 · 14 13 · 2 12 · 11 3 · 5 139 · 13 9

7 12 · 1 0 · 5 1 · 13 26 · 1 29 · 4 3 · 1 7 · 7 3 · 1 6 · 5 2 · 2 59 · 5 6

ulating benzene, EPA, OSHA, and CPSC "adopted different risk-assessment principles, relied on different types of scientific evidence, and reached different conclusions about the extent of benzene-related health hazards."[136] OSHA's ethylene dibromide standard allows residual risks more than 1,000,000 times greater than the level at which EPA banned some uses of the same substance. In short, federal regulatory agencies have failed to offer any sensible and coherent program of carcinogen control.

Amidst this inconsistency, uncertainty, and inaction, however, some overriding regulatory principles and policies have emerged. Although different agencies employ different statutes and varying administrative assumptions, the resulting rules reflect some remarkably universal themes. For example, some cancer risks are so small that no agency ever regulates them, regardless of statutory mandate. Conversely, other risks are so large that agencies will act to reduce them regardless of cost. A recent article surveyed 132 federal carcinogen control regulations that included quantitative risk assessments, and the authors discovered:

First, every chemical with a risk above 4×10^{-3} ... was regulated. Second, except for one FDA decision ... , no action was taken to reduce individual lifetime risks that were below 1×10^{-6}.[137]

Where a particularly large population was exposed, the authors found that agencies regulated all risks exceeding 3×10^{-4}. With small exposed populations (less than 1,000), agencies have ignored all risks below 1×10^{-4}. The study of agency practice left a significant "gray area" of risk, in which regulation may or may not result. In this gray area, the regulatory decision appears largely driven by cost concerns:

In the region between the de manifestis and de minimis levels, substances with risk reduction costs of less than $2 million per life saved were regulated; substances that cost more were not regulated.[138]

These conclusions applied to regulations by OSHA, FDA, CPSC, and the various regulatory divisions of EPA.

The empirical predictability of carcinogen regulation should not be overstated—the authors reviewed a limited number of regulations over a limited time period, without consideration of all the variables that could influence agency decisions. The study does demonstrate that agencies will bow to political and practical realities, even at the expense of ignoring their authorizing statute's literal mandates.

Indeed, the delay, ineffectiveness, and inconsistency of regulatory decisions result from discordance between the organic statutes and administrative reality. Experience with FDA's Delaney Clause, OSHA's aborted cancer policy, EPA's section 112 practice, and other developments shows that agencies have expended more resources attempting to rationalize carcinogen regulation under their organic statutes than they have spent on actual positive regulation. New legislation, which is more realistic and comprehensive, might offer the optimal solution. The prospect for legislative reform is not good, however. Even under current statutes, agencies can improve their carcinogen regulation. A proposed outline for future, more effective regulation is set forth in the following chapter.

NOTES

1. 29 U.S.C. Sec. 655(b)(5) (1970).

2. 29 U.S.C. Sec. 652(8).

3. 37 *Fed. Reg.* 11318 (1972).

4. Industrial Union Department, AFL-CIO v. Hodgson, 499 F.2d 467 (D.C. Cir. 1974).

5. 38 *Fed. Reg.* 10929 (1973).

6. Dry Color Manufacturers' Association v. Brennan, 486 F.2d 98 (3rd Cir. 1973).

7. 39 *Fed. Reg.* 3755 (1974).

8. Synthetic Organic Chemical Manufacturers' Association v. Brennan, 506 F.2d 385 (3d Cir. 1974), cert. denied, 423 U.S. 830 (1975).

9. 39 *Fed. Reg.* 35889 (1974).

10. Society of the Plastics Industries, Inc. v. OSHA, 509 F.2d 1301 (2d Cir. 1975).

11. 41 *Fed. Reg.* 46750 (1976).

12. American Iron and Steel Institute v. OSHA, 477 F.2d 825 (D.C. Cir. 1978).

13. 39 *Fed. Reg.* 20494 (1974).

14. 40 *Fed. Reg.* 3392 (1975).

15. 43 *Fed. Reg.* 19584 (1978).

16. Shiela Sage Jasanoff, "The Misrule of Law at OSHA." In *The Language of Risk,* ed. D. Nelkin (1985), 159.

17. 45 *Fed. Reg.* 5004 (1980).

18. 45 *Fed. Reg.* 5011 (1980).

19. 43 *Fed. Reg.* 5918 (1978).

20. American Petroleum Institute v. OSHA, 581 F.2d 493 (5th Cir. 1978).

21. Industrial Union Department, AFL-CIO v. American Petroleum Institute, 448 U.S. 607, 653 (1980).

22. Id., 641.

23. Asarco, Inc. v. OSHA, 647 F.2d 1 (9th Cir. 1981) (*per curiam*).

24. 43 *Fed. Reg.* 2586 (1978).

25. 43 *Fed. Reg.* 45762 (1978).

26. 46 *Fed. Reg.* 61671 (1981).

27. 48 *Fed. Reg.* 1866 (1983).

28. 40 *Fed. Reg.* 47652 (1975).

29. 48 *Fed. Reg.* 51085 (1983).

30. 51 *Fed. Reg.* 22612 (1986).

31. Building and Construction Trades Department, AFL-CIO v. Brock, 838 F.2d 1258 (D.C. Cir. 1988).

32. Public Citizen Health Research Group v. Auchter, 554 F. Supp. 242 (D.D.C.), *aff'd*, 702 F.2d 1150 (D.C. Cir. 1983).

33. *52 Fed. Reg.* 34459 (1987).

34. *53 Fed. Reg.* 20960 (1988).

35. *53 Fed. Reg.* 21349 (1988).

36. 42 U.S.C. Sec. 7412(b) (1982).

37. *38 Fed. Reg.* 8819 (1973).

38. *40 Fed. Reg.* 59531 (1975).

39. David Doniger, "Federal Regulation of Vinyl Chloride: A Short Course in the Law and Policy of Toxic Substances Control," *Ecol. L. Q.* 7 (1978): 500, 566.

40. Frank Cross, *Beyond Benzene: Establishing Principles for a Significance Threshold on Regulatable Risks of Cancer,* 35 EMORY L.J. 1, 23 (1986).

41. *44 Fed. Reg.* 76739 (1979).

42. Sierra Club v. Gorsuch, 17 Env't Rep. (BNA) 1748 (N.D. Cal. 1982).

43. *48 Fed. Reg.* 15075 (1983).

44. "EPA Won't Issue Radiation Limits," *New York Times,* October 24, 1984, p. 17, col. 1.

45. *48 Fed. Reg.* 33112 (1983).

46. *51 Fed. Reg.* 27956 (1986).

47. *42 Fed. Reg.* 29332 (1977).

48. *45 Fed. Reg.* 83558 (1980).

49. *49 Fed. Reg.* 8391 (1984).

50. *50 Fed. Reg.* 1184 (1985).

51. Natural Resources Defense Council v. EPA, 824 F.2d 1146, 1165 (D.C. Cir. 1987).

52. Congressional Hearings, *Hearing on EPA's Air Pollution Control Program Before the Subcomm. on Oversight and Investigations of the House Comm. on Energy and Commerce,* 98th Cong., 1st Sess., 1983, 19.

53. 33 U.S.C. Sec. 1317(a)(2) (1982).

54. 33 U.S.C. Sec. 1311, 1314 (1982).

55. Natural Resources Defense Council v. Train, 8 Env't Rep. Cases (BNA) 2120 (D.D.C. 1976).

56. *52 Fed. Reg.* 42522 (1987).

57. 33 U.S.C. Sec. 1314 (1976).

58. 33 U.S.C. Sec. 1321 (1976).

59. *44 Fed. Reg.* 15925 (1979).

60. *45 Fed. Reg.* 46097 (1980).

61. Environmental Defense Fund v. EPA, 598 F.2d 62 (D.C. Cir. 1978).

62. 5 U.S.C. Sec. 2603(f) (1982).

63. 5 U.S.C. Sec. 2605(a) (1982).

64. Congressional Hearings, *Formaldehyde: Review of Scientific Basis of EPA's Carcinogenic Risk Assessment: Hearings Before the Subcomm. on Investigations and Oversight of the House Comm. on Science & Technology,* 97th Cong., 2d Sess. (1982): 252.

65. Nicholas Ashford, C. William Ryan and Charles Caldart, *A Hard Look at Federal Regulation of Formaldehyde: A Departure from Reasoned Decisionmaking,* 7 HARVARD ENVIRONMENTAL L. REV. 297, 326 (1983).

66. *49 Fed. Reg.* 21869 (1984).

67. 40 *Fed. Reg.* 59566 (1975).
68. Environmental Defense Fund v. Costle, 578 F.2d 337 (D.C. Cir. 1978).
69. 41 *Fed. Reg.* 28404 (1976).
70. 42 U.S.C. Sec. 300g-1(b)(1)(B) (1986).
71. 42 U.S.C. Sec. 300g-1(b)(3).
72. 44 *Fed. Reg.* 68642 (1979).
73. 50 *Fed. Reg.* 46880 (1985).
74. 52 *Fed. Reg.* 20672 (1987).
75. 7 U.S.C. Sec. 136a(c)(5) (1976).
76. 7 U.S.C. Sec. 136(bb).
77. 45 *Fed. Reg.* 42855 (1980).
78. Cross, 19–20.
79. Office of Technology Assessment, *Identifying and Regulating Carcinogens* (November 1987), 119.
80. 40 C.F.R. 35.501-1.
81. General Accounting Office, *Indoor Air Pollution: An Emerging Health Problem* (1980).
82. 15 U.S.C. Sec. 201 (1988).
83. 40 C.F.R. 763.90(a) (1988).
84. Safe Buildings Alliance v. EPA, 846 F.2d 79 (D.C. Cir. 1988).
85. 21 U.S.C. Sec. 348(c)(3)(A) (1976); 21 U.S.C. Sec. 376(b)(5)(B) (1976).
86. 21 U.S.C. Sec. 346 (1976).
87. 21 U.S.C. Sec. 342 (1976).
88. 40 *Fed. Reg.* 6489 (1975).
89. 42 *Fed. Reg.* 13540 (1977).
90. Monsanto v. Kennedy, 613 F.2d 947, 954 (D.C. Cir. 1979).
91. 38 *Fed. Reg.* 10458 (1973).
92. 39 *Fed. Reg.* 42748 (1974).
93. 39 *Fed. Reg.* 42750 (1974).
94. 43 *Fed. Reg.* 8808 (1978).
95. Cross, 40.
96. 47 *Fed. Reg.* 33007 (1982).
97. 39 *Fed. Reg.* 30830 (1974).
98. 42 *Fed. Reg.* 17487 (1977).
99. 42 *Fed. Reg.* 17492 (1977).
100. 44 *Fed. Reg.* 38330 (1979).
101. 45 *Fed. Reg.* 61476 (1980).
102. 45 *Fed. Reg.* 72116 (1980).
103. 42 *Fed. Reg.* 19996 (1977).
104. 45 *Fed. Reg.* 36942 (1980).
105. 47 *Fed. Reg.* 14463 (1982).
106. 47 *Fed. Reg.* 57681 (1982).
107. Scott v. FDA, 728 F.2d 322 (6th Cir. 1984).
108. 51 *Fed. Reg.* 28331 (1986).
109. Public Citizen v. Young, 831 F.2d 1108 (D.C. Cir. 1987).
110. 831 F.2d at 1122.
111. 15 U.S.C. Sec. 2056(a)(1) (1982).
112. 15 U.S.C. Sec. 1261 (1976).

113. Aqua Slide N' Dive Corporation v. CPSC, 569 F.2d 831 (5th Cir. 1978).

114. *39 Fed. Reg.* 18115 (1974).

115. *39 Fed. Reg.* 30112 (1974).

116. Pactra Industries, Inc. v. CPSC, 555 F.2d 677 (9th Cir. 1977).

117. *43 Fed. Reg.* 12308 (1978).

118. *42 Fed. Reg.* 63353 (1977).

119. *42 Fed. Reg.* 18849 (1977).

120. Spring Mills, Inc. v. CPSC, 434 F. Supp. 416 (D.S.C. 1977).

121. *43 Fed. Reg.* 21839 (1978).

122. *46 Fed. Reg.* 27910 (1981).

123. *43 Fed. Reg.* 25658 (1978).

124. Dow Chemical, USA v. CPSC, 459 F. Supp. 378 (W.D. La. 1978).

125. *44 Fed. Reg.* 23821 (1979).

126. Richard Merrill, *CPSC Regulation of Cancer Risks in Consumer Products: 1972–1981,* 67 VA. L. REV. 1261, 1270 (1981).

127. *46 Fed. Reg.* 11188 (1981).

128. *47 Fed. Reg.* 14365 (1982).

129. Gulf South Insulation v. CPSC, 701 F.2d 1137 (5th Cir. 1983).

130. *44 Fed. Reg.* 39858 (1979).

131. *49 Fed. Reg.* 21593 (1985).

132. *49 Fed. Reg.* 21595 (1985).

133. *49 Fed. Reg.* 21596 (1985).

134. 3 C.F.R. 127 (1982).

135. Rushefsky, 105.

136. Howard Latin, *Good Science, Bad Regulation, and Toxic Risk Assessment,* 5 YALE J. OF REGULATION 89, 108 (1988).

137. Curtis Travis, Samantha Richter, Edmund Crouch, Richard Wilson, and Ernest Klema, "Cancer Risk Management," *Environmental Science & Technology* 21 (1987): 418.

138. Ibid., 419.

6

FUTURE DIRECTIONS FOR CARCINOGEN REGULATION

The past decade's experience in carcinogen regulation, encompassing both failures and limited successes, offers guidance for more effective future regulation. By avoiding past mistakes, agencies may improve their regulatory record. This chapter proposes future directions for carcinogen regulation, in the form of a series of principles for agency action.

Effective regulation must begin with a sound decision regarding which environmental cancer risks to regulate. Thus I contend that agencies should assess risks honestly and completely, recognizing both the upper bound of risk and the most likely estimate, and that agencies should then prioritize their resources and target the greatest risks. Once this process has focused upon a carcinogen, agencies should pursue a moderate course of risk management regulation, relying upon feasibility analysis whenever legally permitted. Agencies should coordinate and integrate their carcinogen regulations with one another. Finally, Congress, the courts, and the agencies should strive to avoid or restrain judicial review of the resulting regulations. Additional details are set forth below.

ASSESS RISKS HONESTLY

While risk assessment has undeniable limitations and uncertainties, some use of the procedure is essential. Without risk assessment, agencies are incapable of prioritizing regulatory objectives or assessing regulatory benefits. Unfortunately, "dishonest" risk assessment can compromise the innate benefits of the procedure.

First, honest risk assessment means that agencies must openly make and acknowledge the policy assumptions about science that they use in regulation. These policy assumptions should include the absence of a threshold for carcinogens and the characteristics of dose-response relationships for carcinogens. The most conservative, risk-averse assumptions should be incorporated into every risk assessment, though other assumptions may also be used to illustrate the sensitivity of the assessment to the policy assumptions. All risk assessments should include an upper confidence limit (UCL) of maximum plausible risk, as well as a most likely estimate (MLE), which may be based upon less cautious policy assumptions.

In recent years, industry has called for the "separation of science and policy." This perspective abjures the use of conservative assumptions in risk assessment in favor of the most likely point estimate of risk at a given exposure. Then, risk aversion or conservatism may be introduced at the risk management stage of regulation. This approach supposedly protects the purity of the most accurate risk estimates, untainted by unrealistically cautious policy assumptions. Recently, EPA Administrator Ruckelshaus issued a similar call for the separation of science and policy in carcinogen regulation, and EPA's most recent carcinogen guidelines provide that risk assessment should "use the most scientifically appropriate interpretation" of the data and should be "carried out independently from considerations of the consequences of regulatory action."[1]

This proposed program of separation of science and policy is superficially appealing and theoretically logical. Yet the principle of such separation is contrary to both scientific knowledge and sound policymaking. There is no separable pure and conclusive science of carcinogenicity to apply in quantitative risk assessment. The National Research Council of the National Academy of Sciences thus observed:

A key premise of the proponents of institutional separation of risk assessment is that removal of risk assessment from the regulatory agencies will result in a clear demarcation of the science and policy aspects of regulatory decision-making. However, policy considerations inevitably affect, and perhaps determine, some of the choices among the inference options.[2]

Scientific risk assessment is unavoidably infected with policy conclusions. Indeed, many scientists have become political actors, representing various environmental and industrial interest groups. The science of carcinogenicity is yet so primitive that no indisputable "best" scientific estimate is possible. Attempts to produce and rely on a single MLE point estimate of risk merely create illusory and artificial certainty. Policy assumptions exist because of scientific uncertainty, and those assumptions must be used where uncertainty exists in the risk assessment process.

Reliance on a single MLE also yields illogical policy results, which cannot be corrected merely by conservative risk management policies. Consider hypothetical risk assessments for given exposures to two substances, both of which yield MLEs of 10^{-5}, but which have UCLs of 10^{-2} and 10^{-4}, respectively. Although the risk from both may be comparable, as in the MLEs, the first substance presents the possibility of creating much greater public health risk. This possibility should be at least considered in policymaking. Reserving conservative judgments for the risk management stage, however, would irrationally apply the same conservatism to both substances. A more sensible policy would introduce conservative policy assumptions at the risk assessment stage, so policymakers could acknowledge the difference between the two substances.

The need to combine scientific and policy considerations in risk assessment was recently highlighted by Howard Latin, a professor of law at Rutgers. Latin notes that science simply does not possess the answers to most risk assessment questions, and some outside policy consideration is inevitable. He thus writes that the " 'good science' perspective is simplistic and potentially harmful in toxic contexts where the best available science is unreliable."[3] In Latin's view, emphasis on false scientific precision "is likely to result in reduced public protection against potential toxic hazards, increased regulatory decisionmaking costs, and expanded opportunities for obstructive behavior by Agency bureaucrats or private parties hostile to toxic regulation."[4]

Second, honest risk assessment means acknowledging uncertainties and the role of policy assumptions. There is an unfortunate tendency of risk assessors to minimize the uncertainty associated with their estimates. Sometimes, environmental groups call for uniformly conservative policy assumptions to produce a UCL, and then these groups treat the UCL as if it were the most likely or only point estimate of public health risk. Instead, the UCL should be recognized for what it is—a theoretical estimate of maximum plausible risk that likely overstates the unmeasurable actual risk presented by a substance. The full range of risk estimates should be considered by regulators, including any MLEs based on alternative assumptions. Once this range is understood, regulators can make reasoned decisions with an eye to both the most likely risk estimate and the maximum plausible cancer risk resultant from exposures to a substance under consideration. When policy assumptions are employed in risk assessment, their use and significance should be identified clearly. The National Research Council thus argues that "a major contribution to the integrity of the risk assessment process would be the development of a procedure to ensure that the judgments made in risk assessments, and the underlying rationale for such judgments, are made explicit."[5]

This balanced approach—including MLEs and acknowledging uncertainty—contrasts with that of OSHA's proposed cancer policy. OSHA established conservative policy assumptions as irrebuttable presumptions of fact for purposes of regulation. The conservative assumptions are legitimate, but their limitations must be recognized. Thus the OSTP calls for a "*weltschauung* utilizing a balanced approach with an appreciation of all elements of the problem."[6]

Environmentalists object to this case-by-case "balanced approach," which they view as an opportunity for delay as industry proposes a series of unlikely contentions, such as the existence of a carcinogenic threshold. Alternatively, the balanced approach could be manipulated to ideological ends. While both these criticisms are legitimate, neither is compelling.

Considering all the relevant evidence is unlikely to delay regulations overmuch. Carcinogen regulation historically is characterized by extensive delays, which have existed even in the absence of any risk assessment. The amount of time required to assess substance-specific information is trivial compared with these past delays. Indeed, delay may be ascribed largely to political concern over the consequences of zero risk or other extreme regulatory outcomes. A more moderate approach may actually reduce delay through enhanced cooperation. As for the fear of political manipulation of risk assessment, there are many alternative channels for such manipulation should a political administration choose to so act.

Industry will no doubt object to continued use of conservative assumptions as a bias in regulation and as perhaps contrary to administrative law requirements for determining the best evidence. This concern is largely obviated, however, so long as decisionmakers recognize the limited role of the UCL. The UCL should not form the sole basis of prioritization and regulation. Exclusive and complete reliance upon the most conservative assumptions may significantly overestimate risk and render regulations unsustainable under judicial review.

Moreover, conservative assumptions in risk assessment need not necessarily lead to more rigorous regulation. By introducing conservatism in risk assessment, where it belongs, less conservatism may be required in risk management. Once we know the maximum plausible risk at a given exposure, we may feel more secure in considering costs or feasibility and avoid a zero risk paradigm. This approach may ensure adequate public health protection while minimizing regulatory compliance costs, insofar as possible.

Thus risk assessment should produce at least two estimates for a substance, for the most likely level of risk, and for the plausible upper level of risk. If possible, the assessment should also include descriptive evidence indicating the confidence that may be ascribed to the MLE. Concededly, this approach yields only an imprecise range of risk estimates. Precision is not so necessary for the use of risk assessment in priority setting, which is the preferred use for this unavoidably uncertain regulatory tool.

CONTROL PRIORITIZATION

The hundreds of possible carcinogens and the widely varying public health threats presented by these substances suggest the need for effective prioritization of agency regulatory targets. While regulatory efficiency may improve in the future, federal agencies will never be able to address all possible carcinogenic hazards. Seventy thousand chemicals are in commercial use, and FDA alone must deal with over 14,000 food-related chemicals currently in use. Very few of these substances have even been tested for carcinogenicity, much less regulated. Consequently, agencies must prioritize future action so as to address the most serious health threats first.

Limited regulatory resources are a fact of life. Limited personnel, limited investigatory resources, and limited time for the administrator all constrain regulation. No agency has ever been able to adopt more than one or two carcinogen regulations per year. Given this limitation, a "wise regulatory procedure obviously cannot waste these finite administrative commodities chasing after substances that present little risk."[7]

In light of the limited regulatory resources, effective carcinogen control demands that the available resources be concentrated on the most serious solvable problems. Problems do not target themselves. Rather, the regulatory agency first must recognize the problem and then must be motivated to address the problem. Indoor air pollution illustrates the need for prioritization. Indoor air pollution, particularly radon exposure, has long been one of the most serious public health problems in the United States. Yet the problem was not recognized until recently and, even now, federal agencies are not motivated to take significant action to regulate the problem.

Indoor air pollution thus illustrates a failure of prioritization. Such pollution should be given top priority by an agency intent upon maximizing public health protection, but the various federal regulatory agencies have largely lost control of the prioritization process. Instead, priorities are typically set by political pressure from various public or special interest groups. While these groups are properly concerned with public health protection, they have their own constituencies and interests, such as outdoor air pollution or hazardous wastes, and consequently may divert regulatory concern from other more serious problems.

Experience demonstrates that agencies have lost control of the prioritization process. Chapter 4 discloses that most EPA initiatives have been taken in response to citizen petitions. One review thus notes that "EPA has had great difficulty in setting explicit risk-based priorities, especially for the agency as a whole, across program lines."[8] Similarly, OSHA regulation is almost entirely in reaction to labor union pressure. Two expert students of regulation thus observed:

The Environmental Protection Agency (EPA) constantly changed its priorities during the 1970s on the basis of current concerns and media headlines. Under this "carcinogen of the month" policy, many major risks were neglected in favor of transient public concerns.[9]

Limited regulatory resources have been wasted in pursuit of trivial cancer risks.

The administrative process of setting standards for carcinogens requires considerable money and man-hours in accumulating information on health effects, analyzing control options, applying legal standards, drafting defensible rules, and complying with the gauntlet of procedural requirements imposed by courts. It is estimated that setting an OSHA carcinogen standard requires approximately $2 million in agency funds. OSHA's annual budget for standard-setting is approximately $5 million. Given the large number of carcinogens found in an occupational setting, trade-offs are inevitable, and OSHA's efforts to "develop a permanent standard for vinyl chloride within six months required dropping everything else."[10] Rather obviously, OSHA has little money to waste and should focus its resources wisely.

Federal misprioritization of funds for carcinogen control is exemplified by EPA's budgetary priorities. In the most recent year, the agency devoted nearly $60 million to identifying and correcting problems from asbestos in schools, which causes a handful of cancers at most, and spent only about $6 million on indoor radon exposures, which are thought to be responsible for tens of thousands of cancers. The agency spent over $70 million setting hazardous waste standards, but only $13 million on air pollution standards, though air pollution is clearly a greater threat to public health. OSHA, which confronts one of the greatest carcinogen problems, receives less than $10 million for all aspects of standards development. Currently, carcinogen control resources are badly misallocated. Resources are further misallocated within individual media cancer prevention programs.

Blame for this misallocation of funds is shared by the executive branch and Congress. Administrators should inform the budget-setting process, though, and push political officials toward the greatest risks. EPA's recent announcement regarding the threat of indoor radon exposure received considerable media attention and belatedly commenced mobilization of control resources.

Some public involvement in agency priority setting is unavoidable and probably beneficial. Structurally, the "operational priorities of agencies in a democratic government arise from politics."[11] Yet agencies must go beyond such "democratic" inputs and employ their specialized expertise in prioritization. Given the widespread public misperception of risk and the specialized concerns of powerful interest groups, too much deference to public input will compromise effective carcinogen regulation. "EPA's experience in the 1970s makes clear that being 'too responsive' can waste opportunities and fail to protect the public."[12]

Any effective prioritization system must begin with significant risk. If we are to maximize public health protection, agencies should direct their limited resources to the greatest health hazards. Thus agencies should adopt a program of identifying and ordering the quantitatively greatest cancer risks and addressing those risks in some systematic manner. Quantitative comparison of risks thus becomes paramount.

This logical ordering of cancer risks for regulation will be attacked from both ends of the spectrum. Industry interests emphasize that agencies also should consider the feasibility and cost-effectiveness of risk reduction, in order truly to maximize health protection. Such an approach has been proposed by Richard Stewart and Bruce Ackerman, two leading professors of environmental law.[13] While theoretically sound, widespread utilization of these considerations is likely to stall regulation through overanalysis. The effectiveness of risk reduction might appropriately be incorporated in prioritization for some problems, but in most cases agencies should simply use risk significance as the prioritizing tool.

Some environmentalists have contended that risk assessment is too uncertain even for use in prioritization. One commentator suggested that risk assessment uncertainty was comparable to "not knowing whether one has enough money to buy a cup of coffee or pay off the national debt."[14] Latin considers a structuring ordering of risks for prioritization to be "not merely 'fanciful,' but fantastic."[15]

Yet this criticism of risk assessment is too easy and superficial. Some means must be used to prioritize regulatory action. Risk assessment is sufficiently accurate to identify the most substantial carcinogenic hazards. We can be certain, for example, that indoor radon exposures present a risk far in excess of individual outdoor pollutants. Likewise, few if any scientists would dispute that mycotoxins are a far greater hazard than color food additives. When epidemiology identifies an excess risk, such as that found around arsenic smelters or among pottery workers, we can be confident that the risk is a substantial one worthy of priority attention.

Risk assessment may also promote valuable prioritization among sources of a given pollutant. For example, benzene emissions from coke ovens far exceeded those from benzene storage vessels. The relative risk from the former source was 100 times higher. Yet EPA chose to propose regulation for storage vessels before coke ovens. Better-controlled prioritization would add rationality and effectiveness to this regulatory program. The Harvard Scientific Conflict Mapping Project emphasized this point, after studying regulatory experience, observing that:

agencies tend to react to petitions from interest groups and then seek scientific advice on a case-by-case basis. We believe that if federal agencies sought and utilized more external scientific advice on the comparative risks of various chemicals, they would be able to expend their limited resources in a way that provided greater public health benefits.[16]

The proposed prioritization approach would employ significant risk to order chemical hazards for regulation, with consideration given to the feasibility and cost-effectiveness of control technology in some limited number of cases. Qualitative evidence of carcinogenicity might also be incorporated into this prioritization framework. Every federal agency should be legally allowed to employ this prioritization, as courts have generally deferred to administrative priority setting. For example, while the Supreme Court has precluded OSHA use of cost/benefit analysis in risk management standard-setting, the Court has expressly authorized at least some cost considerations in OSHA's prioritization of targets for regulation. EPA's air toxics program has had some limited recent success with prioritization, identifying the greatest hazards from airborne carcinogens and focusing regulatory attention on these substances.

PURSUE A MODERATE COURSE OF RISK MANAGEMENT

Too often, the debate over carcinogen regulation is polarized between environmentalists striving to eliminate all carcinogen exposure and representatives of industry seeking to avoid all regulation. Environmentalists point to the thousands of preventable cancer deaths as a compelling call to dramatic action. Industry representatives emphasize that science is unable conclusively to link most environmental exposures to any such cancer deaths. The disagreement between these two camps is partly scientific but largely grounded in policy assumptions and values.

Both environmental and industry groups have some truth to their respective positions. Continued cancer deaths command some regulatory action, before science can conclusively prove the cause of such deaths. Yet the relative insignificance of many environmental exposures as a cause of cancer and the undeniable costs of regulation caution against precipitous and radical regulatory requirements. A moderate regulatory course seems the wisest.

The pragmatic case for moderation in regulation is even more compelling. When government has attempted extremely strict and rigid carcinogen regulation, its program has typically backfired and produced little effective regulation. Conversely, when government has avoided regulating carcinogens, public backlash has compelled a more active course of regulation.

The political environmental commitment of the administration in power has had surprisingly little effect on carcinogen regulation. Exhibit 6-1 reviews the regulatory successes of the Carter administration and the two terms of the Reagan administration, identifying proposed and final rules for carcinogens under three leading sources of statutory authority. Regulations that failed judicial review are not counted. Exhibit 6-1 seems to suggest that the Reagan administration has done more to control carcinogens than the Carter administration, even though the officials appointed by Carter were unquestionably more committed to environmental

Exhibit 6-1
Carcinogen Regulation by Administration

AGENCY ACTION	CARTER	REAGAN I	REAGAN II
OSHA			
Final Rules	Acrylonitrile Arsenic	Ethylene Oxide	Asbestos Formaldehyde
Proposed Rules	Acrylonitrile	Asbestos Ethylene Oxide Ethylene Dibromide	Benzene Formaldehyde Air Contaminants
EPA Air			
Final Rules			Arsenic Radionuclides Coke Ovens
Proposed Rules	Benzene	Arsenic Coke Ovens Radionuclides	Radionuclides Benzene
TSCA			
Final Rules		Asbestos PCBs	Asbestos
Proposed Rules	Asbestos	PCBs	Asbestos

and occupational safety regulation. This conclusion may be too strong—most of the Reagan actions were compelled by outside public pressure or court action. The exhibit strongly suggests, though, that political commitment to regulation is insufficient for effective action against environmental carcinogens.

Some of the Carter administration failure must be ascribed to overregulation, and the Reagan administration's efforts at avoiding regulation have failed. Agencies must eschew both overregulation and underregulation. The hazards of these extreme courses and a proposed moderate approach are elaborated below.

Avoid Overregulation

However desirable it might seem to abolish all human exposure to environmental carcinogens, this approach is unnecessary and unworkable. The zero risk paradigm is theoretically nonsensical, for reasons discussed in chapter 4. Zero risk is also practically ineffective as an approach to carcinogen control. If the zero risk paradigm were ever to succeed, the Delaney Clause would demonstrate such success. The Delaney Clause governs only intentional food additives, which are economically unnecessary and may practically be eliminated. Even in this best case for zero risk, however, administrative practicalities have destroyed the approach. FDA has struggled to avoid the zero risk paradigm of the Delaney Clause, and this provision has made no meaningful contribution to cancer prevention.

Nevertheless, some public health and environmental groups continue to press for a zero risk approach to carcinogen control. In slightly more moderate form, these groups may simply fight any cost consideration in regulation or insist upon extremely low residual risk levels in regulation. Such efforts are doubtless well-motivated, but attempts to impose highly restrictive controls on carcinogens have a history of failure. Like zero risk, such a rigorous control program may even become counterproductive.

Overly stringent control regimes chill the promulgation of regulations. When an agency "is compelled to regulate more strictly than it would prefer, it will probably become even more reluctant to undertake new standards."[17] This danger has been realized under the Clean Air Act, where "the potentially extreme language of section 112 has frightened EPA away from making any significant use of that authority."[18] FDA has had similar experience with the Delaney Clause. Rather than promoting carcinogen regulation, the Delaney Clause has focused FDA efforts' on avoiding its application in regulation. FDA saccharin regulation is also instructive. One commentator thus noted:

Anticipating the storm of criticism that would accompany a ban of the only dietetic sweetener remaining on the market, the FDA delayed all meaningful regulation of [saccharin] for at least ten years after evidence of its potential carcinogenicity began to accumulate. Like all politically sensitive organizations, the FDA balks at remedies it sees as disproportionate to the ill needing cure.[19]

Of course, once FDA finally did attempt to ban saccharin, political forces overturned its action.

Not only may the fear of statutorily compelled overregulation chill agency action, but extremely stringent controls on any given substance may obstruct the control of additional substances. A program of "intense focusing...on a single or very few substances" will "delay recognition, assessment and some degree of control over the full range of potential carcinogens."[20] Adoption of very stringent regulatory controls requires more agency time to identify and justify controls, while simultaneously provoking added resistance from the industry to be regulated, which in turn requires still more agency resources in response. A review of experience at OSHA and EPA concluded that in "the larger political arena," there are "long-run trade-offs between intensity and scope" of toxic chemical regulation.[21] There is an inexorable depth vs. breadth trade-off that must be addressed by regulators. Given the numerous environmental carcinogenic hazards of roughly comparable risk, regulators should begin to opt for breadth of regulation, at the sacrifice of depth or stringency.

Even when very stringent environmental regulations are adopted, enhanced public health protection may not necessarily result. Regulations must be enforced to be effective. For example, industrial sources frequently violate water pollution NPDES permits, often without penalty. The enforcement process is riddled with discretion, and study of the administrative process has shown that agencies will not vigorously enforce rules that are perceived as unreasonable. Conversely, when regulatory demands are more moderate and achievable, voluntary compliance increases, and enforcement is more vigorous and evenhanded.

Thus moderation is critical in carcinogen regulation. The current situation of environmentally induced cancer is not so serious as to require radical action. Moreover, well-meaning efforts at stringent carcinogen regulation are likely to set back overall protection, as a practical matter. Even the "union staff who are most involved in health and safety issues are aware that overregulation can be counterproductive."[22] A cross-national comparison of regulation in Great Britain and the United States likewise concluded that "the American experience demonstrates that overregulation can readily lead to underregulation."[23]

Avoid Underregulation

The danger of underregulation became a realistic concern during the first term of the Reagan Administration. EPA, OSHA, and other federal agencies seemed emasculated and withdrew as many proposed regulations as they issued. Procedurally, underregulation often takes the form of cost/benefit analysis, which at minimum delays regulatory action and may be manipulated to avoid action altogether. Alternatively, regulatory demands for absolute scientific certainty in causation may also stifle action. Howard Latin argues that "a typical consequence of requiring regulators to address currently unanswerable scientific questions is agency paralysis, not improved decisionmaking."[24] In addition, underregulation results from certain risk assessment procedures, such as assuming the existence of thresholds. These procedures may lead to the stultification of all regulation of environmental carcinogens.

The most obvious argument against underregulation or government inaction is the public health toll of cancer in the United States today. Some environmental sources contribute significantly to these cancer deaths. Experts may quibble over whether air pollution causes 1,000 or 10,000 deaths, but either scenario justifies regulatory control. One court observed that "[i]f regulation were withheld until the danger [from carcinogens] was demonstrated conclusively, untold injury to public health could result."[25] There is a widespread public consensus that environmental exposures to carcinogenic chemicals require some measure of regulation.

There remain, of course, some "true believers" who question whether any cancer deaths are caused by environmental pollutants and who contend that the costs of environmental regulation invariably outweigh the benefits. This group is a minority, however, and its policy prescriptions are ultimately self-defeating.

In the early days of the Reagan administration, with such prominent appointees as James Watt, Anne Burford and Thorne Auchter, the antiregulatory minority largely held sway. Before long, however, this group was discredited and public pressure drove the administration back toward a more centrist environmental policy. A "combination of scandals within EPA plus strong congressional and public support for continued environmental protection created an environment in which cancer policy development moved back toward the consensus (among the agencies, at any rate) enunciated during the Carter Administration."[26] Underregulation, or the perception of underregulation, may poison even moderate standards issued by regulatory agencies. A pattern of unconcern creates skepticism about all actions of an agency. Thus, "[j]udicial mistrust of Reagan's deregulation effort also helped to derail the [OSHA] cotton dust and lead standards."[27]

Rely Primarily on Feasibility Analysis

To be effective, carcinogen regulation should rely primarily on feasibility analysis for risk management. The zero risk paradigm is unrealistic and ineffective. The significant risk paradigm offers advantages in prioritization but is too imprecise for use in setting regulatory control levels. Cost/benefit analysis is also too imprecise and too subject to manipulation and delay.

As discussed in chapter 4, feasibility analysis is perhaps the most illogical risk management approach, when viewed in the abstract. In application, however, feasibility analysis has been far more effective than alternative approaches. Former EPA administrator during the Carter administration Douglas Costle testified that "experience with the alternative approaches ... leave[s] us firmly convinced that for the bulk of known or suspected toxics of concern, technology-based standards established on an industry-by-industry basis are by far the most feasible to implement and administer."[28]

Throughout the federal government, regulatory provisions employing feasibility-based standards have been the most effective. Professor Latin reviewed the Clean Water Act and suggested that "EPA has promulgated more toxic substances standards in the past decade under this one technology-based program than it has under all of its programs that require quantitative risk assessments based on 'good science.' "[29] Similarly, under the Clean Air Act, EPA "has been much more effective in developing [technology-based] NSPSs than in promulgating NESHAPS under section 112" for carcinogens.[30]

INTEGRATE CARCINOGEN REGULATION

Truly effective carcinogen regulation requires consistency of policy both among and within the federal regulatory agencies charged with this responsibility. Consistency can be achieved through integrating risk assessment and management policies through interagency cooperation. Given conflicting statutory mandates, total consistency is unachievable. Considerable progress can be made, however, through maximizing the level of coordination and consistency enabled by law.

Integrate Risk Assessment Policies

The varying statutory directives given agencies are almost exclusively limited to risk management, leaving the agencies considerable discretion in their adoption of principles for risk assessment. In the past, different agencies have taken very different policies on risk assessment issues, with some adopting uniformly conservative assumptions and others relying more on central estimates of risk. Nothing in the different jurisdictions of the regulatory agencies justifies such disparities in risk assessment policy.

Integrative consistency in risk assessment is essential to fair and effective regulation of carcinogens. When EPA and CPSC take widely varying views of the science of formaldehyde carcinogenicity, for example, the system not only appears illogical, it is illogical. Former EPA Administrator William Ruckelshaus complained that the "public interest is not served by two federal agencies taking diametrically opposed positions on the health risks of a toxic substance and then arguing about it in the press."[31] There is no reason why the federal agencies charged with carcinogen regulation cannot agree upon principles for use in risk assessment and apply these principles in regulatory decisions.

The National Research Council has appealed for such consistency, calling for government-wide guidelines, because they "help[] to ensure fairness and rationality by precluding the arbitrary application of selected inference options that differ from one time to the next."[32] The Council also emphasized that consistent guidelines can make regulations more defensible in litigation challenging the adoption of carcinogen controls. Like the National Academy of Sciences (NAS), the American Medical Association Council on Scientific Affairs has declared that "a uniform policy with uniform decision-making criteria should be applied by the several relevant federal agencies."[33] The Administrative Conference of the United States has also urged that "agencies responsible for regulating carcinogens should adhere to common criteria for evaluating and interpreting health effects data."[34]

Consistent risk assessment principles also offer valuable predictability to regulated industries. Industry can plan its own testing and development programs in reliance on established government policy. Otherwise, "a regulated party may have to call on the agencies for judgments on numerous issues and have no assurance that the judgments will not change unexpectedly or that one agency's judgment will be consistent with another's."[35] The presence of inconsistent or even erratic responses frustrates voluntary action by industry and may encourage industry to undertake additional challenges to individual agency actions.

Consistent risk assessment practices offer additional benefits as well. Interagency consistency fosters credibility, both in overall federal action and in individual regulations. True consistency would also provide economies of scale and avoid repetition when different agencies must regulate the same substance.

Some progress has been made in integrating risk assessment among the federal agencies. The IRLG demonstrates that the agencies can agree on general principles. The developing OSTP cancer guidelines could provide the principles essential for integrated risk assessment. At the present time, however, the OSTP policy is too vague and has not been entirely adopted by any of the agencies commissioned with carcinogen regulation.

Intermedia Integration

Integration of carcinogen control among various exposure media (air, water, food, etc.) has been largely lacking. Congress authorized different regulatory programs for different media, in its program of media-specific statutes. With the exception of the Toxic Substances Control Act, the leading carcinogen controls statutes are predominantly limited to a specific media of exposure. Administrative control efforts have been divided roughly parallel to this underlying statutory authorization. Most environmental media are regulated by EPA, however, and that agency could compel additional consideration of intermedia effects in all its regulation.

Intermedia integration is directly important to the protection of public health. For example, an air pollution rule prohibiting or regulating incineration of wastes may cause greater use of land or water disposal of such wastes, which themselves threaten health. Water quality regulations have for years removed toxic pollutants from water and disposed of them in landfills, some of which promptly leached into groundwater. EPA occasionally has recognized and addressed this problem. In the agency's recent water effluent guidelines for the chemicals industry, it noted that "available information strongly indicated that biological treatment systems fail to treat substantial portions of volatile and semi-volatile pollutants but rather transfer them to the air."[36] Even after recognizing this problem, the agency elected not to control air emissions in the context of a water quality standard but postponed consideration for subsequent regulation under the Clean Air Act. Regulatory history suggests that applicable air quality regulations may be a long time in coming, however. Consequently, EPA has promulgated expensive water quality control requirements that may offer little public health benefit. The agency may even have exacerbated the health problem, as air emissions may cause greater exposure and present a greater hazard through inhalation.

All agencies therefore should consider the intermedia effects of their regulations. The problem is particularly pronounced at EPA, where intermedia transfer of cancer risks is especially likely. Rather than use this risk transference as an excuse for inaction, however, EPA should initiate cross-media regulation for the greatest cancer hazards. Nothing prevents EPA from taking a substance such as vinyl chloride and combining air, water, and land disposal regulations into a single rulemaking proceeding.

Indeed, EPA has made some progress in intermedia assessment for environmental pollutants. The agency has formed an Integrated Environmental Management Program that operates upon the following lines:

Exposures through all media (for example, air, drinking water, or food) from all significant toxic chemical sources in the area are modeled and the associated risks are estimated. The risks from various control options are also estimated. Through additional modeling it is then possible to arrive at the most efficient way of reducing total risk for any desired expenditure.[37]

EPA's integrated risk management program is encouraging but has showed little in the way of results. Agency regulations continue blithely to ignore the intermedia consequences of carcinogen control.

Interpollutant Integration

In regulating carcinogenic chemical exposures, agencies have sometimes focused on an industry category but more often have addressed specific individual pollutants, regardless of their sources. Concededly, the latter approach appears more consistent with statutory authorizations, which often call for specific pollutants to be "listed" or otherwise identified prior to regulation. Experience suggests, however, that broad regulation by industry category offers greater promise for effective and efficient carcinogen regulation.

Former EPA Administrator Costle testified that industry-by-industry feasibility standards were the most practical to set. These standards can balance the various risks presented by a source category and adopt the most cost-effective controls. Coke ovens, for example, produce a number of carcinogens, some of which have been regulated in separate proceedings. Surely a combined proceeding to address carcinogenic hazards of coke ovens more comprehensively offers economies of scale and more efficient and effective regulation.

Industry-based standards also offer substantial spillover benefits—application of an emission reduction action will typically control emissions of many pollutants beyond the one in question. Air pollution control provides an ironic example of this effect. Various common ambient air pollutants (such as carbon monoxide, ozone, and particulates) are controlled through state emission control requirements under section 110 of the Clean Air Act. While these requirements are not based on carcinogenic effects, the section 110 standards have incidentally done more to prevent exposure to airborne carcinogens than have all the section 112 standards combined. According to EPA, the effect of the ambient standards on carcinogens "far exceeds the impact of section 112 regulation."[38]

Integrate Risk Management Policies

Full integration of risk management is prevented by statute. Some statutes compel cost/benefit analysis, while others prohibit the tool. Some risk management integration is still possible, however. Former EPA administrator William Ruckelshaus stresses that "even at the management stage there is no reason why the approaches cannot be coordinated to achieve the goal of risk avoidance or minimization with the least societal disruption possible."[39] At least those agencies employing cost/benefit analysis could use the technique consistently. For example, OSHA regulations have implicitly valued human life saving from $200,000 to $20 million, while EPA air pollution controls have spent in excess of $100 million per life saved. Similar disparities appear throughout federal health protection regulation. While some disparity is an unavoidable consequence of varying statutory regimes, minimizing the disparity can contribute to more rational and effective carcinogen regulation.

Inconsistencies likewise appear in agency use of significant risk principles. Unfortunately, little or no effort has been given to establishment of uniform federal policies of risk significance. Dr. Roy Albert has thus complained that "the current carcinogen standards of the Occupational Safety and Health Administration entail lifetime cancer risks as high as 1 percent to 2 percent [10^{-2}], which is completely out of balance with the attempts to control environmental exposure to lifetime risk levels of 10^{-6}."[40]

Inconsistency in risk regulation compromises its effectiveness, and Dr. Albert went on to suggest that, in part for this reason, "there has never been a federal cancer regulatory policy that really works."[41] Moreover, inconsistency can undermine the "perceived equity" of regulatory decisions, resulting in a loss of confidence that can cause "paralysis" in "risk management decisionmaking."[42] By contrast a coherent and consistent policy could offer considerable benefit. Creating "a predictable regulatory environment would be a powerful incentive to conform business decisionmaking to politically sanctioned social policy," thereby producing extra-regulatory benefits in the form of voluntary "substitution of less hazardous substances in industrial processes or the adoption of more efficient technology that is also safer for workers and less damaging to the environment."[43]

In addition to consistent regulatory policies, agencies should cooperate among themselves in regulatory initiatives. An action by one agency may influence the concerns of another. For example, when EPA restricted the carcinogenic pesticide ethylene dibromide, only phosphine and methyl bromide were available as substitutes. Yet both these substances presented a much greater occupational risk than did ethylene dibromide. In effect, the EPA rule produced a "redistribution of risk from the general public to the workers—imposed risks that may be substantial."[44] Perhaps EPA was correct in banning certain uses of ethylene dibromide, but there is no justification for the agency ignoring the risks of substitutes, simply because those risks were outside EPA jurisdiction. A joint action with OSHA might have better protected overall public and worker health.

In addition, different federal agencies may have overlapping jurisdiction with respect to a given health problem. When this occurs, a judgment must be made regarding which agency will assume regulatory responsibility for the problem. Because agencies have differing resources and expertise, this judgment may critically affect the success of carcinogen control. Making such a principled judgment based on relative abilities and resources will further contribute to effective regulation.

Jurisdictional overlaps are most common between OSHA authority to regulate occupational exposures and EPA TSCA authority to control all sources of exposure. Congress anticipated jurisdictional disputes and included section 9 in TSCA, which permits the EPA administrator to refer hazards to other agencies, such as OSHA, for regulation. In operation, however, this authority has been primarily used to avoid regulation. EPA has referred seven carcinogenic chemicals to OSHA, none of which have been yet regulated and only one of which, formaldehyde, has seen even a proposed regulation.

In a sense, the current interagency cooperation and integration is backwards. Rather than avoiding use of TSCA, the federal government should be making greater use of that statute. TSCA offers greater flexibility and greater regulatory power than the Occupational Safety and Health Act or most other federal statutes. TSCA alone permits simple and complete integration of intermedia exposures as well. Greater reliance on TSCA regulation is the most promising source of integrated carcinogen risk management.

EPA may now be inching toward this desired regulatory integration under the Toxic Substances Control Act. The agency has created a new Office of Pollution Prevention to provide a broader perspective and promote overall minimization of waste streams.[45] EPA has recently used TSCA to regulate air emissions of hexavalent chromium, because TSCA offered better control options than those provided in the Clean Air Act. In preparing for future regulation of chlorinated solvents, the agency is first seeking out the optimal control measures and only then choosing which statute to use for regulation. These developments foreshadow a more integrated and effective approach to carcinogen regulation within EPA.

RESTRAIN JUDICIAL REVIEW

Rather obviously, judicial review has obstructed carcinogen regulation. Numerous rules have been vacated and remanded for agency consideration. This action has delayed carcinogen controls for years and, in some cases, has forestalled regulation altogether. Steps should be taken to reduce the intrusiveness of judicial review.

Some judicial review, of course, is necessary. Only this review can ensure compliance with law and prevent bureaucratic arbitrariness. And in some instances, judicial decisions facilitate future regulation. Too often, though, judges immerse themselves in scientific decisions and policy judgments and second-guess the choices made by agency officials. In these cases, judges are stepping beyond their role and capability.

Judge Bazelon of the D.C. Circuit Court of Appeals put it well when he cautioned that "substantive review of mathematical and scientific evidence by technically illiterate judges is dangerously unreliable."[46] Judges should instead defer to administrative judgments. While this conclusion would seem unexceptional, it is largely lacking in adherents. Industry groups, of course, favor judicial review, which they have used to their advantage. Environmentalists frequently call for judicial deference to agency regulatory decisions, but then demand judicial activism in response to decisions not to regulate. Even Judge Bazelon was unable to eschew such an activist stance in citizen action against the Nuclear Regulatory Commission. Judicial deference should be evenhanded, respecting agency policy judgments to regulate and those not to regulate.

The greatest concern involves judicial review that makes carcinogen regulation difficult, if not impossible. An archetypical example of inappropriate judicial review can be found in *Gulf South Insulation v. CPSC*, which struck down the Commission's ban on formaldehyde insulation.[47] In *Gulf South*, the court closely scrutinized the scientific record, concluded that the Commission had relied on the wrong studies, and required much more data. Quite obviously, this holding intruded deeply into administrative policy judgments. Professor Latin concludes that this opinion "reflects insensitivity to the protective goals of the organic regulatory legislation and a fundamental misunderstanding of the limited evidence on which most risk assessments of carcinogens are based."[48] Latin goes on to complain that "[u]nrealistic judicial requirements for comprehensive agency assessments of all potentially relevant factors and for a high degree of scientific precision have substantially emasculated environmental control programs in the past decade."[49] The history of carcinogen regulation summarized in chapter 5 provides numerous examples of this effect.

A less severe, but still problematic, type of judicial intrusion is when the courts compel regulation of a substance or substances. When courts step in to force regulatory action, the agency program is disrupted. Environmentalists, of course, can point to numerous instances where judicial review was essential to compel regulatory action against a carcinogen, such as the toxic water pollution consent decree. This perspective, however, overlooks the opportunity benefits forgone when agencies diverted resources to compliance with court decrees.

On balance, the history of judicially compelled regulation is not encouraging. When courts required EPA section 112 regulation of radionuclides and established a deadline, the agency had to take personnel from development of new source performance standards, which probably would have provided more overall health protection. Even the value of the toxic water pollutant consent decree may be questioned. One commentator has suggested that "[l]itigation generated by the statutory deadlines [enforced by the court] consumed scarce resources that might otherwise have been directed to the promulgation of regulations."[50] One court has acknowledged that the "delay required to give meaningful consideration to the technical intricacies of promising control mechanisms may well speed achievement of the goal of pollution abatement by obviating the need for time-consuming corrective measures at a later date."[51]

The importance of judicial restraint was well expressed in a very recent D.C. Circuit Court decision involving automobile safety investigation and enforcement, in which the court wrote:

While safety is an indispensable element of the decision not to investigate, [the National Highway Traffic Safety Administration] can and does consider such "nonsafety" factors as its available resources, enforcement priorities, the likelihood of uncovering sufficient evidence to establish the existence of a defect, and the prospect of ultimately succeeding in any necessary enforcement litigation. The regulation *sub judice* provides the court no way to second-guess the weight or priority to be assigned these elements. In particular, it would be unwise, and inconsistent with the broad mandate of the agency under the governing statute, to infer a mandatory allocation of the agency's limited resources.[52]

Consequently, the court denied a public petition to compel agency investigatory and enforcement action. While this decision only involves judicial deference to agency inaction, courts should also respect the terms of agency actions, in recognition of courts' limited expertise in the substance of carcinogen regulation.

The need for judicial restraint is greater and more defensible, should agencies adopt the prioritization and risk management proposals set forth above. Under the present system, one can sympathize with environmentalist frustration over regulatory inaction and, sometimes, with industry's complaints against arbitrary agency action. Regulatory adoption of a systematic, integrated program of prioritization, assessment and management of carcinogenic risks eliminates much of the need for judicial review.

Pursuit of moderate risk regulation may itself restrain judicial intrusion into administrative decisionmaking. Some regulations may never reach the courts; "[i]f political conflict between pro- and anti-regulation groups could be reduced, court appeals would be less frequent and less serious."[53] Industry is less likely to appeal more reasonable regulation, and environmental groups are less likely to litigate when agencies are regulating more substances. When courts have overturned agency actions, invoking procedural shortcomings, those decisions frequently masked the judges' discomfort with the substantive extremity of the appealed rule. Courts are more likely to defer to moderate regulation, so long as agencies avoid obvious and unambiguous procedural or substantive violations.

The courts may still make some contribution to carcinogen regulation, by setting the "rules of the game" for future carcinogen regulation. Consider the Supreme Court decision in *Industrial Union Department, AFL-CIO v. American Petroleum Institute,* which vacated OSHA's benzene standard and required a finding of significant risk precedent to regulation.[54] Environmentalists and Professor Latin have complained that this decision reflects judicial intrusiveness into agency decisionmaking. But the decision simply required an agency finding of significant risk and left considerable discretion for making such a finding. Combined with a subsequent decision holding that OSHA must use feasibility analysis rather than cost/benefit analysis, the Court established a framework of rules for

OSHA regulation. Since these decisions, OSHA has been far more effective in regulating carcinogens than before. If one recalls the failures of OSHA during the Carter Administration, the benzene decision may be regarded as facilitating regulation.

Courts also must ensure that fair procedures are used in regulation. This role also must be limited, however. Virtually any substantive intrusion, such as that in *Gulf South*, may be couched in procedural terms. The amount of information necessary to determine a significant risk, for example, is a substantive matter that should not be overturned by the judiciary. Federal agency regulation of carcinogens has certainly had its shortcomings, but "intensive judicial second guessing, which leads to the wholesale transfer of policy-making discretion to the judiciary, only aggravates the problem."[55]

CONCLUSION

Past carcinogen regulation often has been termed a failure. Fortunately, most environmental contaminants present only a modest health risk, and the lack of regulation is not as serious as it might be. Recent evidence, however, reveals some unregulated major health risks, particularly indoor air pollution. Enhanced future regulation is essential, promising to avert thousands of cancers.

Some simple steps can provide valuable improvements in regulatory effort. Most critically, sensible prioritization of government resources, informed by honest and accurate risk assessment and coordinated among relevant agencies, can ensure that the greatest hazards are addressed by the proper agencies. Then, a moderate and feasibility-based risk management program will enable agencies to promulgate final regulations within a more reasonable period of time. Finally, a measure of judicial restraint will permit those regulations to take effect and protect the public from carcinogens.

NOTES

1. 51 *Fed. Reg.* 33992 (1986).
2. National Research Council, *Risk Assessment in the Federal Government: Managing the Process* (1983), 33.
3. Howard Latin, *Good Science, Bad Regulation, and Toxic Risk Assessment*, 5 YALE J. REG. 89, 134 (1988).
4. Latin, 90.
5. National Research Council, 49.
6. 49 *Fed. Reg.* 21597 (1985).
7. Frank Cross, *Beyond Benzene: Establishing Principles for a Significance Threshold on Regulatable Risks of Cancer*, 35 EMORY L. J. 1, 11 (1986).

8. Milton Russell and Michael Gruber, "Risk Assessment in Environmental Policy-Making," *Science* 236 (April 17, 1987): 287.

9. Daniel Byrd and Lester Lave, "Narrowing the Range: A Framework for Risk Regulators," *Issues in Science and Technology* (Summer 1987): 95–96.

10. J. M. Mendeloff, *The Dilemma of Toxic Substance Regulation* (Boston, Mass.: MIT Press, 1988), 112.

11. Russell and Gruber, 287.

12. Byrd and Lave, 296.

13. Bruce Ackerman and Richard Steward, *Reforming Environmental Law,* 37 STAN. L. REV. 1333, 1360 (1985).

14. C. Richard Cothern, William Coniglio, and William Marcus, "Estimating a Risk to Human Health," *Envtl. Science & Tech.* 20 (1986): 115.

15. Latin, 107.

16. John D. Graham, Laura Green, and Mark J. Roberts, *Seeking Safety: Science, Public Policy and Cancer Risk* (to be published by Harvard University Press).

17. John Mendeloff, "Does Overregulation Cause Underregulation?," *Regulation,* (1981): 49.

18. Frank Cross, *Section 111(d) of the Clean Air Act: A New Approach to the Control of Airborne Carcinogens,* 13 B.C. ENV. AFFAIRS L. REV. 215, 228 (1986).

19. Peter Huber, *The Old-New Division in Risk Regulation,* 69 VA. L. REV. 1025, 1071 (1983).

20. Paul Deisler, "Dealing with Industrial Health Risks: A Stepwise Goal-Oriented Concept," in *Risk in the Technological Society* (Boulder, Colo.: Westview, 1982), 244.

21. Mendeloff, 50.

22. Mendeloff, 163.

23. David Vogel, *National Styles of Regulation* (Ithaca, New York: Cornell University Press, 1985), 192.

24. Latin, 106.

25. Environmental Defense Fund v. EPA, 598 F.2d 62, 89 (D.C. Cir. 1978).

26. Mark E. Rushefsky, *Making Cancer Policy* (New York: State University of New York Press, 1986), 139.

27. Mendeloff, 171.

28. *Implementation of the Federal Water Pollution Control Act: Summary of Hearings on the Regulation and Monitoring of Toxic and Hazardous Chemicals Under the Federal Water Pollution Control Act,* 95th Cong., 1st Sess. (1977), 26.

29. Latin, 127, n.191.

30. Cross, 239.

31. William D. Ruckelshaus, "Science, Risk, and Public Policy," *Science* 221 (1983): 1028.

32. National Research Council, 70.

33. Council on Scientific Affairs, "Carcinogen Regulation," *J. Am. Med. Assoc.* 246 (1981): 256.

34. Administrative Conference of the United States, *Federal Regulation of Cancer-Causing Chemicals,* Recommendation 82-5 (adopted June 18, 1982), 4.

35. National Research Council, 71.

36. 52 *Fed. Reg.* 42558 (1987).

37. Russell and Gruber, 287.

38. EPA Office of Policy, Planning and Evaluation, *The Air Toxics Problem in the United States: An Analysis of Cancer Risks for Selected Pollutants* (May 1985), 88.

39. Ruckelshaus, 1028.

40. Letter from Dr. Albert, *Science* 219 (1983): 798.

41. Ibid., 796.

42. Jay Sorenson, "The Assurance of Reasonable Toxic Risk," *Natural Resources J.* 24 (1984): 549, 566.

43. Marguerite Connerton and Mark MacCarthy, *Cost-Benefit Analysis and Regulation: Expressway to Reform or Blind Alley?*, National Policy Paper No. 4 (October 1982), 21–22.

44. Aaron Wildavsky, *Searching for Safety* (London: Transaction Books, 1988), 202.

45. 19 *Environment Reporter* (BNA) (Current Developments) (July 22, 1988), 384.

46. Ethyl Corporation v. EPA, 541 F.2d 1, 67 (D.C. Cir.) (Bazelon, C. J., concurring) *cert. denied*, 426 U.S. 941 (1976).

47. 701 F.2d 1137 (5th Cir. 1983).

48. Latin, 131.

49. Latin, 133.

50. Alden Abbott, *Case Studies on the Costs of Federal Statutory and Judicial Deadlines,* 39 ADMIN. L. REV. 467, 471 (1987).

51. Natural Resources Defense Council v. Train, 510 F.2d 692, 712 (D.C. Cir. 1975).

52. Center for Auto Safety v. Dole, 846 F.2d 1532, 1535 (D.C. Cir. 1988).

53. Mendeloff, 13.

54. 448 U.S. 607 (1980).

55. Graham et al.

Part III

COMMON LAW LIABILITY FOR ENVIRONMENTAL CARCINOGENS

However strong and effective federal regulatory cancer prevention efforts may become, some individuals will suffer cancer as a consequence of environmental exposures. These individuals may obtain damages for their costs and suffering through the traditional common law tort system. The tort system has twin goals: (1) providing compensation to those injured, by forcing payments from responsible parties who have violated some legal standard; and (2) inducing those responsible parties not to cause future harms, by making them pay the consequences of such harms. This part will discuss both goals, but will focus mainly on the compensation objective. The second goal of deterring future harm is largely derivative and achievable only if accurate compensation succeeds.

Chapter 7 begins by discussing the ability of a cancer victim to sue as plaintiff and establish the liability of some defendant to pay for the plaintiff's cancer harms. Under present rules, establishing liability is quite difficult. The plaintiff must show that the defendant violated some legal standard and that this violation caused plaintiff's cancer harms. Both these tasks are made more difficult by the very high costs of litigation and the frequent unavailability of essential evidence. Even more problematically, the unique features of carcinogenesis make it extraordinarily difficult for plaintiffs to prove that any given exposure "caused" their cancer. The common law currently creates other substantial barriers to plaintiffs' recovery as well, including statutes of limitations, difficulty identifying defendants capable of paying damages, and rules of evidence and proof that may preclude a plaintiff's best case. Tort recovery for environmental cancer is not impossible, but it is quite difficult.

Establishing liability is only the first of a plaintiff's tasks, however. Plaintiffs must also prove their damages, which is discussed in chapter 8. If a plaintiff has suffered cancer and can establish a defendant's liability, he or she will be able to recover for costs and suffering. Waiting out cancer's latency period, however, makes establishing liability far more difficult. Now, plaintiffs increasingly sue immediately after exposure and seek damages for their risk of incurring future cancer, for their fear of future cancer, and for the costs of medical surveillance necessary to detect any future cancer. The availability of these damages is still somewhat uncertain, and necessary proof varies considerably by state of jurisdiction.

Chapter 9 proposes future directions for common law liability for cancer. While some have advocated replacing the courts with an administrative compensation bureaucracy, this "solution" does not address the substantive difficulties of carcinogenesis (especially proof of causation) and offers no answer in itself. Many of the obstacles to effective common law compensation could be eased by allowing plaintiffs to recover for a future risk of cancer resulting from recent exposures. This recovery, proportional to their degree of risk, could be used to insure against any future cancer that might develop. Other procedural difficulties could be ameliorated by providing a greater administrative role in compensation. This could take the form of a new administrative compensation system, but it could also be largely accomplished through court reliance on administrative risk assessments for carcinogens, rather than relying on costly, lengthy, duplicative, and inexpert risk assessment by jury.

There is no panacea for compensating the victims of environmentally induced cancer. The special problems of carcinogenesis described in chapter 1 have no easy solution. The directions proposed in chapter 9 should improve the system and make accurate and fair compensation more sure and less costly.

7

ESTABLISHING LIABILITY

For those suffering cancer or the risk of future cancer due to environmental exposures, traditional common law principles hold out some promise of compensation. Americans are aware of their ability in tort law to recover losses caused by a careless driver or by other negligent actions and similarly look to courts to recover damages caused by environmentally induced cancer. The use of tort law to recover for such harms has increased markedly and has created a new field of law, commonly known as "toxic torts." The complexity and uncertainty of carcinogenesis, however, make common law recovery for cancer far more difficult than for automobile accidents.

The plaintiff suing to recover for cancer, like all other tort plaintiffs, must meet certain traditional legal requirements in order to establish liability. First, the plaintiff must demonstrate that the defendant being sued violated some standard of care or other legal responsibility in a way that created the hazard complained of. Second, the plaintiff must show that this unlawful action or omission by the defendant caused the harm suffered by the plaintiff. Along the way, the plaintiff must overcome other legal obstacles, such as the admissibility of evidence and standards of proof required by courts. The above tasks are very difficult ones for plaintiffs seeking recovery for environmentally induced cancer.

The special complexities of cancer remain problematic for the court system. The system has received widespread criticism, as exemplified by the following commentary:

It doles out compensation in inconsistent amounts, leaving many without remedy because they have been struck down by natural forces or a penniless actor or because they can't identify the person who harmed them. On the other hand, leaving matters to lay jurors can impose enormous risks and uncertainty on providers of goods and services. Moreover, tort litigation can be very expensive for all and can leave the injured party uncompensated to the extent that his lawyer takes a share....[1]

This chapter summarizes the applicable legal requirements for toxic tort recovery, the difficulties created, and the law's response, if any, to the unique characteristics of carcinogenesis.

STANDARD OF LIABILITY

Initially a plaintiff must prove that the defendant violated some legal standard of liability, such that the defendant might be required to compensate the plaintiff for his or her injuries. Tort law does not compensate all injuries but only those resulting from defined sources of liability. The most common potential sources of liability for cancer are negligence and strict liability, although some other liability standards may also be used.

Negligence

One obvious and well-established standard of liability in tort is negligence. Negligence is typically defined as behavior that "falls below the standard established by law for the protection of others against unreasonable risk of harm."[2] This definition, of course, contributes little, because the key question involves what "standard" should be established by law and what risk is "unreasonable." In applying a negligence standard, courts typically employ a "reasonable person" standard. The defendant's behavior is measured against what the hypothetical reasonable person would have done in the same circumstances. Yet there is considerable room for debate about what a reasonable person would do in many situations.

The vague standard for negligence has been fleshed out somewhat in the course of judicial decisions. The classic formulation of negligence was propounded in 1947 by Judge Learned Hand, who wrote:

Possibly it serves to bring this notion into relief to state it in algebraic terms: if the probability [of harm] be called P; the injury, L; and the burden [of preventing harm], B; liability depends upon whether B is less than L multiplied by P.[3]

A negligent act is therefore a failure to take precautions where the cost of preventing harm is less than the harm done, discounted by the probability of its occurrence. This formulation, which is still widely employed, is theoretically quite similar to the cost/benefit analysis paradigm discussed in chapter 4. Unlike the sophisticated quantification of administrative cost/benefit analyses, however, common law judicial balancing tends to be extraordinarily rough and imprecise. Seldom will a court perform anything approximating a typical administrative cost/benefit analysis. For example, a common law court will not attempt to value human life as part of this analysis. The judicial common law standard for negligence has largely devolved into a requirement not to do unnecessary harm to others, with unnecessary harm meaning that which may be feasibly prevented without exorbitant cost.

In order to maintain a negligence action, the plaintiff must thus show that his or her cancer risk resulted from defendant's irresponsible lack of care. At minimum, the plaintiff probably will be required to prove that the defendant knew or should have known that he or she was creating a cancer risk. This may require plaintiff to demonstrate that the substance in question was a known carcinogen at the time of release and exposure. In addition, the plaintiff will likely be required to demonstrate that the risk was avoidable and was significant enough to justify whatever precautions would have prevented the hazard.

This required showing will necessitate an extensive fact-finding inquiry by plaintiffs. One commentator summarized the demands of bringing suit against a leaking hazardous waste disposal site:

Since the nature and quantity of the waste materials and the actual disposal practices have rarely been recorded by generators, haulers, or site owners, plaintiffs may have to initiate and bear the cost of private on-site "digging expeditions," which, depending on the site's age and the attending circumstances, may or may not prove a fruitful source of information. They may also have to arrange and pay for water and air samples to be taken from properties surrounding the site and analyzed at qualified laboratories. Interviews with employees, past and present, of the many different business enterprises that could be involved in the creation and maintenance of the disposal site may have to be conducted.[4]

This elaborate on-site factual investigation may be so difficult that "the cost of developing the information necessary to pursue a cause of action in negligence may be prohibitive."[5] Moreover, a plaintiff must engage in other investigations, regarding the scientific evidence of carcinogenicity at the time of exposure and the availability and practicality of measures to reduce the risk at that time. The burden of proof may be "very hard for plaintiffs to meet, because victims will rarely have access to evidence concerning defendants' actions, which may have occurred twenty years earlier."[6] Even when this evidence is available, "it is extremely difficult for a toxic waste victim to prove either that the defendant's conduct was unreasonable or that the plaintiff's harm was foreseeable."[7] Moreover, "the plaintiff will inevitably be faced with delay in the system which will be extremely prejudicial to the plaintiff's interest."[8]

The difficulty of bringing a negligence case will not always be so bleak as portrayed above, however. For risks from hazardous waste sites, the federal government has itself identified and investigated the largest sites under Superfund. The government may therefore have performed much of the necessary site-specific research groundwork precedent to negligence actions. For other routes of exposure, such as air and water pollution, government investigation is not so extensive, but government records nevertheless will frequently provide valuable information regarding emissions and ambient contamination levels.

In proving a defendant's lack of care, plaintiffs may also be aided by a doctrine known as negligence *per se*. This doctrine states that when a defendant has violated a statutory requirement, the defendant's conduct will automatically be adjudged negligent for failing to comply with the law. Accordingly, where a defendant operates in violation of EPA or other government regulatory requirements, negligence will often be presumed. The doctrine of negligence *per se* offers more promise for the future than for the present, however. Today's cancers are typically founded in exposures twenty years past, and at that time there were relatively few legal requirements proscribing environmental pollution.

In addition, when a defendant complies with applicable government requirements, such compliance may be considered evidence of non-negligence. Perhaps the leading torts authority declaimed:

Where there is a normal situation, clearly identical with that contemplated by statute or regulation, and no special circumstances or danger are involved, it may be found and can be ruled as a matter of law, that the actor has done his full duty by complying with the statute, and nothing more is required.[9]

When government has enacted licensing or other regulations to protect public health, compliance with those rules may insulate defendants from negligence actions. This defense is not perfect—"[c]ompliance with a legislative enactment or an administrative regulation does not prevent a finding of negligence where a reasonable man would take additional precautions," especially when special circumstances exist.[10] In one important case, compliance with federal pesticide labeling requirements was held inadequate and a defendant was held liable for negligent failure to warn of pesticide hazards beyond the federal regulatory demands.[11]

While bringing a negligence case may be difficult, it is by no means impossible. In one important recent case, *Sterling v. Velsicol Chemical Corp.*,[12] residents sued a chemical corporation for personal injuries, including risk of cancer, allegedly resulting from a chemical waste burial site. The court held that Velsicol owed the nearby residents a duty of care to protect them from "unreasonable harm arising from the dumping of chemicals."[13] The court also found that Velsicol had breached this duty because the company had failed to investigate the geological suitability of the site, failed to install proper monitoring procedures at the site, and failed to respond to government warnings that chemicals at the site were leaking. Velsicol was found liable in negligence.

The *Velsicol* decision illustrates the possibility of recovering in negligence. Unfortunately, negligence frequently will fail as a basis for tort recovery from carcinogens. The negligence claim is highly fact-based and dependent upon balancing uncertain costs and risks, characteristics that make the claim a difficult and expensive one for plaintiffs to prove.

Strict Liability

Strict liability permits a plaintiff to recover from a defendant even in the absence of negligence. When strict liability applies, the plaintiff need not demonstrate that the defendant failed some duty of reasonable care. This source of liability is increasingly used in toxic tort cases. Strict liability is not always available, however. The two primary relevant circumstances in which strict liability applies are the conduct of certain ultrahazardous activities and when personal injurie result from the use of products.

Virtually all states now recognize that strict liability will apply to certain activities that are considered ultrahazardous or abnormally dangerous. The theory behind liability seems to be that individuals who engage in unavoidably dangerous activities should be prepared to pay the costs of harm done by such activities. There is no simple test for determining whether an activity is ultrahazardous, however. Typically, the courts will balance the following factors:

a. existence of a high degree of risk and some harm to the person, land or chattels of others;

b. likelihood that the harm that results from it will be great;

c. inability to eliminate the risk by the exercise of reasonable care;

d. extent to which the activity is not a matter of common usage;

e. inappropriateness of the activity to the place where it is carried out; and

f. extent to which its value to the community is outweighed by its dangerous attributes.[14]

A plaintiff need not meet all these criteria—they are simply factors to be considered in a court's discretion. A literal and exhaustive application of these factors would require significant risk analysis, feasibility analysis, and cost/benefit analysis. Courts, however, have not required elaborate analyses of the criteria for strict liability, but have permitted rather generalized showings of hazard. On occasion, carcinogen-producing activities may be considered ultrahazardous under the above tests. Courts remain divided on this issue. Some have applied strict liability to carcinogen producers, while a number of other courts "have refused to apply strict liability to the disposers and generators of hazardous waste."[15] Some states have statutorily created strict liability for some toxic torts. When strict liability does apply, a plaintiff's burden of proof will be somewhat easier than under negligence.

A second source of strict liability is found in product liability. Tort law throughout the states provides that anyone who sells a defective product that is unreasonably dangerous is strictly liable for personal injuries caused by the defective product.[16] A product may be considered defective if it contains a flaw from production, if it was defectively (unsafely) designed, or if the manufacturer simply failed to warn consumers of the hazards associated with the product. Whether a product is unreasonably dangerous is usually determined through a risk/utility test, comparing the risk from the product with the benefits of the product in its present state. Once again, this seems to call for a rough cost/benefit analysis. When carcinogen exposure results from a product, such as a pesticide or food product, strict liability may be available to plaintiffs. Even houses may be considered products to which strict liability applies.[17]

The benefit of strict liability to plaintiffs has been reduced somewhat by the "state-of-the-art" defense. Some courts have held that a defendant is not liable, even under strict liability, when that defendant employed the best existing state of the art for safety in its activities. For example, if a harm was unknowable at the time of the activity or if the defendant used the best available technology to control that harm, the defendant would be exonerated. Reliance on the state-of-the-art defense has been criticized for reducing strict liability to something like negligence. In a famous New Jersey case holding a manufacturer liable to an employee for asbestos exposure, a court rejected the state-of-the-art defense, holding that the "burden of illness from dangerous products such as asbestos should be placed upon those who profit from its production and, more generally, upon society at large, which reaps the benefits of the various products our economy manufactures."[18] This decision did not foreshadow the abolition of the state-of-the-art defense, however, even in New Jersey. A subsequent case involving harm from exposure to medical drugs restored the state-of-the-art defense. Many jurisdictions are likely to apply the state-of-the-art defense to strict liability claims. A relatively rare case seeking damages for indoor radon failed due to this defense.[19] A court held that builders had no "reason to know of the dangers of radon gas" in 1969, at the time of construction.[20]

Plaintiffs in the *Velsicol* case discussed above also sued in strict liability. The district court again ruled in their favor, finding that the hazardous waste site constituted an ultrahazardous activity. In applying the factors for strict liability, the court found that there was "a high degree of risk of some harm to the person," that there "was a likelihood that the harm that results would be great, such as the increased risk of many diseases including cancer," that the risk could not be eliminated through use of reasonable care, and that the dump site was in an inappropriate location and "not a matter of common usage."[21] In addition, the court held that the disposal site's value to the community was "none," while the risk from the site was "great."[22] The *Velsicol* decision also recognized the state-of-the-art defense but held that defendant had violated the prevailing state of the art.

Strict liability is probably the most promising standard for plaintiffs' seeking to recover for environmentally induced cancer, and the decisions in *Velsicol* and other cases demonstrate the potential success of this theory. As courts apply the standards for strict liability and the state-of-the-art defense, however, they increasingly reduce strict liability to a test similar to negligence. This practice places an added evidentiary burden on plaintiffs that will often be difficult to sustain. An expert task force on hazardous waste disposal site liability reported to the Congress that "[c]ommon law strict liability, as generally applied, involves balancing and notions of fault that create substantial barriers to plaintiffs' recovery...."[23]

Additional Theories

While negligence and strict liability represent the overriding liability theories open to plaintiffs, other theories may also be available. When a tangible pollutant enters onto the land of a person, that person may sue for trespass. Traditional trespass does not require the balancing inherent in other theories of liability. In many jurisdictions, however, the person must prove that the trespass resulted from negligence, intentional action, or an ultrahazardous activity. Moreover, trespass will only avail those plaintiffs who were exposed to carcinogens on land that they possess.

Still another source of liability is nuisance law. Private nuisance occurs when a defendant unreasonably interferes with a plaintiff's use and enjoyment of his land. Carcinogenic pollution could theoretically qualify as such a nuisance. The test for whether interference is "unreasonable," however, is another cost/benefit balancing test. Like trespass, private nuisance only protects harms occurring on land in the possession of the plaintiff. The *Velsicol* court also found the defendant liable for both trespass and nuisance.[24]

A related doctrine, public nuisance, protects against more general harms to a community. Generally, public nuisance requires a finding of some law violation. Plaintiffs are also limited in damages recoverable after a finding of public nuisance. A plaintiff can recover for personal injuries only when his or her harm differs in kind from that suffered by the public as a whole. In cases involving carcinogens, the harms are not likely to be so distinct. Frequently, "establishing the existence of the public nuisance and the presence of special injuries not shared by the general public will often be barriers to recovery" under this theory.[25]

Depending upon the circumstances of carcinogenic exposure, still other theories of liability may be available to plaintiffs. When the harm results from consumer products or housing, the plaintiff may have a contract theory, such as violation of warranty. No liability theory is perfect for carcinogen exposure, and all theories place considerable burdens upon plaintiffs. Nevertheless, a plaintiff in possession of adequate resources for investigatory fact-finding will sometimes be able to demonstrate liability, as illustrated by the decision in *Velsicol*.

CAUSATION

Probably the largest barrier to recovery for environmentally induced cancer is the need to prove legal causation. Such causation is required under any legal theory that plaintiffs might employ. The unique characteristics of cancer, detailed in chapter 1, make it quite difficult for plaintiffs to prove that a given cancer was caused by any definite source of exposure.

Consider the following scenario. A manufacturing company accidentally releases a high level of an airborne carcinogen into the surrounding community of 10,000 people over a material period of time. This release is later discovered and scientists testify that this high level violates government standards and creates an additional risk of lung cancer of 1 in 100 (1 x 10^{-2}) to individuals in the community. Given the size of the community, this means that 100 individuals will contract lung cancer from the release. As readers of the previous chapters will recall, this risk is far greater than that produced by the vast majority of environmental pollutants. Then suppose that a member of the local community contracts lung cancer some twenty years after being exposed to the carcinogenic releases. The individual desires to sue the company for the damages resulting from her cancer.

The above hypothetical situation is far more favorable to plaintiffs than the typical case of environmentally induced cancer. The plaintiff will have little difficulty proving negligence or strict liability on the part of the defendant. We have assumed away the plaintiff's responsibility of proving exposure and identifying the responsible party. We have also assumed away any disputes over risk assessment of the chemical's hazard. Moreover, the high risk level creates a greater suggestion of causation than is usual for environmentally induced cancers. Nevertheless, the hypothetical plaintiff will have great difficulty in recovering.

The difficulty in tracing any lung cancer to the toxic release is obvious. The community, if it has ordinary characteristics, would naturally expect nearly 1,000 of its residents to succumb to lung cancer. Thus, even if the 100 cancers traceable to the toxic release actually occur, they will be submerged in this much larger number of expected lung cancers. Conclusively determining which of these lung cancers were caused by the toxic release and which have other causes is a task beyond present scientific capabilities.

The task is even more daunting when viewed from the plaintiff's perspective. Her lung cancer has innumerable potential causes, and science cannot trace her specific cancer to any given cause. She is limited to attempting to prove causation through relative probabilities.

Her attempt to prove causation through probabilities will confront great difficulty. Initially, the court may be reluctant to admit even uncontroverted risk assessment evidence derived from animal tests (a problem discussed below). Even if this evidence is admitted, it may be unpersuasive. The 1 in 100 risk from the toxic release is unusually high for environmental contaminants but still represents only a 1 percent risk of lung cancer. The ordinary standard of proof in civil tort cases requires a plaintiff to prove causation and other issues with a preponderance of the evidence. This standard is usually described as showing that causation is "more likely than not" and equated with a greater than 50 percent probability of truth. Plaintiff's 1 percent probability falls far short of this standard. While we "know" (to the best of science's ability) that 100 individuals will contract cancer from the release, none of those individuals will be capable of demonstrating probabilistic causation to the satisfaction of a court.

Some of the shortcomings of current concepts of causation are illustrated in major litigation over Agent Orange, a defoliant used in Vietnam that allegedly caused a wide variety of harms to exposed individuals and their descendants. First, plaintiffs had difficulty even demonstrating their degree of exposure, as the judge noted that it was "impossible to measure accurately the actual herbicide exposure a veteran may have received."[26] Potency assessment was a more substantial problem. After reviewing available evidence, the presiding judge was sufficiently persuaded of the dangers of Agent Orange that he would have upheld government action limiting the defoliant's use. The judge emphasized that in a toxic tort case, however, "a far higher probability" of harm is required.[27] Consequently, the judge approved a settlement that was widely regarded as highly favorable to the defendants.

At least in theory, defendants may also suffer from this legal system of causation. Suppose 100 individuals contract cancer, after being exposed to a 55 percent risk from a single defendant and lesser risks from other individuals. Logically, that defendant should be responsible for fifty-five of the cancer cases, but every one of the cancer victims can pass the "more likely than not" test for legal causation, and the defendant will be responsible for all 100 cases. Any more-than-doubling of a cancer risk "will result in every cancer victim recovering 100 percent of his damages from the toxic leaker, even though many have acquired cancer for reasons unrelated to the leak."[28]

The present legal system thus creates an unavoidable "causation paradox," that guarantees inaccurate conclusions regarding causation. A 51 percent probability will be 100 percent compensated, while a 49 percent probability means zero compensation. This inaccuracy inheres in even a perfectly informed and functioning factual and procedural environment for litigation. In the certain absence of such perfect information and in the presence of numerous practical problems faced by plaintiffs, the inaccuracy created by current concepts of causation will snowball.

Indeed, the abstract theoretical difficulties of demonstrating causation are probably dwarfed by practical difficulties of proof. Simply proving that a plaintiff has been exposed to a carcinogen may be a daunting task. Even today, monitoring records for environmental contaminants are spotty, and such records were largely nonexistent decades in the past. In many circumstances, even monitoring of emissions will not demonstrate plaintiff's exposure. For example, "in the case of groundwater contamination, defining the migration patterns of toxic substances through the soil frequently presents complicated problems."[29]

Even when sufficient records exist to prove exposure, the plaintiff will have considerable difficulty proving the extent of his or her personal exposure. For example, a Texas worker who sued for cancer from radiation exposure failed because he wore no measurement device for two years and because the device that he did wear had demonstrated inaccuracies.[30] This plaintiff failed even though his exposure occurred occupationally (where monitoring records are more readily available) and even though he wore a personal exposure monitor (obviously not present in most exposure situations). The typical environmental exposure case will have far less supporting exposure evidence than this failed case. The alleged exposure must also be tracked to a specific defendant, a substantial difficulty discussed later on in this chapter.

Even assuming that exposure can be demonstrated precisely, the plaintiff will face the difficulty of assessing the risk from such exposure. As demonstrated in chapter 3, potency assessment is a highly uncertain procedure, fraught with unprovable assumptions. For some substances, underlying scientific data may be insufficient to construct a reliable risk assessment. Even when data are available, the results of such potency assessments may vary widely. A plaintiff must find favorable scientific experts to testify about risk and must combat the defendant's experts, who doubtless will present conflicting assessments. Such plaintiffs are unlikely to have the benefit of conservative assumptions employed by regulatory agencies, and a plaintiff must somehow persuade a judge or jury to accept his or her assessment of risk.

A plaintiff's practical difficulties are significantly compounded by the substantial financial resources required to demonstrate the above facts, even assuming it is possible to do so. One commentator has referred to the "enormous costs of developing a hazardous waste private damages case."[31] Investigatory studies and expert testimony are not inexpensive. Additional litigation costs may also arise. The cost of bringing a toxic tort action is often in the hundreds of thousands of dollars. One plaintiff "testified he was 'economically bludgeoned out of the courtroom' when his lawyer told him the grim economic facts of appealing his unexpectedly low trial award."[32] While this situation is not unique to toxic tort litigation, the relative complexity of such litigation exacerbates the ordinary concern for litigation costs.

Litigation costs may be ameliorated somewhat by a contingency fee arrangement, whereby the plaintiff's attorney initially bears these costs in exchange for a percent of the ultimate award. This tool is no panacea, however:

Even where the attorney accepts a contingent fee and advances litigation costs to the plaintiff, the plaintiff must eventually repay the costs so advanced. Given that chances for success on the merits are small in most toxic torts cases, plaintiffs and attorneys alike will no doubt find such an arrangement unsatisfactory.[33]

Plaintiffs have also sought to reduce individualized costs through the procedural tool known as a class action, whereby numerous plaintiffs join in a single suit, thereby spreading the costs of litigation. Class actions are only allowed, though, when "fact[s] common to the members of the class predominate over any questions affecting any individual members."[34] In toxic tort cases, key factual issues will involve the nature and extent of the plaintiffs' exposure, which will be individualized determinations that may not lend themselves to a class action lawsuit or may significantly reduce the size of the plaintiff class allowed by judges. Plaintiffs alleging harms from hazardous waste disposal at Love Canal, for example, were denied class status.[35]

In short, the difficulties associated with proving causation in toxic tort cases are considerable. Some authors gloomily conclude that "the level of certainty required by the legal system may be impossible to attain."[36] An expert report to Congress likewise reported that "it is clear that proof of the causal connection between exposure and injury is an almost overwhelming barrier to recovery, particularly in smaller cases (regardless of their merit) because the cost of mounting the massive probative effort and the arrays of technical and scientific evidence will be prohibitive."[37] This conclusion reflects a virtually universal consensus.

On some occasions, proof of causation may be more practical. Workers exposed to high levels of asbestos have consistently recovered for their resulting cancers. The asbestos cases, however, have very unique circumstances. Asbestos causes a relatively rare form of cancer, not produced by other substances. In addition, these workers were exposed to unusually high risks, as documented by extensive data on asbestos-induced cancer. Such favorable causation circumstances are unlikely to be found in many other toxic tort cases.

The plaintiffs in *Velsicol* overcame some causation difficulties through a different approach. These plaintiffs sued before contracting cancer, seeking damages for their future risk of cancer. This new approach is discussed in chapter 8, but it is not widely recognized.

In most typical toxic tort cases, causation will be an almost insurmountable obstacle for plaintiffs. Proof of exposure and resultant risk will either be unavailable or extremely costly to obtain. Even when such data are accumulated, the resulting risk will ordinarily fall well below the 50 percent threshold required for recovery under traditional concepts of causation.

ADDITIONAL BARRIERS TO RECOVERY

Establishing liability and causation are fundamental and universal substantive requisites to a plaintiff's action. Certain procedural characteristics of tort litigation may create further significant barriers to a plaintiff's success. The leading additional barriers are (1) the difficulty of identifying responsible and solvent defendants; (2) the presence of statutes of limitations that preclude untimely actions; and (3) problems of evidence and proof under established legal rules.

Identifying Solvent Defendants

Even when a plaintiff has identified his or her exposure to a hazardous substance and can link that exposure to cancer, the plaintiff still must determine the source of the substance in the environment. Tracking the source of pollutants may be quite difficult. This was illustrated by a recent episode:

The recent discovery of toxic blobs on the bed of Ontario's St. Clair River illustrates some of the difficulties in establishing the first element of causation. Some scientists contend that nearly eight billion litres of chemical wastes, pumped into wells near Sarnia, Ontario between 1958 and 1976, are the source of the St. Clair's contamination. Others point to an estimated 41 litres of waste that Dow Chemical deposited beneath its plant on the edge of the river. Adding to the confusion, industry spokesmen and Environment Ministry officials attribute the toxic blobs to still other sources such as incidental spills and illegal dumping by unknown persons. While there is much speculation, therefore, no one is certain where the blobs have come from.[38]

The problem is likely to be greater in the case of air pollution, where cars, major stationary sources, and minor private sources all contribute to the "urban soup" of pollutants found in the ambient air. The historic lack of emission records adds to a plaintiff's difficulties, and covert, illegal disposal practices will not show up in what limited records do exist. Thousands of hazardous waste sites, for example, have been abandoned over the past decades.

The above problem is compounded further by mixing of pollutants. Chemicals in the air and water may combine or separate to form new compounds, which may be untraceable to any original source. When such new compounds combine synergistically to elevate a cancer risk, the causation burden is all the more intractable.

Should a plaintiff be unusually fortunate in ability to precisely determine the source of the carcinogenic exposure and the causation of disease, recovery may still be impossible. The relevant exposure may have occurred years in the past and the identified defendant company may no longer be in existence at the time of the ultimate cancer. If the relevant companies still exist, they may lack the resources to compensate all of the injured plaintiffs. In many cases, the polluters will be small businesses or even private citizens. Remember, for example, that wood stoves are a leading source of carcinogenic air pollution. Large companies may be bankrupt, and the tort system may even "provide an incentive for hazardous actors to stay in business for only a few years, and then reorganize or declare bankruptcy to avoid potential upcoming liabilities."[39]

Plaintiffs and courts have developed new theories for ameliorating the problem of identifying responsible defendants. The most remarkable and controversial of these theories is market share liability, applied in the leading case of *Sindell v. Abbott Laboratories.*[40] In *Sindell*, the plaintiff was suing for cancer allegedly caused by her mother's ingestion of a drug known as DES. While the plaintiff was able to trace her cancer to DES ingestion, she was entirely unable to identify the drug manufacturer that produced the DES taken by her mother. The plaintiff sued all the major DES producers. The court did not require the plaintiff to identify the responsible defendant but shifted the burden of proof to individual company defendants to demonstrate that they were *not* the source of the DES taken by plaintiff's mother. In the absence of such proof, the court assigned liability for a percentage of plaintiff's damages correlative with each company's market share at the time of ingestion.

While *Sindell* offers substantial benefits to many plaintiffs, the decision has been criticized and has not been widely followed in subsequent cases. Moreover, even *Sindell* will not avail many toxic tort plaintiffs. Unlike the drug scenario, environmental pollution has no defined market shares and may involve an excessively large number of potential defendants who had emitted carcinogens. Imagine an air pollution plaintiff suing every citizen who possessed a wood stove, in addition to every industry, and perhaps every person who drove a car in the plaintiff's vicinity.

In the *Velsicol* case, used as an example for this chapter, a few plaintiffs lived near a waste disposal site that was owned and operated by a major chemical corporation. Only Velsicol disposed of wastes at this site. While the plaintiffs had some causation problems, they were readily able to identify Velsicol as the source of the chemicals in question. Most cases will not present such ready identification of solvent defendants, however. Identifying defendants, especially solvent defendants able to pay for plaintiff's injuries, remains a major barrier in toxic tort litigation.

Statutes of Limitations

All states have statutes of limitations for torts, which specify the maximum amount of time in which a plaintiff may bring an action. Thus a plaintiff must bring an action within a certain time after suffering from a tort or lose his or her legal claim. Defendants therefore need not worry forever about the prospect of litigation and the difficulty of defending against a stale suit. In most jurisdictions, the statute of limitations for tort claims is four or five years.

The statute of limitations presents obvious problems in the case of carcinogens, which have roughly a twenty-year latency period. If the statute of limitations begins to run at the time of the tortious action of carcinogenic exposure (the traditional rule), potential plaintiffs will not suffer their cancer until well after the statute of limitations will have already run.

Courts have not ignored this obvious problem in applying the statute of limitations to toxic torts involving carcinogenesis. An alternative application uses the "discovery rule," under which the statute of limitations does not begin to run until the plaintiff discovers or should have discovered the injury complained of. Thus a plaintiff would have four or five years from the date when a reasonable person would have discovered the cancer. Some form of the discovery rule has been adopted by courts in the vast majority of jurisdictions.

The discovery rule is not a panacea for cancer injuries under the statute of limitations, however. Discovery is a somewhat ambiguous term. Discovery might be deemed to occur at the first symptom of a disease, regardless of whether the disease were diagnosed. Cancer may develop slowly and erratically, however, and the first sign of disease "would not necessarily put an injured party on notice as to what he is suffering from and, consequently, he may not be cognizant of the fact that he has a claim, or of the identity of the potential defendant."[41] Discovery of the disease may yield no clues regarding its cause. Statutes of limitations remain a problem for plaintiffs:

Even the emergence of the "discovery rule," ... may not be sufficient to save a plaintiff's cause of action. Plaintiffs will still be at the mercy of the formulation of the "discovery rule" adopted by the jurisdiction where they reside or where their injuries occurred, a fortuitous circumstance at best. Moreover, most of the so-called "liberal" limitations rules still bar plaintiffs who discover the fact of injury but are unable to pin point a specific cause for many years.[42]

In many circumstances, even the discovery rule will not avail toxic tort plaintiffs.

Some jurisdictions have liberalized the discovery rule even further, defining "discovery" as the time when the victim knows or should know the source of the cancer. In *Velsicol*, the plaintiffs sued prior to incurring cancer, and thereby avoided statute of limitations problems. The statute of limitations is not the great problem that it once was for toxic tort plaintiffs, but these statutes may still prevent recovery in some cases in some states.

In addition, several states have enacted statutes of repose as well as statutes of limitations. Statutes of repose set a maximum number of years for initiation of a lawsuit and by definition begin running at the time of defendant's tortious conduct, even in states using the discovery rule for the statute of limitations. While statutes of repose allow plaintiffs more time to sue, their typical period is twelve years—still too short to offer relief to cancer victims.

Evidentiary Proof Problems

Regulatory agencies, with their considerable resources and substantial judgmental discretion, still have difficulties identifying and assessing the general public risk from carcinogens. Courts, limited by time and established rules of evidence, face much greater difficulties in adjudicating individual cases of carcinogenesis. A court may be required to conduct a factual inquiry that can become overwhelmingly voluminous. Even the best available evidence on carcinogenicity may not meet judicial standards of evidence and may be excluded from consideration. Explaining and condensing the evidence for a judge or jury also may represent a surpassingly difficult task.

As described previously, it is impossible to trace the cause of a given cancer. Plaintiffs therefore must present a risk assessment, suggesting a high probability that given exposures will produce cancer. A jury might then infer that the plaintiff's cancer was attributable to his or her past exposures.

Any such risk assessments must derive from animal bioassays, extrapolated to humans, or epidemiological studies. Considerable uncertainty attends such risk assessments, however. In light of this uncertainty, judges may deem the risk assessment inadmissable as evidence in a toxic tort case, thereby depriving a plaintiff of the only valid method of suggesting causation. Courts now are split on the admissibility of such evidence, but one major decision has refused admissibility.[43] Commentators have argued that "[a]nimal studies are not reliable predictors of the effects of toxic substances upon humans and thus should not be allowed into evidence for the purpose of proving causation."[44] Some courts have rejected epidemiological evidence as sufficient proof of causation. If this argument is heeded, and risk assessments are deemed inadmissible, plaintiffs will be denied the only reasonable available tool for proving causation.

Even if risk assessments are admitted as evidence, courts are not promising adjudicators of the accuracy of such assessments. Any risk assessment by a plaintiff is sure to be rebutted by a defendant's experts, who undoubtedly will suggest the presence of a lesser risk. Inexpert judges and juries will be called upon to sort through this expert testimony and ascertain scientific truth. Tort law places juries "in the position of determining the answers to questions that even scientists cannot answer with certainty."[45]

There is good reason to question the institutional capability of judges and juries to resolve such scientific controversies. Fear is expressed that "the complex technical aspects of animal studies may overwhelm the ability of jurors to comprehend the evidence, thereby preventing the jury from using the evidence in an informed manner."[46] A Texas case involving occupational radiation exposure illustrates this problem. A plaintiff was denied compensation for his cancer because "the other causes such as natural radiation, virus, and infection [were not] designated improbable by either the expert testimony or the circumstances of plaintiff's cancer."[47] Yet such proof is scientifically impossible at the present time, and the court thereby denied the possibility of a worker ever recovering from radiation exposure. The *Parker* court also rejected such "esoteric scientific theories" as the one-hit, no threshold hypothesis for carcinogenesis.[48] It may be unreasonable to expect courts to demonstrate a high degree of scientific sophistication regarding cancer, but the current tort system demands such sophistication for accurate adjudication.

Whatever the ability of a court to resolve complex scientific controversy, the trial forum is a poor and inefficient context for such resolution. Expert federal regulatory agencies commanding vast resources for scientific fact-finding have taken over a decade to work through risk assessment disputes. Rearguing these controversies before a possibly uneducated jury with very limited time and resources, limited by rules of evidence and the adversary system, scarcely seems a method designed to encourage accurate science. This is especially so when the debate must be repeated in every one of the tens of thousands of lawsuits claiming damages from cancer.

The cost in time is exemplified by *Allen v. United States*, a case involving lung cancers allegedly caused by nuclear fallout.[49] Ten representative plaintiffs filed their claim in 1979, on behalf of over 1,000 exposed individuals. The case took years to come to trial, the trial consumed three months, and the judge required seventeen more months to pore over the evidence and reach a verdict, some five years after filing. The judge issued a remarkable and detailed 225-page opinion. Three years later, the verdict for plaintiffs was overturned on appeal. The eight-year long *Allen* case reviewed and capably analyzed many key scientific and medical issues regarding environmentally induced cancer, but a new case would have to start from the beginning and reenact the lengthy *Allen* proceedings by relitigating most of these issues before a new judge or jury.

In one recent case, a plaintiff alleged cancer from groundwater contamination, based upon a risk assessment based on the carcinogenicity of trichloroethylene in mice. The defense, which ultimately prevailed, emphasized that the mice in the study were given such high doses that in order to ingest a comparable amount, "a human would need to consume almost a ton-and-a-half of the chemical."[50] This sort of argument may be highly persuasive to an untrained judge or jury. Yet extrapolation from high doses is a scientific necessity (as discussed in chapter 3). Litigation of such issues encourages sophistic arguments. One leading scientist bemoans the tort system's susceptibility to defendants' "[m]ythologies and pseudoscience."[51] And it seems foolish to reargue such universal principles in each and every cancer case.

Plaintiffs in the *Velsicol* case had the benefit of a relatively liberal judge who admitted extensive evidence on risk, permitting quantitative assessment of the hazard to plaintiffs. The court expressly held that "the use of animals is a valid and scientific basis to identify potential human carcinogens and to attempt to quantify such a risk."[52]

Risk assessment in *Velsicol* required elaborate expert testimony. One expert, relying on "conservative" exposure assessment and using both animal and human risk data, estimated an elevated cancer risk of 10 percent for the plaintiffs. Another expert estimated a 16 percent increase. Yet another expert employed different assumptions to estimate an excess cancer risk of as much as 40–50 percent. This expert candidly acknowledged the uncertainty of her estimate, though, testifying "[i]t could be a ten percent increased risk. It could be twenty, thirty, forty, fifty."[53] The judge did not engage in any detailed scientific scrutiny but merely concluded that the increased risk was at least 25 percent to 30 percent. The trial was quite lengthy, requiring the judge to evaluate expert testimony on such issues as a threshold for carcinogens, extrapolation of animal data, and other complex scientific issues. The judge required 132 pages for his opinion. Moreover, the *Velsicol* plaintiffs had to wait seven and one-half years for their district court victory, which was partially overturned two years later on appeal.

OVERVIEW OF ESTABLISHING LIABILITY FOR TOXIC TORTS

This chapter has focused on the difficulties confronting cancer victim plaintiffs in establishing the liability necessary to recover for their injuries, especially in the area of causation. These difficulties are indeed substantial and bar many potential plaintiffs from recovering compensation. Commentators have bluntly stated that "[r]ules and causes of action that developed from traditional, individualized wrongs do not allow recovery by toxic waste victims."[54] This complaint is overstated, however, and the prevailing tort liability system creates some serious problems for defendants as well. Numerous companies have their financial resources sapped by defending toxic tort litigation, including some frivolous cases, and these costs have even bankrupted some otherwise healthy major United States corporations. A recent review concluded that "[p]laintiffs and defendants alike have found the tort system inefficient and unfair."[55]

The history of asbestos litigation is illustrative. Up until 1973, plaintiffs had little success in recovering for occupational asbestos–induced cancer. A modest success in that year marked a key turning point that opened the floodgates of litigation. More than 30,000 such asbestos cases have been filed and, ultimately, over 50,000 are projected. Over $1 billion have been spent on these asbestos cases, which bankrupted Johns-Manville, among other companies. The cost of litigation and compensation of asbestos claims may reach tens of billions over the next few decades. While plaintiffs have won large awards in many of the asbestos cases, a study by Rand Corporation discovered that plaintiffs actually received only thirty-nine cents out of each dollar awarded, after litigation costs were taken out.[56] The judge in the Agent Orange litigation lamented this situation and concluded that if "much of a recovery will go to attorneys and experts rather than to those injured, then traditional tort remedies may be so ineffective as to put in doubt their utility in particular types of cases."[57]

The economic consequences of liability may have an even more severe impact upon future plaintiffs, who were only recently exposed to carcinogens. As defendants pay out very large awards, "tort litigation diverts both financial resources and attention from business operations whose continuity is essential for the payment of these [future] claims."[58] Even limited victories for today's plaintiffs may obliterate the possibility of victories for tomorrow's plaintiffs.

One of the most frustrating aspects of tort law is its disturbing and seemingly irrational randomness. Tobacco is by far the greatest cancer hazard faced by Americans, yet only one smoker suffering lung cancer had obtained a single modest tort recovery from tobacco companies by summer 1988. Meanwhile, other plaintiffs had received massive awards for being subjected to much smaller cancer risks from other sources. Another disturbing pattern involves a series of plaintiffs suing over a particular source of cancer, with many subsequently failing, in the urgent hope that a single plaintiff will eventually succeed. Once the first favorable precedent is created, subsequent plaintiffs have a much greater likelihood of success. This pattern occurred in the occupational asbestos exposure context, and commentators predict similar developments in tobacco litigation. To have a plaintiff's chances of success depend so heavily on the timing of his or her action, rather than its merits, is irrational and surely frustrating to plaintiffs and defendants alike.

The tort system has produced some obviously irrational results and does not discriminate sensibly among sources of cancer hazards. Plaintiffs have brought many more cases complaining of indoor air pollution from asbestos or formaldehyde than for the much more hazardous radon exposure. Similarly, plaintiffs have and will find it relatively easier to recover for cancer from hazardous waste disposal than from air pollution, because air pollution is relatively less traceable and usually causes the more common lung cancer. Air pollution, though, is almost certainly responsible for more cancer than waste disposal. Companies seeking to avoid liability may shift disposal to incineration and other sources of air pollution, which may actually create a greater risk to public health than land disposal. Others suggest that "the tort system inherently discriminates against new technologies, stressing their risks without giving adequate weight to the reduction of risk that results when they displace more dangerous technologies."[59]

The great variability of state laws and jury inclinations produces further inequity. Congressional testimony has suggested that "[v]ictims who happen to reside or be injured in Texas or New Jersey stand far greater chances of recovering . . . than someone with a substantially identical suit from South Dakota or Ohio."[60] Seemingly erratic damage awards further compound this problem.

The tort system contains yet another serious source of even greater unfairness. Proof of liability may depend on the presence of past records, thereby penalizing those companies that kept accurate records on their wastes and unfairly rewarding irresponsible companies that kept no records or secretly dumped their wastes. Plaintiffs also have a considerable incentive to proceed against large firms with significant cash reserves, even when these firms are not the companies most at fault in the plaintiff's injuries. Companies may be penalized simply for having greater assets or more of a social conscience.

Others express fear that toxic tort litigation will undermine the court system. As courts become more open to plaintiffs, toxic tort suits may proliferate and overburden the courts. Toxic tort cases are especially long and burdensome for courts. One single asbestos case in San Francisco involved more than 1,000 attorneys and necessitated over $200,000 in renovations on an auditorium to accommodate the trial. A leading attorney has warned that if "we do not halt the current trend toward more and more litigation, and do not find better means for resolving these problems, the whole process will choke on itself, leaving our environment despoiled, those injured uncompensated, our courts hopelessly overburdened and our economy gravely threatened."[61]

The above picture of the current toxic tort system is certainly a gloomy one, which has caused numerous commentators to suggest that it be jettisoned in favor of some administrative recovery system. The common law of torts is the only institutional structure currently available for compensating most cancer victims, however, and it should not be tossed aside lightly. Moreover, many of the system's failings have less to do with any inherent failings of the common law of torts and the judiciary than with the nature of carcinogenesis, which presents apparently intractable problems such as causation. Prospects for future change are discussed in chapter 9.

NOTES

1. Richard Marcus, "Apocalypse Now?" 85 MICHIGAN L. REVIEW (1987): 1267, 1277.

2. Restatement (Second) of Torts, Section 282, (1965): 9.

3. United States v. Carroll Towing Co., 159 F.2d 169, 173 (2d Cir. 1947).

4. William Ginsberg & Lois Weiss, *Common Law Liability for Toxic Torts: A Phantom Remedy,* 9 HOFSTRA L. REV. (1981): 859, 896.

5. Id.

6. Note, *Administrative Remedies for Hazardous Waste Victims: Prospects for U.S. Action in an International Perspective,* 12 NORTH CAROLINA JOURNAL OF INTERNATIONAL LAW AND COMMERCIAL REGULATION (1987): 277, 287.

7. Note, *Developments in the Law: Toxic Waste Litigation,* 99 HARVARD L. REV. (1986): 1458, 1611.

8. Anthony Roisman, "Common Law Toxic Tort Litigation: Strengths, Weaknesses, Reforms, Alternatives," in *Toxic Tort Litigation* (1984), 81.

9. D. Prosser, *Law of Torts,* Section 36, 203–204 (4th ed. 1971).

10. Restatement (Second) of Torts, Section 288 (1976).

11. Ferebee v. Chevron Chemical Co., 736 F.2d 1529 (D.C. Cir.), *cert. denied,* 105 S.Ct. 545 (1984).

12. 647 F. Supp. 303 (W.D. Tenn. 1986).

13. 647 F. Supp. 316.

14. Restatement (Second) of Torts, Section 520 (1976).

15. Note, *Developments in the Law,* 1610.

16. Restatement (Second) of Torts, Section 402A (1965).

17. Frank Cross & Paula Murray, *Liability for Toxic Radon Gas in Residential Home Sales,* NORTH CAROLINA L. REV. (1988): 687, 703.

18. Beshada v. Johns-Manville Products Corp., 447 A.2d 539, 549 (N.J. 1982).

19. Feldman v. Lederle Laboratories, 479 A.2d 374 (N.J. 1984).

20. Wayne v. Tennessee Valley Authority, 730 F.2d 392, 396 (5th Cir. 1984).

21. 647 F. Supp. 316.

22. Id.

23. *Injuries and Damages From Hazardous Wastes—Analysis and Improvement of Legal Remedies,* Report to Congress by the Superfund Section 301(e) Study Group (September 1982), 130–131.

24. 647 F. Supp. 319–320.

25. Superfund Section 301(e) Report, 109.

26. In re "Agent Orange" Product Liability Litigation, 597 F. Supp. 740, 780 (E.D.N.Y. 1984).

27. 597 F. Supp. 781.

28. Robert Bush, Between Two Worlds: The Shift from Individual to Group Responsibility in the Law of Causation of Injury, UCLA L. REV. (1986): 1473, 1486-1487.

29. Ora Harris, Jr., *Toxic Tort Litigation and the Causation Element: Is There Any Hope of Reconciliation?,* SOUTHWESTERN L. J. (1986): 909, 940.

30. Parker v. Employers Mutual Liability Insurance Co., 440 S.W. 2d 43 (Tex. 1969).

31. Mark Seltzer, "Personal Injury Hazardous Waste Litigation: A Proposal for Tort Reform," 10 ENVIRONMENTAL AFFAIRS (1982–1983): 797, 824.

32. Note, *Hazardous Waste Liability and Compensation: Old Solutions, New Solutions, No Solutions,* CONN. L. REV. (1982): 307, 323 n.88.

33. Note, "Administrative Remedies," 281.

34. Federal Rule of Civil Procedure 23(b)(3).

35. Snyder v. Hooker Chems. & Plastics Corp., 429 N.Y.S.2d 153 (N.Y. Sup. Ct. 1980).

36. Ginsberg & Weiss, 922.

37. Superfund Section 301(e) Report, p.71.

38. John Forstrom, *Victim Without a Cause: The Missing Link Between Compensation and Deterrence in Toxic Tort Litigation,* 18 ENVIRONMENTAL LAW 151, 154 (1987).

39. Leslie Gara, *Medical Surveillance Damages: Using Common Sense and the Common Law to Mitigate the Dangers Posed by Environmental Hazards,* 12 HARVARD ENVIRONMENTAL L. REV. (1988): 265, 293.

40. 607 P.2d 933 (Cal. 1980).

41. Note, *Discovering Justice in Toxic Tort Litigation: CPLR 214-c,* 61 ST. JOHN'S LAW REVIEW (1987): 262, 270 n.44.

42. Note, "Administrative Remedies," p.284.

43. Lynch v. Merrell-National Laboratories, 646 F. Supp. 856 (D. Mass. 1986).

44. Bert Krages, *Rats in the Courtroom: The Admissibility of Animal Studies in Toxic Tort Cases,* ENVIRONMENTAL LAW AND LITIGATION (1987): 229, 253.

45. Charles Chadd & John O'Malley, SUPERFUND AMENDMENTS OFFER HOPE FOR PLAINTIFFS IN TOXIC TORT ACTIONS, NATIONAL L. J. (March 21, 1988): 18.

46. Id., 244.

47. Parker v. Employers Mutual Liability Insurance Co. of Wisconsin, 440 S.W.2d 43, 48 (Tex. 1969).

48. Id., 49.

49. 588 F. Supp. 247 (D. Utah 1984).

50. Peter Lynch, Amanda Benton & James Pagliaro, *On the Frontier of Toxic Tort Liability: Evolution or Abdication?,* 6 TEMPLE ENVTL. L. & T. J. 1, (Summer 1987): 13.

51. Samuel Epstein, "The Role of the Scientist in Toxic Tort Case Preparation," 17 *Trial* (July 1981).

52. 647 F. Supp. 480.

53. 647 F. Supp. 478.

54. Note, *The Inapplicability of Traditional Tort Analysis to Environmental Risks: The Example of Toxic Waste Pollution Victim Compensation,* STANFORD L. REV. (1983): 575, 580, quoted by Harris, 909.

55. Note, "Administrative Remedies," 279.

56. J. Kakalek, P. Ebener & W. Felstiner, *Costs of Asbestos Litigation* (1984).

57. 597 F. Supp. 842.

58. Feinberg, *The Toxic Tort Litigation Crisis: Conceptual Problems and Proposed Solutions,* 24 HOUSTON L. REV. (1987): 155, 164.

59. Marcus, 1278.

60. *Superfund Reorganization: Judicial and Legal Issues: Oversight Hearings Before the Subcomm. on Administrative Law and Governmental Relations of the House Comm. on the Judiciary,* 99th Cong., 1st Sess. 416 (1985) (statement of Janet Hathaway, staff attorney of Public Citizen's Congress Watch).

61. Hazardous Substance Victim's Compensation Legislation: Hearings Before the Subcomm. on Commerce, Transportation, and Tourism of the House Comm. on Energy and Commerce, 98th Cong., 1st Sess. 146 (1983) (statement of George Freeman).

8

COMMON LAW REMEDIES

In the field of toxic torts, remedies have received relatively little attention, as scholarship has been primarily directed to the difficulty of establishing the existence of liability. The plaintiff's main interest in a lawsuit, however, lies in the remedy. Success or failure in establishing liability means little if remedies are incomplete. Moreover, the choice among remedies may itself have a powerful influence on the process of proving a defendant liable.

This chapter addresses the primary remedies available to compensate for environmentally induced cancer or the risk thereof. The most common and obvious remedy is recovering the medical and related costs of cancers incurred. Plaintiffs are increasingly seeking new, more novel remedies, however, in advance of the development of an actual cancer. These include damages for a future risk of cancer, the costs of medical surveillance to detect the development of any future cancer, and recompense for mental anguish associated with the risk of such future cancer. In addition, many plaintiffs seek punitive damages against defendants who have recklessly exposed them to cancer hazards. This chapter discusses the requirements and availability of these various common law remedies.

DAMAGES FOR CANCER INCURRED

To date, most toxic tort litigation has involved a plaintiff who has already suffered cancer and who is suing for personal damages resulting from this cancer. Most of chapter 7, discussing establishment of liability, assumes this form of case. If a plaintiff can overcome the substantial barriers described in that chapter and prove the defendant's liability, that plaintiff almost certainly can recover damages for his or her cancer.

In tort cases, the amount to be recovered for cancer is not specifically defined by law. Recovery will vary with the plaintiff's age and occupation, extent of suffering, and medical costs. As an example of possible recovery, an asbestosis victim received an $800,000 award, which was ruled to be reasonable on appeal.[1] There are quite a number of damage awards for cancer incurred, and precedents suggest that damages of up to $1 million are common and considered reasonable. One plaintiff, though, received an award of $2.75 million, which a court found excessive and reduced to $1.2 million.[2] In other cases, juries have awarded much smaller sums for cancer.

While there is no uniform recovery for cancers that have been suffered, many plaintiffs will recover considerable sums if they can prove that named defendants were legally responsible for their disease. As described in the preceding chapter, this proof of liability is a major obstacle to many plaintiffs who have cancer. Consequently, prospective plaintiffs have sought recovery for other types of damages, even before their cancer develops.

RISK OF FUTURE CANCER

Currently, many individuals exposed to carcinogens are unwilling to wait the twenty or more years of cancer's latency to sue for the potential adverse consequences of this exposure. Whether it be due to simple impatience or to these individuals' recognition of the considerable difficulties in potential future litigation of decades-old exposures (addressed in chapter 7), plaintiffs are increasingly suing for the risk of future cancer resulting from current exposures to carcinogens. The courts are still divided and uncertain in their response to these cases. These cases can be broken down into two groups—those that seek recovery for a purely future risk of cancer and those that seek recovery for a manifest present harm that can cause such a future cancer risk. Should courts recognize cases for probabilistic risk of future cancer in either context, the plaintiffs' burden in establishing liability will be eased considerably.

"Pure" Future Risk of Cancer

In traditional tort law, individuals sued for injuries already incurred. A traffic accident victim might thus recover for those injuries that resulted from the accident. Once these injuries occurred, however, the plaintiff might also recover for any demonstrable and probable future losses. Thus, if the accident made the plaintiff significantly more susceptible to some future harm, the plaintiff could recover for any such provable latent harms. In this way, courts avoid repeated relitigation of a single accident as new harms develop.

Traditionally, there must be some present injury to recover for such future harms. Only after the plaintiff has demonstrated an existing harm may the plaintiff seek recovery for future harms. When no injury is yet manifest, plaintiffs historically have been prevented from suing for purely future risks of harm. In a classic formulation, "the mere fact of risk without an accompanying physical injury is insufficient to state a claim."[3]

Plaintiffs in many toxic tort cases are now asking courts to rethink this traditional rule. Recent critics contend that the "seemingly flippant disregard of a recognizable, albeit latent, injury is becoming a less tenable judicial attitude for a number of reasons."[4] The characteristics of environmentally induced cancer, where plaintiffs face great difficulty in *post facto* recovery, argues for recognition of future risks as compensable injuries.

Courts have advanced reasons not to accept future risks in cancer cases, however. Some courts have emphasized that "[a]llowing recovery of risk of cancer damages not only encourages anticipatory lawsuits but runs counter to the desirable goal that cases be decided on the best quality evidence available."[5] Other courts have cautioned that "[t]o permit recovery for possible risk of injury or sickness raises the spectre of potential claims arising out of tortious conduct increasing in boundless proportion."[6]

While opinions are divided over recovery for future risk of cancer, a majority of decisions deny recovery when plaintiffs allege only future adverse consequences. Courts have denied relief to plaintiffs seeking recovery for future expected cancers from parental DES exposure,[7] for future cancers from exposure to nuclear fallout,[8] for future cancers from exposure to Agent Orange in Vietnam,[9] for future risk due to air pollution,[10] and for future cancers from drinking water contaminated by hazardous wastes,[11] among other contexts. A majority of jurisdictions adhere to the traditional rule, which does not recognize purely future injuries.

Some courts, though, have begun to suggest that the traditional rule requires change. In litigation over alleged cancer risk created by the Three Mile Island accident, for example, the plaintiffs were allowed to present evidence of their future risk of cancer, though in this case it was decided that the future risk was miniscule. Judges of the New Jersey and West Virginia Supreme Courts have vigorously argued that courts should recognize future risk of cancer as a compensable harm, as has the influential federal appellate judge Richard Posner. A few cases, including occupational asbestos claims, have accepted this argument.

Even when plaintiffs have been allowed theoretically to recover for future risks of cancer, their prospects are limited under current precedents. Courts have required proof of future cancer by a preponderance of the evidence, which translates into a requirement that plaintiffs demonstrate a probability of future cancer before being allowed to recover anything. Thus, plaintiffs must show a "greater than 50 percent chance" of the future cancer.[12] This is sometimes called the "reasonable certainty standard." Requiring proof of such a 50 percent or greater probability will preclude recovery for all but a small fraction of toxic tort plaintiffs. As discussed in chapters 2 and 3, environmental and occupational carcinogen exposures very seldom are high enough to produce a risk in excess of 50 percent. This test is sometimes called the "reasonable medical certainty rule" and "equate[s] a forty-nine percent chance of disease formation with speculation, yet treat[s] a fifty-one percent probability as reasonably certain."[13] Obviously, this rule is arbitrary and precludes most plaintiffs from recovering for risks of future cancer, even in those limited jurisdictions that recognize such a remedy.

Risk of Future Cancer Plus Present Harm

Plaintiffs have yet another avenue to recover for future risks, however, under the "extent of the injury rule." This rule, which is accepted throughout the United States, permits a plaintiff to sue for future risks when they arise out of a present manifest injury. Thus, if an accident causes damage to a person's head, and that trauma increases the likelihood of future cancer, the person may recover for the risk of the future cancer. Plaintiffs can recover all the demonstrable adverse future consequences of a present injury.

Allowing such future recovery is virtually required by procedural characteristics of the tort system. Plaintiffs are precluded from "claim-splitting," which involves two or more lawsuits arising from a given tort. Under this principle, a party suing for present damages is precluded from bringing a second future action for subsequently realized damages resulting from the same episode. Thus, a plaintiff, who can sue only once for injuries, must include all foreseeable damages, including future damages, in that single suit.

For individuals exposed to toxic substances, the ability to demonstrate a present harm may allow them to bootstrap a claim for risk of future cancer. In some instances, carcinogenic substances may also have immediate acute toxic effects on exposed individuals. If so, there is a greater prospect of recovery for future risks.

Even in the absence of such acute effects, creative plaintiffs are alleging that exposure to carcinogens itself creates a present harm. Some have argued that ingestion or inhalation of a carcinogenic substance itself should be considered harm, although this has been rejected in the asbestos liability cases.

A more promising theory relies upon new scientific techniques that can detect subcellular chromosome damage in human cells, of the type that may be caused by a carcinogen. Some plaintiffs now contend that such identifiable subcellular chromosomal damage should suffice as a present harm. As described in chapter 1, cancer development is a lengthy multistage process. In the early stages, exposure to an initiating carcinogen may produce immediate alterations in a cell's chromosomes. These alterations are the first step in a process that may ultimately develop into a malignant cancer. The alterations themselves might be considered a present physical harm to the exposed individual.

Present chromosomal harm was alleged in a recent case seeking damages for high levels of exposure to indoor radon, in which the plaintiffs claimed that this exposure caused "immediate, present damage to their cellular and subcellular structures."[14] The court accepted this contention, writing that "experts are able to conclude with a reasonable degree of medical probability" that chromosome damage has resulted and that this damage could "deprive the plaintiffs of a degree of immunity."[15] This demonstration meant that the " 'trigger' of a cancer change has been cocked," which was sufficient to represent a present manifest harm.[16]

If chromosomal damage is accepted to be a manifest present harm, those exposed to carcinogens will have a cause of action for future risk of cancer. The no-threshold hypothesis suggests that any exposure to any initiating carcinogen, no matter how small, may cause subcellular injury. One federal court has noted that "the overwhelming weight of currently available scientific evidence supports the view that at *any* exposure level, ionizing radiation causes *some* degree of biological damage."[17] There appears to be a trend to recognition of subcellular carcinogenic damage as a present injury, and one commentator has suggested that "[a]s the development of medical science makes chromosomal damage as readily visible as broken legs," the damage will be increasingly recognized at law.[18]

Recognition of chromosal damage as a present injury has been criticized, because this "damage" has no immediate adverse effect on a plaintiff's life activities. One court has ruled that "cellular damage" represents only the "possibility of some future harm."[19] Many individuals who suffer chromosomal damage will never contract a malignant cancer. What's more, "this exception could swallow the present injury rule in cancer cases,"[20] and virtually everyone exposed to an environmental carcinogen would obtain an immediate cause of action for risk of future cancer.

Notwithstanding these concerns, courts seem increasingly to be accepting some degree of chromosomal damage as a present manifest injury that authorizes plaintiffs to sue for future risks of cancer. Whether all degrees of future risk are recoverable, however, is yet unsettled. In general, courts have allowed plaintiffs with manifest present injury to recover for future cancer risks with probabilities of less than 50 percent. Courts in some jurisdictions have permitted recovery for only those risks that "reasonably are to be expected to follow, so far as human knowledge can foretell"[21] or other similar formulations suggesting that plaintiffs must prove a high probability of future cancer. Many cases, however, have permitted recovery for risks of less than 50 percent. Courts have permitted "recovery for lesser probabilities in cases involving the occurrence of epilepsy as a result of collision, paralysis from bullet wound, cancer from medical malpractice, cancer from burns in an accident, and cancer from hazardous waste sites."[22]

Allowing recovery for less-than-50 percent probability of future cancer in the present injury cases is virtually mandated. The procedural doctrinal prohibition against claim-splitting means that plaintiffs suing for present injury may not later return to court to sue for subsequent related injuries. If a hypothetical plaintiff with a present injury and a 20 percent future risk of cancer is denied any recovery for the risk in a trial over the present injury, that plaintiff could never recover for the subsequent cancer, if it developed. Such a result is inequitable and does nothing to discourage defendants from releasing carcinogens into the environment.

Plaintiffs suing for risk of future cancer resulting from present injuries under the "extent of the injury" rule should be able to recover for cancer probabilities well below 50 percent. The minimum percentage risk requirement for recovery in these cases has not been definitively established, but plaintiffs in past cases have recovered for risks of future epilepsy as low as 3 to 5 percent. If chromosomal damages are recognized as a present harm, most plaintiffs should be able to proceed on a claim for risk of future cancer from environmental exposures to carcinogens.

If plaintiffs are allowed such recoveries for a future risk, the measure of the recovery must still be defined. Logically, plaintiffs should be able to recover their percentage probability of future cancer multiplied by the anticipated future costs and suffering of any future cancer. While this computation might be difficult, the estimation is already performed by insurance industry actuaries, who must set current premiums in policies that protect against the risk of future cancer. The best measure of future damages for a risk of cancer may be the present cost of insuring against that degree of risk.

The plaintiffs claiming injuries from a hazardous waste site in the *Velsicol* site sought recovery for future risk of cancer. The district court in this case allowed such recovery, holding that "enhanced susceptibility is an existing condition and not a speculative future injury."[23] While the *Velsicol* plaintiffs had proved present injuries, including liver and kidney disease, the court apparently would have permitted recovery for a risk regardless of such present injuries. The court accepted plaintiffs' evidence of a 25 to 30 percent cancer risk and awarded the various plaintiffs damages ranging from $75,000 to $250,000 for this risk, depending on their degree of exposure to the carcinogenic wastes.

On appeal, however, the appellate court reversed these awards for risk of future cancer. The appellate court stressed that plaintiffs must prove damages with "reasonable medical certainty" and that a 25 to 30 percent risk was "a mere probability or speculation."[24] Furthermore, the court required a 50 percent or greater probability even in the presence of manifest existing injuries. At the present time, the prospect of recovery for future cancer risks is uncertain, but the appellate decision in *Velsicol* bodes ill for such recoveries in at least some jurisdictions.

FEAR OF FUTURE CANCER

Some plaintiffs have sued for their present emotional distress caused by the fear of incurring cancer in the future. The compensability of such fears is still somewhat uncertain. Historically, courts have been uncomfortable granting money damages for many psychological harms. This reluctance is largely borne of a concern for "burdening either the judicial system or individual defendants" with damages for injuries that are "trivial, evanescent, feigned or imagined."[25] Proof of mental distress and its magnitude is obviously less clear than proof of a broken leg or other physical injury.

The possibility of genuine mental distress cannot be ignored, however. "Numerous studies illustrate the reality and severity of the emotional distress that can accompany exposure to a long term risk of uncertain magnitude."[26] We know that many people have a particular fear of dying from cancer, sometimes called "cancerphobia," which is now a medically recognized condition. The law recognizes that some mental anguish claims are legitimate and cognizable in damages. As a rule, plaintiffs cannot recover for "temporary fright, nervous shock, nausea, grief, rage and humiliation" but may recover for "long continued mental disturbance, as for example in the case of repeated hysterical attacks, or mental aberration...."[27]

In an attempt to distinguish legitimate claims, many states limited mental anguish recoveries to those arising out of or resulting in a demonstrable physical injury, such as fear that epilepsy might develop some decades after an automobile accident.[28] Many more recent cases, however, have tended to recognize serious and genuine mental distress or fear as a compensable injury, even in the absence of contemporaneous physical harm. Jurisdictions remain split on this issue.

Even in jurisdictions where contemporaneous physical injury is prerequisite to recovery for mental anguish, plaintiffs may recover for fear from exposure to carcinogens. Chromosomal damage may suffice as the "slight impact and injury" necessary to present mental distress claims.[29] Other courts have recognized the mere ingestion of toxic substances as "sufficient physical impact or injury to support a mental distress claim."[30]

Courts have specifically recognized the compensability of cancerphobia, permitting recoveries for asbestos exposure, medical malpractice, and DES exposure that created a risk of future cancer. In one recent case, a court allowed recovery grounded in psychic damages for the transportation of nuclear waste over plaintiff's land.[31] As a rule, courts have been willing to compensate plaintiffs for demonstrable fears of future cancer attributable to a defendant's misconduct.

Not all instances of even genuine cancerphobia should be compensable, however. Some plaintiffs may have patently unreasonable fears of future cancer. The public misperceives many cancer risks, exaggerating some while underplaying the significance of others. Defendants should not be liable for damages simply because some individuals become unreasonably scared. For example, both the hazardous waste disposal site at Love Canal and the accident at Three Mile Island yielded extensive press attention that produced considerable public fear. After Three Mile Island, 22 percent of all easterners were "extremely worried about self or family's safety."[32] Yet the best scientific evidence shows that the cancer risk for those living very near Love Canal or Three Mile Island is miniscule. The cancerphobia is more a creature of press attention than scientific reality. Defendants should not be required to compensate those individuals who are unduly frightened by the media or others. There is some danger that unrestricted emotional distress damages for fear of future cancer "could expose companies to unforeseeable and potentially crippling liability even when it was ultimately determined that their conduct had not caused any tangible harm."[33]

Plaintiffs should only be compensated for cancer fears that are reasonable under the circumstances. Recovery may be denied when physicians "assured appellant she did not have cancer and that there was no cause for concern."[34] While a few courts have compensated plaintiffs without looking into the scientific reasonableness of the cancer fear, the better view would require a "reasonable fear" standard for recovery. To be reasonable, however, the feared cancer need not necessarily be probable. One might sensibly fear even a 5 percent risk of future cancer, for example. Where the fear is scientifically plausible, even relatively small probabilities should form the basis for cancerphobia compensation. Many cases do not quantify the future risk, but fear of future epilepsy has been compensated, when the medically estimated risk of such epilepsy was as low as 2 to 5 percent.[35] In a number of toxic tort cases, plaintiffs might recover some damages for genuine, seriously felt fear of future cancer.

One further barrier may exist to recoveries for fear of cancer. Recovery may depend upon the liability standard employed by a plaintiff. Courts have been willing to grant emotional distress damages when exposure to carcinogens was the result of a defendant's negligence. If a plaintiff proceeds under strict liability, however, "there is little precedent for compensating mental distress such as fear of future cancer."[36] While some precedent exists for denying emotional distress damages in strict liability actions, other courts have suggested that such damages may be obtained. At the present time, the availability of damages for fear of cancer in strict liability actions is uncertain and may vary by jurisdiction.

The amount of money that may be recovered for cancerphobia is also uncertain. Unlike physical injuries, which have establishable medical care costs and lost wages for compensation, the suffering of mental anguish is primarily internalized. When psychiatric care is required, those costs should be recoverable. In addition, juries have traditionally placed a price tag on demonstrable pain and suffering. When a prisoner was needlessly exposed to carcinogenic benzidine, he received $60,000 in compensatory damages for his fear of developing cancer and some unquantified risk of future cancer.[37] When members of a household were exposed to a toxic pesticide in their water supply, they each received nearly $7000 for their mental anguish.[38]

The *Velsicol* plaintiffs also sought damages for mental anguish arising out of fear of future cancer. The trial court accepted this claim, finding that "plaintiffs are entitled to recover for fear, distress or emotional injury because that fear or distress reasonably or naturally flowed or resulted from the disclosure of the nature and possible effects of those chemical contaminants."[39] After examining the nature and extent of the distress, the court emphasized that "the medical and scientific evidence provided justifies the conclusion that such fear and apprehension has continued after disclosure and/or will continue into the future."[40] Consequently, the court awarded the various plaintiffs damages for emotional distress ranging from $50,000 to $250,000. The court also awarded damages up to $250,000 for a specific psychological problem known as "post traumatic stress disorder."

The emotional distress damages awarded in *Velsicol* were challenged on appeal. The appellate court specifically recognized the theoretical legitimacy of cancerphobia as a compensable form of mental anguish. While the appellate court stressed that "there must be a reasonable connection between the injured plaintiff's mental anguish and the prediction of a future disease," that court accepted the trial court's determination that the plaintiffs had a "reasonable fear."[41] The specific amounts of damages awarded by the trial court, however, were deemed excessive, because "plaintiffs failed to prove at trial that they have a significant increased risk of contracting cancer and other diseases."[42] The appellate court reduced the damages to a range of $18,000 to $72,000. While the court expressly recognized that a plaintiff need not prove probability of future cancer to recover for mental distress from cancerphobia, the lesser probability provided reason for substantially reducing the amount awarded in damages. The appellate court rejected all the damages for post traumatic stress disorder, because consumption of contaminated water "does not rise to the level of the type of psychological trauma that is a universal stressor."[43]

FUTURE MEDICAL SURVEILLANCE

Individuals exposed to carcinogens may sue for another type of damages, for future medical surveillance, without awaiting the decades-long latency before cancer actually develops. Since exposure to cancer-causing substances will produce an elevated risk of cancer, plaintiffs have sought to recover the costs of medical monitoring of their condition, so that any cancer that might result could be detected at an early stage. Such early detection greatly enhances the prospects for effective treatment of the cancer.

The general availability of damages for medical surveillance following tortious injury is well-established in some older cases involving accidents.

Congress, too, has recognized the worth of such surveillance, as the Occupational Safety and Health Act compels employers to provide medical surveillance "to employees exposed to such hazards in order to most effectively determine whether the health of such employees is adversely affected by such exposure."[44]

Granting damages for the costs of medical surveillance also makes logical sense. When an individual is at risk of cancer, early detection of the cancer can substantially improve prospects for survival. Courts have recognized that early detection will "lead to improved prospects for cure, prolongation of life, relief of pain, and minimization of disability."[45] Medical surveillance damages overcome the causation problem, because plaintiff need only show an elevated risk and need not link a specific cancer to a specific source. Moreover, the costs to defendants of providing such surveillance are not great and are clearly cost-effective. Once again, the cancer context presents difficulties and questions, however, regarding the availability of medical surveillance cost recovery.

Some courts have virtually prohibited recovery for such medical surveillance damages. In one asbestos case, the judge precluded plaintiff's attorneys from even presenting any evidence on a future increased risk of cancer, on the grounds that the evidence could unfairly prejudice the jury in plaintiff's favor.[46] Other decisions have placed barriers in the way of recovery of medical surveillance costs. Some courts have required that plaintiff prove a present manifest injury, as in the risk of cancer cases. As discussed above, growing recognition of subclinical chromosomal damage as a present harm should help overcome this obstacle.

A still uncertain question involves the degree of increased risk necessary to justify a requirement of compensation for future medical surveillance. One case permitted recovery of such costs whenever future surveillance was considered "medically advisable."[47] Another court suggested that plaintiff must demonstrate a "reasonable probability" or a "greater than average risk" of developing a future cancer.[48]

The uncertainty regarding the appropriate test for recovery of future medical surveillance costs is amply illustrated by the series of decisions in a New Jersey hazardous waste case. The trial court permitted recovery for such damages, after holding that plaintiffs did not have to show a "reasonable probability" of cancer but only need to show some increased risk and that surveillance would be necessary to "properly diagnose the warning signs of the development of the disease."[49] This decision implied that almost any increased cancer risk, however small, would justify future surveillance cost damages, and the court awarded a total of more than $8 million to 352 plaintiffs suing as a class.

On appeal, the court rejected all the future medical surveillance damages. The court emphasized the "admitted inability of the [plaintiff's] expert witness to quantify the increased risk," which raised the possibility "that such increase is so microscopically small as to be meaningless."[50] The court held that plaintiff's proof fell short of the "reasonable probability" required by its legal standard.[51]

Plaintiffs appealed this rejection of their claim and the New Jersey Supreme Court reversed again, upholding the trial court's determination on medical surveillance damages. The court emphasized the presence of "competent expert testimony . . . [that] a program of regular medical testing and evaluation was reasonably necessary and consistent with contemporary scientific principles."[52] The court further reasoned that "[e]ven if the likelihood that these plaintiffs would contract cancer were only slightly higher than the national average," future medical surveillance was justified.[53] This decision clearly authorized medical surveillance damages without requiring plaintiffs to show a more-than-50-percent probability of developing future cancer. The case only controls the law of one state, however, and other states may be less open to medical surveillance cases. In Illinois, for example, a court has required evidence that the possible future harm is "reasonably certain" to result, before plaintiffs can recover their medical surveillance costs.[54] The promise of recovery for costs of medical surveillance will vary by jurisdiction, for the time being at least.

Even in jurisdictions where medical surveillance damages are theoretically promising, plaintiffs may face difficulty in bringing their case. Awards for future medical surveillance are relatively small, averaging under $25,000 per successful plaintiff. This small recovery may not justify trial costs. One commentator has noted:

> Claims for medical surveillance damages are different from personal injury compensation claims in yet another way—they often result in smaller damage awards. Because of the expense usually incurred in developing competent evidence that a plaintiff's health has been endangered, it may be difficult to persuade attorneys to represent individuals seeking only medical surveillance damages.[55]

This problem can be overcome in part by bringing class actions on behalf of a large number of plaintiffs. Because medical surveillance damages only require general proof of cancer risk, they present fewer individualized causation questions, and courts may be more willing to grant class action status to plaintiffs seeking surveillance damages.

Medical surveillance damages also conjoin well with other damage claims. If medical surveillance costs are sought in tandem with future risk and cancerphobia claims, the same evidence on risk will inform the court's decision on all the claims. Indeed, future surveillance may actually reduce plaintiff's recovery for future risk and cancerphobia, by protecting plaintiff against the most severe consequences of future cancer. If courts allow plaintiffs to recover for medical surveillance at the time of exposure and then recover later for cancers actually incurred, the surveillance itself will facilitate the later trial. The period of testing will provide "progressive evidence . . . of great value to a factfinder in determining whether a resulting injury . . . is causally linked to the defendant's hazard."[56]

Although the plaintiffs in *Velsicol* did not even seek recovery for future medical testing, there appears to be a trend in favor of granting damages for future medical surveillance in environmental cancer tort actions. This recovery should be readily available to any plaintiffs exposed to a meaningful excess risk of cancer, but the amount of damages for such surveillance is likely to be small.

PUNITIVE DAMAGES

Some of the largest awards in toxic tort cases have taken the form of punitive damages. Punitive damages fundamentally differ from other forms of damages that are designed only to compensate the plaintiff for his or her losses. Punitive damages go beyond such compensation and provide plaintiffs with something of a windfall of extra damages, in order to punish the tortious behavior of a defendant.

The leading purposes of punitive damages, which now are recognized by virtually every state, are "punishing the defendant," "deterring the defendant from repeating the offense," and "deterring others from committing the offense."[57] This common law punishment and deterrence has been limited to cases where a defendant's behavior has been particularly egregious. Typically, punitive damages are only awarded when the defendant's actions are "malicious" or particularly "reckless." Plaintiffs increasingly seek punitive damages, and juries have been more willing to grant substantial punitive damages. One study found that the average punitive damage verdict increased more than a hundredfold over a recent twenty-year period.[58] There has been some backlash against these increasing awards, and some states have placed statutory ceilings on the size of punitive damage recoveries. Nevertheless, punitive damages still offer many plaintiffs a source of substantial potential recovery.

Punitive damages are awarded rather frequently in toxic tort cases, as opposed to other litigation. Many toxic torts involve a relatively wealthy defendant, who may have recklessly endangered innocent individuals. Juries may be frustrated by this disregard for human health and well-being and feel driven to punish such defendants. In practice, punitive damages may also be used to reward sympathetic plaintiffs who are unable to meet the difficult causation burden in toxic tort litigation.

Punitive damages create some problems in application and have been subject to much recent criticism. Rather than deterring future misconduct, high punitive damage awards may drive defendants into insolvency. One leading commentator explains:

Where a single defendant's misconduct has caused mass disaster, or injury to many persons, there is a clear possibility that the defendant could be utterly ruined by the addition of punitive damages to his normal liability. Furthermore, if litigation takes place in many different courts, it is unlikely that damages awards could be coordinated at all. One result of heavy, multiple, and uncoordinated puntive awards in this situation, might be that the defendant's assets are exhausted by the awards made to the first claimants, leaving later, but equally injured claimants uncompensated. An award of punitive damages to claimant number one, in say, New York, is certainly not desirable if it results in depriving claimant number two, say, in California, of even a compensatory recovery.[59]

This danger is not merely hypothetical but has largely come to pass in the case of Johns-Manville, which declared bankruptcy as a consequence of numerous asbestos claims and punitive damage awards. One court has declined to award punitive damages in a case involving a drug that injured over 5,000 persons, because the court feared that punitive damages could be excessive and destroy the defendant company.[60]

Others worry that punitive damages permit juries to vent their prejudice and irrationality without regard to the facts of a case "since there is no measure nor any objective basis" for assessment of such damages.[61] The propriety of punitive damages is difficult to scrutinize on appeal. This danger may be of special concern in toxic torts, where a jury may force a defendant to pay punitive damages to a cancer victim plaintiff, simply because the defendant can afford to do so. To help avoid this eventuality, there is a traditional requirement that punitive damages may be awarded only when a plaintiff has proved that a defendant has caused some actual harm justifying compensatory damages. This rule may offer little protection, however, from jury caprice. In one recent Illinois case involving a spill of hazardous chemicals from a tank car, the jury awarded each plaintiff $1 in actual health-related compensatory damages and then awarded a total of $16.25 million in punitive damages.[62]

Punitive damages were hotly contested in the *Velsicol* case. The district court awarded $7.5 million in punitive damages, which was its estimate of the profits that Velsicol derived from the operation of the hazardous waste site challenged by plaintiffs. The court based its award on two factors. First, the court ruled that Velsicol's operation of the waste site involved "gross, wanton and willful disregard for the health and well-being of the plaintiffs."[63] Second, the court held that Velsicol's trial defense that the plaintiffs themselves were contributorily negligent and responsible for their own exposures was so "outrageous as to subject the defendant to punitive damages."[64] The appellate court rejected the second basis for punitive damages, holding that it could "chill an attorney's advocacy" of client interests.[65] That court accepted the first basis for punitive damages, however, and ordered the trial judge to recompute those damages without punitive consideration of defendant's trial arguments.

Punitive damages are troublesome in toxic tort cases, because of the risk of bankruptcy and the danger of jury prejudice. Punitive damages suffer from an even more fundamental flaw, however. The acknowledged purpose of these damages is to influence or even direct the future behavior of the defendant and similarly situated companies with respect to carcinogen releases. This is especially clear in the recent "judicial bargaining" of punitive damages. In a Kansas case, a judge awarded $10 million in punitive damages for pollution of a groundwater aquifer but offered to reduce or eliminate the damages if the defendant restored the aquifer to its unpolluted condition.[66] Punitive damages are regulatory in nature, rather than compensatory.

Courts and juries are ill-suited to implement such regulatory actions, however. Chapters 3–6 elaborate the complexity of carcinogen regulation. Total elimination of carcinogenic emissions is unrealistic, and the degree of reduction to be required by society is a complex one. The carcinogenic hazard must be assessed, a matter of great scientific complexity. The emission reduction may be grounded in cost/benefit analysis, feasibility analysis, or other procedures properly left to the democratically chosen representatives of the people. Regulatory decisions are difficult, even given the expertise and resources of regulatory agencies. Courts are rather clearly incapable of making informed and wise regulatory decisions when they are constrained by time, rules of evidence, and limited knowledge of the subject. Judicial use of punitive damages to deter or otherwise direct the behavior of polluting defendants risks improper or excessive regulatory effect. Such excessive control of specific carcinogens in specific media may have a counterproductive effect and compromise public health.

Regulation is best left to regulators. Punitive damages should be unavailable in instances where Congress or agency officials have established applicable requirements for carcinogenic emissions and where a defendant has complied with all such rules. There may be some proper scope for punitive damages when a defendant has violated the law, but even in this case enforcement should be left primarily in the hands of government authorities and punitive damages should be limited in amount and to cases where the defendant's liable activities were particularly and remarkably egregious.

NOTES

1. Cathey v. Johns-Manville Sales Corp., 776 F.2d 1565 (6th Cir. 1985).
2. Pruitt v. Suffolk Ob-Gyn Group, P.C., 644 F. Supp. 593 (E.D.N.Y. 1986).
3. Mink v. University of Chicago, 460 F. Supp. 713, 719 (N.D. Ill 1978).
4. Allen Kanner, *Emerging Conceptions of Latent Personal Injuries in Toxic Tort Litigation,* 18 RUTGERS L. J. (1987): 343, 350.
5. Eagle-Picher Industries v. Cox, 481 So.2d 517, 523 (Fla. Dist. Ct. App. 1985).

6. Ayers v. Township of Jackson, 461 A.2d 184, 187 (N.J. Super. 1983).

7. Reingold v. E. R. Squibb & Sons, Inc., No. 74-3420 (S.D.N.Y> Oct. 14, 1975).

8. Laswell v. Brown, 683 F.2d 261 (8th Cir. 1982).

9. In re "Agent Orange" Product Liability Litigation, 635 F.2d 987 (2d Cir. 1980).

10. Diamond v. General Motors Corp., 20 Cal. App. 3d 374 (1971).

11. Ayers v. Jackson Township, 461 A.2d 184 (N.J. Super. 1983).

12. Jackson v. Johns-Manville Sales Corp., 781 F.2d 394 (5th Cir.) (en banc), *cert. denied*, 106 S. Ct. 3339 (1986).

13. Note, *Increased Risk of Disease from Hazardous Waste: A Proposal for Judicial Relief,* 60 WASHINGTON L. REV. (1985): 635, 639.

14. Brafford v. Susquehanna Corp., 586 F. Supp. 14, 17 (D. Colo. 1984).

15. 586 F. Supp. 17–18.

16. 586 F. Supp. 18.

17. Allen v. United States, 588 F. Supp. 247, 419 (D. Utah 1984).

18. Kanner, p.352.

19. Laswell v. Brown, 683 F.2d 261, 269 (8th Cir. 1982).

20. Frank Cross & Paula Murray, *Liability for Toxic Radon Gas in Residential Home Sales,* 66 NORTH CAROLINA L. REV. (1987): 687, 728.

21. Anderson v. W. R. Grace & Co., 628 F. Supp. 1219, 1230 (D. Mass. 1986).

22. Cross & Murray, 730.

23. 647 F. Supp. 303, 322 (W.D. Tenn. 1986).

24. Sterling v. Velsicol Chemical Corp., 22 Env't Rep. Cases 1985, 1999 (6th Cir. 1988).

25. Payton v. Abbott Labs, 437 N.E.2d 171, 179 (Mass. 1982).

26. Robert Bohrer, *Fear and Trembling in the Twentieth Century: Technological Risk, Uncertainty and Emotional Distress,* 1984 WISCONSIN L. REV. (1984): 83, 84 n.2.

27. *Restatement (Second) of Torts,* Section 436(A) (1979).

28. Figlar v. Gordon, 53 A.2d 645 (Conn. 1947).

29. Herber v. Johns-Manville Corp., 785 F.2d 79, 85 (3d Cir. 1986).

30. Cross & Murray, 731.

31. Texas Electric Service Co. v. Nelon, 546 S.W. 2d 864 (Tex. Civ. App. 1977).

32. Bohrer, p.84 n.2.

33. Daniel Farber, *Toxic Causation,* 71 MINNESOTA L. REV. 1219, 1224 n.21 (1987).

34. Winik v. Jewish Hospital, 293 N.E.2d 95, 95 (N.Y. 1972).

35. Heider v. Employers Mutual Liability Insurance, 231 So.2d 438 (La. Ct. App. 1970).

36. Cross & Murray, 733.

37. Clark v. Taylor, 710 F.2d 4 (1st Cir. 1983).

38. Laxton v. Orkin Exterminating Co., Inc., 639 S.W.2d 431 (Tenn. 1982).

39. 647 F. Supp. 321.

40. Id.

41. 27 Env't Rep. Cases at 1999.

42. 27 Env't Rep. Cases at 2000.

43. 27 Env't Rep. Cases at 2002.

44. 29 U.S.C. Section 655(b)(7) (1982).

45. Ayers v. Jackson Township, 525 A.2d 287, 304 (N.J. Super. 1985).

46. Jackson v. Johns-Manville Sales Corp., 727 F.2d 506 (5th Cir. 1984).

47. Hagerty v. L & L Marine Services, 788 F.2d 315, 319 (5th Cir. 1986).

48. Herber v. Johns-Manville Corp., 785 F.2d 79, 83 (3d Cir. 1986).

49. Ayers v. Township of Jackson, 461 A.2d 184, 190 (N.J. Super. 1983).

50. Ayers v. Township of Jackson, 493 A.2d 1314, 1323 (N.J. Super. 1985).

51. Id.

52. Ayers v. Township of Jackson, 525 A.2d 287, 308–309 (N.J. 1987).

53. 525 A.2d at 312.

54. Morrissy v. Eli Lilly & Co., 394 N.E. 2d 1369, 1376 (Ill. 1979).

55. Leslie Gara, *Medical Surveillance Damages: Using Common Sense and the Common Law to Mitigate the Dangers Posed by Environmental Hazards,* 12 HARVARD ENVIRONMENTAL L. REV. (1988): 2231, 295.

56. Gara, 270.

57. Dorsey Ellis, *Fairness and Efficiency in the Law of Punitive Damages,* SOUTHERN CALIFORNIA L. REV. (1982): 1, 3.

58. M. Peterson, *Punitive Damages: Preliminary Empirical Findings* (1985).

59. D. B. Dobbs, *Law of Remedies* (West Pub., 1973): 212.

60. Roginsky v. Richardson-Merrell, 378 F.2d 832 (2d Cir. 1967).

61. Dobbs, 219.

62. Kemner v. Monsanto Co., No. 80-L-970 (1987).

63. 627 F. Supp. at 323.

64. Id.

65. 27 Env't Rep. Cases at 2007.

66. Miller v. Cudahy Co., 656 F. Supp. 316 (D. Kan. 1987).

9

FUTURE DIRECTIONS IN COMMON LAW RECOVERY

Currently, there is widespread acknowledgment that mechanisms for common law toxic tort recovery for environmentally induced cancer are seriously flawed. Both plaintiffs and defendants suffer the shortcomings of this system, and both argue for modifications. Experience under the present system, combined with an understanding of the special problems presented by the features of environmentally induced cancer, should enable a positive restructuring of compensation systems. Ideally, this restructuring should serve the mutual interests of plaintiffs, defendants, and society as a whole.

Creation of an effective compensation system is vital to any ethical government system dealing with environmentally induced cancer. Regulation cannot prevent all environmental cancer risks, and government must therefore allow some public exposure to carcinogens and some level of environmentally induced cancer. Such a system is defensible if the eventual victims are fairly and adequately compensated. If victims must go uncompensated, however, the system devolves into one that places the costs of economic and social progress on a small and largely defenseless subgroup of the population ultimately victimized by cancer. Such a system would be unacceptably inequitable. Hence, fairness demands improvements in the compensation system for environmental cancer.

Many proposals have been put forth to remedy the shortcomings of the present common law compensation system. This chapter reviews and analyzes the proposals, in an attempt to produce a useful solution. First, the procedural reform of administrative, rather than judicial, compensation will be considered. Second, various substantive reforms will be reviewed and evaluated. While many of these reform proposals are inadequate or unfair, some changes warrant attention.

PROCEDURAL REFORM—ADMINISTRATIVE COMPENSATION

A leading focus of reformers has been the elimination of the common law tort recovery system for toxic substance injuries and its replacement by a simpler administrative procedure for compensation. Administrative compensation could take one of two different forms. The first would simply substitute an administrative tribunal for the courts, imposing liability directly upon defendants found responsible for disease. The second would establish a fund, probably through taxes imposed upon hazard-producing industries, and then disburse this fund to victims of environmentally induced cancer. Whichever form is chosen, administrative compensation could reduce the costs of litigation and avoid some rigid procedural and evidentiary requirements of the courts. Proponents promise that administrative compensation could provide swifter and more equitable compensation for victims of toxic torts such as cancer.

Abolition of tort recovery should be taken only cautiously. While the tort system has substantial and undeniable shortcomings, it does slowly respond to new problems, such as that presented by carcinogenesis. Insurance industry testimony has thus suggested that "the success rate of claimants under both workers' compensation and the tort system in hazardous substance—related cases is improving steadily, as innovative counsel develop, and sympathetic courts adopt, new theories of liability."[1] Proponents of new administrative compensation should carry a burden of proof, before wholesale changes are made in existing procedures for victim compensation.

Fortunately, administrative compensation systems are not untested but are already employed in the United States for various categories of injuries. The workers compensation system, the black lung disability compensation program for miners and the veterans compensation system are among the best known of these administrative systems. In addition, Japan and New Zealand have adopted administrative compensation systems for injuries caused by environmental pollution. The promise of a shift to administrative compensation can in part be judged by reference to these systems.

Review of existing administrative compensation systems suggests that they work well when dealing with relatively simple injury scenarios, when causation is relatively clear. The promise of administrative compensation in the more complex situation of environmentally induced cancer is much less clear. Indeed, current administrative programs have struggled with cancer damages every bit as much as have the courts.

The Agent Orange experience provides valuable insight into the limitations of administrative compensation for cancer and related genetic diseases. Veterans sued in federal court for compensation, with mixed success. Veterans also sought compensation from the Veterans Administration but had no better results. The Veterans Administration (VA) initially stonewalled the problem, rejecting any association between Agent Orange and alleged harms. After confronting political pressure from influential veterans' groups, the VA agreed to study the problem but has yet to provide compensation. Plaintiffs have complained of inadequate representation under VA structures and "[s]everal veterans, who claimed that they had contracted cancer due to exposure to radiation in the service and that without the help of a lawyer they could not gather evidence and present their complex claims effectively," challenged the constitutional fairness of the system.[2] Veterans also have claimed that "VA employees randomly denied claims in order to achieve high performance ratings."[3] A federal judge ultimately confirmed some of these allegations and sanctioned the Veterans Administration.[4] More recently, a congressional oversight committee charged that the VA "has been unfair to thousands of veterans and has concealed its own findings of 'error and bias.' "[5]

The workers compensation system has also struggled with occupational cancer claims. Workers compensation may have been less successful than the courts in properly compensating cancer victims. A Texas plaintiff who suffered asbestosis, for example, was denied relief because he failed to sue within three years of the harmful exposure.[6] Administrative compensation schemes like workers compensation must grapple with statutes of limitations and other problems, just as the courts must.

Causation has been a particular problem for worker compensation recovery for occupationally induced cancers. A number of states do not offer workers compensation recovery for diseases such as lung cancer, which are common to the general population, but limit coverage to rare cancers like mesothelioma, which are generally caused only by a substance found in the workplace. Causation has barred recovery for scores of employees seeking workers compensation recovery.[7] Even when cancer recovery is allowed, the "[a]gencies have made many awards clearly inconsistent with scientific knowledge of cancer."[8]

The Japanese and New Zealand compensation systems also have faced difficulties. In Japan, for example, cancer is not covered by the system, and environmentally induced cancer is unlikely to be covered in the future due to causation proof difficulties. "Scientific conservatism and political inertia have inhibited the expansion of the statute's coverage to a comprehensive level."[9] The Japanese system has also been criticized "because many victims are either over- or under-compensated by the law's benefit provisions."[10] Japan's administrative compensation does not cure the causation paradox and "the ability of the Japanese statute to isolate the appropriate target group for compensation is doubtful."[11] The New Zealand law also fails to cover diseases such as cancer and has been criticized for inadequate payments to victims.

A purely procedural answer to cancer compensation is doomed to failure. The critical difficulties in framing a compensation system are largely substantive, particularly involving the causation issue. Perhaps an administrative compensation scheme offers benefits, but it is no panacea and must be joined to substantive reforms to effectuate a fair system for recovery of cancer damages.

MISGUIDED SUBSTANTIVE REFORM PROPOSALS

Many experts have proposed remedies for the substantive shortcomings of the toxic tort recovery system. While some problems, such as statutes of limitations, may be readily resolved with relatively minor tinkering with the prevailing legal rules, causation remains particularly intractable. The leading proposals for revision, therefore, focus on the causation problem. While most of the reform proposals address recovery for injuries from hazardous waste disposal, their principles are readily applicable to other sources of environmentally induced cancer. Such proposals must be examined critically. As discussed below, many of these reform proposals are misguided due to scientific inaccuracy or structural inequity.

Rebuttable Presumptions

Plaintiffs' difficulty in proving causation may be overcome through a procedural device called "rebuttable presumptions." Under this framework, a plaintiff who has suffered cancer need only prove a certain specified exposure to a carcinogen, and then the decisionmaker "presumes" that the exposure was the actual cause of the cancer. The presumption is rebuttable because defendants are allowed to introduce evidence to prove that they were not the actual cause of the plaintiff's cancer. A system of rebuttable presumptions is currently used in a federal administrative system to compensate certain miners who suffer from black lung disease and in some state workers compensation systems.

The best-known proposal for rebuttable presumptions is found in the Superfund Section 301(e) Report, drafted by a group of experts to reform the toxic tort compensation system.[12] This report proposed a two-tier system, including both administrative and judicial compensation. Under the administrative compensation proposals of the Section 301(e) Report, the rebuttable presumption would work as follows. First, a claimant (plaintiff) would be required to show that the defendant was engaged "in the production, transportation or disposal of hazardous wastes"; second, that the "claimant was exposed to such hazardous waste by proximity, contact, ingestion, inhalation or by some other form of exposure"; and third, that "the claimant suffered death or the kind of injury or disease which is known to result from such exposure. . . ."[13] Once this showing is made, the study group creates a rebuttable presumption that the defendant is responsible for the claimant's death, injury, or disease.

Critics of the study group report immediately assumed that any exposure to a hazardous waste would trigger the presumption of liability and broadcast the unfairness of this approach. Most environmental exposures to carcinogens, especially in the hazardous waste context, produce only a very small increase in relative cancer risk (such as 1 in 100,000). Other sources, particularly those involving personal lifestyle, produce much greater relative risks. Triggering a rebuttable presumption with any exposure to an environmental carcinogen is thus scientifically inaccurate and would make defendants potentially liable for the hundreds of thousands of cancers that were in fact attributable to smoking, dietary practices and other causes unrelated to environmental contaminants. In the toxic tort context, a "larger percentage of potential claims—perhaps even the vast majority—would involve sufficient causal uncertainty that indulging in presumptions would be factually unwarranted."[14]

The rebuttability of the presumption helps avoid unfairness, but provides only limited relief. The study group does not propose a specific standard of proof for rebutting the causation presumption, but the burden to prove that a substance did *not* cause cancer is even more onerous than the present plaintiffs' burden to prove the substance did cause cancer. In scientific theory, proving such a negative is impossible. In practical application, such proof will be exceedingly difficult. Insurance representatives asserted that the Section 301(e) recommendation would be uninsurable for companies because it "would so weaken the evidentiary and burden of proof requirements of the common law as to place upon defendants and their insurers the impossible task of identifying which of the millions of Americans with long-latency diseases and other health problems did not contract them through exposure to hazardous substances and therefore are ineligible for compensation."[15]

Indeed, such a rebuttable presumption, unfounded in scientific fact, could violate the due process clause of the United States Constitution. A group of coal mine operators challenged the constitutionality of the retroactive causation presumptions of the black lung compensation system in *Usery v. Turner Elkhorn Mining Co.*[16] In this case, the Supreme Court upheld the act's presumptions, but only because of the close causal nexus between coal mine work and black lung. The Court suggested that a statute would be unconstitutional if it imposed liability on a mine operator for harm "that is due to causes other than the operator's conduct."[17] Quite recently, the Supreme Court cut back on the Black Lung Act's presumptions, requiring disabled miners in some circumstances to support their causation claim with a preponderance of the evidence.[18] The Supreme Court has carefully limited presumptions under the law to circumstances when an inference of causation is scientifically supported and reasonable. A toxic compensation presumption unrelated to a high probability of causation therefore might well violate constitutional due process.

Moreover, even the constitutional, scientifically supportable causation presumptions of the black lung compensation program have had unanticipated consequences. A chemical industry commentator has observed:

The Black Lung Act provides an example of what can happen when a compensation system is not well thought out. A General Accounting Office report issued in January 1982 found that 84 percent of claims were paid without adequate medical evidence.

The result: in 1969, Congress estimated that the total program would cost between $40 million and $385 million. By 1972, costs to the federal government alone amounted to $33 million per month. In 1979, such costs amounted to $1.5 billion and reached $2 billion in 1982. The total cost of the program, including benefits paid directly by industry, is unknown.[19]

The Black Lung Act also illustrates the risk that presumptions "can serve as a politically expedient method of manipulating the scope of a program," without regard for scientific fact.[20] Creation of presumptions may enhance compensation of cancer victims, but at potentially enormous cost and unfairness to some companies.

Clearly, a rebuttable presumption that *any* exposure to an environmental carcinogen is the cause of a subsequent cancer is indefensible. This system would make a few industries pay for every cancer in the United States, whatever the cause. The Section 301(e) Report is not so ridiculous, however. Indeed, the report acknowledged that in "the creation of presumptions, a reasonable judgment of probabilities is the most important consideration."[21] Consequently, the report's rebuttable presumption apparently would apply only when plaintiff provided a certain "level of exposure," as defined in administratively prepared Toxic Substance Documents.[21] The harsh unfairness and scientific inaccuracy of the rebuttable presumption could be largely cured by setting a "level of exposure" trigger that is sufficiently high as to imply a probability of actual causation by defendants.

While this approach to rebuttable presumptions may remedy the unconstitutionality and unfairness of the approach, it also seriously undermines the victim compensation benefits that the approach may offer. If the trigger for the presumption is set at the exposure level that would yield a "more than 50 percent" probability of cancer, the system reverts back to the basic causation rules of the existing tort system. While the administrative system may provide some procedural benefits, such a "reform" offers little substantive help to plaintiffs. If the trigger is set at a lower level, however, the results will be patently unfair to defendants, requiring them to pay for a large number of cancers that they did not cause or even contribute to. Neither system addresses the paradox of the probabilistic causation problem. In short, rebuttable presumptions cannot provide a fair and effective answer to the causation difficulties found in toxic tort compensation.

Substantial Factor Test

Some commentators have proposed to settle causation problems by employing a traditional common law test for causation, called the substantial factor test. Under this test, a plaintiff need not prove that a defendant's conduct was the only cause of the plaintiff's injuries but need simply prove that the defendant's conduct was a substantial factor in creating the injuries.

One of the earliest and best-known applications of the substantial factor test was a Minnesota case where a defendant set a fire, which merged with another fire from another source, and the combined fires burned down plaintiff's property.[23] The defendant contended that he should not be liable, because the independently caused fire was the—or at least a—contributing cause of the damage. The court found the defendant liable, based on causation analysis imposing liability for injury whenever the defendant was "a material element and substantial factor in bringing it about."[24]

Advocates of tort reform have suggested use of the substantial factor test for the uncertain causation in cases of toxic torts for cancer damages. These commentators must still define what substantial factor means in this context. One such proponent has suggested that "if the evidence, including scientific evidence, reaches the level of reasonable probability, the requisite causal relationship for awarding compensation should exist."[25] According to this author, "reasonable probability" may be "50 percent or less" and "will vary with the facts."[26] If the standard is set at 50 percent, however, the substantial factor test contributes nothing new. If the standard is set lower, why should a lower level of proof suffice, and how much lower? If the standard varies with the facts of individual cases, why should this be so and what facts should be dispositive? This formulation cannot answer the causation dilemma in toxic tort cases.

Still another advocate of the substantial factor test rests upon "qualitative causation" as an answer.[27] Under this standard, a defendant would be liable whenever his or her conduct "was a substantial potential cause, or substantially increased the risk, of plaintiff's disease. . . . "[28] This showing would be relatively easy for plaintiffs to meet. As further defined, the plaintiff must simply show that "the substance was 'hazardous,' " that "the exposure was 'substantial,' " and that "the injury was 'consistent with the exposure.' "[29] While one must still define "substantial exposure," the author emphasizes that " 'substantial' should certainly not be defined as a probability greater than 50 percent or any other arbitrary level."[30]

The above incarnation of the substantial factor approach may be characterized as the "hunch" theory of carcinogenic causation. The test would assign liability whenever the jury intuits that a defendant was a source of the plaintiff's cancer. A recent major case involving cancer victims of radioactive fallout seemingly adopted this approach when it rejected the 50 percent rule and held that a plaintiff simply must show that "the defendant significantly increased or augmented the risk of somatic injury."[31]

This notion of qualitative causation should be perceived as troublesome. Why should a jury be allowed to intuit causation, when such a hunch may fly in the face of sound, even unrefuted, scientific evidence to the contrary? What possible factual basis could form the foundation for this sort of hunch? The concept suggests an "open season" on defendants, permitting juries to find causation without regard to scientific fact.

One need not be an expert in jury psychology to predict that causation under the above standard will be based largely upon how sympathetic the plaintiff appears and how callous the defendant seems. Some commentators are quite frank about this effect, suggesting that "[c]ourts could also lower the burden of proof where the defendant's action appears especially reprehensible, so as to allow plaintiffs to recover by showing that causation is possible, or conceivable, rather than probable."[32] This is akin to a concept called "negligence in the air," when a party is negligent but fortuitously injures no one.

This remarkable position removes causation from the field of factual questions and transfers it to a subset of a negligence standard of liability finding. In so doing, it transforms jurors from fact-finders into policymakers, who may redistribute wealth from chemical companies to cancer victims based upon intuitive notions of fairness rather than factual causation. One might just as easily and rationally require the negligent chemical companies to compensate the homeless, however. Once the requirement of factual causation is eliminated, the courts are transformed into mini-legislatures empowered to render redistributive and potentially arbitrary "justice" without regard for factual causal inquiries.

Fact-based causation plays a key role in our liberal system of justice. As described by one of the foremost advocates of toxic tort plaintiffs:

> The rule denying liability for "negligence in the air" taps fundamental values of fairness and forgiveness. If someone is wrongfully injured, blame and compensation are entirely in order; but when a potential victim has suffered no loss, no breach of entitlements has occurred. Punishing every error in judgment regardless of whether it has caused harm might result in excessive liability and could lead not only to overbearing and discriminatory enforcement, but also to a fearful and overcautious society.[33]

Such a compensation system would functionally empower juries as "negligence police," seeking out and punishing negligent behavior regardless of its consequences. Granting juries this power will yield arbitrary if not tyrannical results.

Any such negligence in the air approach also violates fundamental notions of fairness. Consider a person who is negligently speeding down an interstate highway. Simultaneously, a nearby pedestrian is struck by lightening. Most Americans will recoil from a system that makes the motorist pay for the pedestrian's damages, based on proximity rather than causation. As discussed above under rebuttable presumptions, some measure of causation requirement is enshrined in the due process clause of the Constitution.

Some proponents of the substantial factor test attempt to resolve the causation paradox by effectively eliminating a causation requirement. Such radical surgery on the tort system is dangerous and unnecessary. Others, who would require at least a probabilistic causal nexus under the substantial factor test, fail to resolve the existing causation paradox.

The substantial factor test may have some proper role in cancer causation judgments. Where two carcinogens act synergistically to increase a risk exponentially, rather than additively, the substantial factor test is more sensible. This is somewhat analogous to the merging fires case. This situation is not common, however, and should be limited to instances when the two or more synergistic carcinogens can be established as the cause in fact of a plaintiff's eventual cancer.

Post Facto Proportional Liability

There is a growing consensus among legal scholars that toxic tort cancer causation determinations must be proportional, based on probability, rather than relying on the traditional all-or-nothing preponderance of the evidence test. It is scientifically impossible to determine the one true cause of a cancer. Cancer causation simply does not lend itself to the traditional test, which produces the paradox of unfairness described in chapter 7.

Post facto proportional liability is one response to this consensus.[34] Consider a lung cancer victim, who was exposed to a 5 percent lung cancer risk from a nearby industrial air polluter, and a 51 percent risk from his workplace exposures. The polluter might be required to pay for 5 percent of his lung cancer damages, and his employer would be required to pay for 51 percent of the damages. The remainder would be paid by other established responsible causes of cancer risk or borne by the plaintiff himself. This seems more equitable than requiring the employer to pay for all the damages under the preponderance of the evidence test. This system also benefits plaintiffs in the more common case, where no single defendant can be proved more than 50 percent responsible for a cancer risk.

Post facto proportional compensation thus avoids the causation paradox for probabilistic cancer risks, without disregarding scientific facts or compelling defendants to pay for cancers they did not cause. This approach, however, contains a logical fallacy when it applies *pre facto* probabilities in a *post facto* manner. At the time of an exposure, the probability of future cancer may be 5 percent. Later, when cancer has occurred, the overall probability of cancer is obviously 100 percent, and the causal probability of any particular carcinogenic exposure is often 0 percent or 100 percent, depending upon whether it was the responsible agent.

To illustrate this fallacy, consider the hypothetical example of a "boy in a bubble." This person, for whatever reason, lives in rather sterile conditions and has been exposed to only one lung carcinogen in his life. Risk assessment tells us that this exposure created a 1 percent chance of lung cancer. If the boy contracts lung cancer, however, we may be confident that this relatively small exposure is responsible for the entirety of the boy's damages. It is unfair to compensate him for only 1 percent of his damages, simply because he was a member of the unlucky 1 percent of the population who eventually contract cancer from the small exposure.

For the *post facto* proportionality rule to operate accurately, it must consider all past carcinogenic exposures in retrospect. The courts should examine all the known sources of relevant cancer risk to which a victim was exposed, and apportion liability based upon the relative probability that the plaintiff's cancer was created by each of these sources.

While the latter system of comparative causation would be relatively fair and overcome the causation paradox, it could be hopelessly difficult to effectuate. It is difficult enough for a plaintiff and defendant to trace a single source of carcinogenic exposure and assess the risk from that source. If the law requires the parties to track down every single risk faced by a person in his or her past life, the burden will become totally unwieldy. The expense and delay of toxic tort cases will be multiplied manyfold. A more practical solution must be found.

The proposed solutions described above all fall short of adequately addressing the causation paradox in toxic torts based on environmental carcinogenesis. Equally important, they offer nothing to solve the other problems faced by toxic tort plaintiffs. In particular, the difficulty and expense of proving a case involving a latent disease are not addressed by these proposals. Even the very liberal rebuttable presumption and substantial factor tests offer little help to a plaintiff trying to prove exposure and defendant's conduct twenty or more years after the fact.

A PROPOSED SOLUTION

Although the causation and related problems created by the toxic tort of cancer are indeed difficult, they may be surmounted. While the above flawed solutions focus directly on the problem of establishing liability and causation, an indirect attack on the problem, which focuses on remedies, offers a superior solution. Once courts accept a risk of future cancer as a compensable harm, many of the plaintiffs' problems, including causation, disappear. Remaining toxic tort problems can be ameliorated by procedural reforms that create a role for expert administrative agencies.

Substantive Reform—Permitting Recovery for a Risk

The notion of recovery for a future risk of cancer has been discussed in chapter 8. While courts have not uniformly rejected such recoveries, decisions in many jurisdictions disallow recovery for a risk. Permitting such recovery for future risks, however, will go far to remedy the causation paradox and other problems associated with cancer-based toxic tort litigation.

If recovery is permitted for a risk of future cancer, a plaintiff need not wait the twenty-year latency period for the possible cancer to develop. Rather, a plaintiff could sue as soon as he or she became aware of a material risk of cancer resulting from the liable actions of another. The case would turn on whether the defendant's actions improperly caused a risk of future cancer rather than whether those actions caused an actual cancer.

The plaintiff would still be required to demonstrate that the named defendant violated some legal duty or standard of liability in creating the risk. If successful, the plaintiff would then be called upon to prove the presence of a future cancer risk and to quantify the risk of cancer resulting from the plaintiff's exposure to the defendant's risk-creating activity. This proof could be through accepted principles of quantitative risk assessment, detailed in chapter 3. Once a plaintiff proved the risk of such a future cancer, damages could be awarded. Damages would provide the present value (cost) of the future risk, discounted by its probability. Successful plaintiffs might also be able to recover for medical surveillance costs, emotional damages, and even punitive damages (in the limited circumstances where they are appropriate).

While damage measurement and valuation of future cancer risk under this proposal might appear complex, it need not be so. Actuaries have considerable expertise in assessing the present value of future risks, and these assessments form the basis of the insurance industry. A meaningful valuation of future cancer risk can be readily obtained.

In some limited circumstances, courts already value such proportional future risks. In a set of "lost chance" cases, courts permit recovery for negligent destruction of a chance of future benefit. For example, when a doctor's negligence omits a procedure that would have given a patient a greater future chance of survival or other health benefits, courts permit proportional recovery for the loss of this chance. Future risk is simply the "flip side" of the lost chance precedents.

The concept of recovery for future risk has been considered, and some such form of proportional recovery is now supported by the "great weight of scholarly authority."[35] Some commentators, however, have raised serious criticisms of future risk recovery. The leading criticism appears to be that recovery for risk allegedly both over- and undercompensates real loss, sometimes called the "windfall-shortfall problem."[36] If the plaintiff is fortunate and never actually incurs cancer, the plaintiff will have received compensation without being harmed. Conversely, if cancer does develop, the plaintiff will have recovered only a fraction of his or her actual cancer damages.

Whatever the merits of this criticism of allowing recovery for future risks, it ignores the reality of current toxic tort law. The theoretical appeal of precise *post facto* compensation is lost in application. As one reviewer observed:

Under our system, one plaintiff sues and gets a huge award, including punitive damages. Another plaintiff with substantially the same industrial exposure or substantially the same set of facts sues and gets reasonably decent compensatory damages, but no more. A third plaintiff comes in and gets absolutely nothing. That has happened time and again in the asbestos cases, and it has happened time and again across the board. This is no way to compensate three people who have been equally grievously harmed.[37]

As described in chapter 7, numerous worthy plaintiffs are presently denied any recovery due to unavoidable, artificial barriers contained within the tort system. Excessive fear of undercompensating plaintiffs in a proportional, recovery-for-risk system ignores the reality of substantial undercompensation under current structures. Plus, allowing a possibility of recovery for future risk would not necessarily preclude a plaintiff from forgoing this option and waiting and suing for any actual risk that develops. Undercompensation for environmentally induced cancer is a prevailing reality, and it is by no means clear that recovery for a risk would aggravate this problem.

The concern for overcompensation of those who never suffer cancer is also misguided. Even if cancer never develops, a plaintiff may still be harmed by suffering the uncertainty of a risk. Thus, "proportional recovery need not be conceptualized as compensation for risk as such, but rather as a means of compensating for actual harm given limited information about causation."[38] When actual harm follows a risk quite quickly, as in an automobile accident, the "at risk" period is quite short, and no compensation is necessary. In cancer, when the "at risk" period is lengthy, the risk itself and its attendant uncertainty may be deemed an actual harm. People's willingness to pay to insure against future risks demonstrates that such risks have some monetarily definable present value.

The criticism that recovery for future risk will over- and undercompensate plaintiffs suffers from an even deeper flaw. If insurance markets are well developed and functioning, the presence of such insurance will make future risk compensation much more precise than any available *post facto* compensation. An individual suffering a certain probabilistic future risk of cancer should receive a damage award equivalent to the present cost of adequately insuring against probable future costs associated with the particular risk of cancer suffered. If such an individual purchases the insurance, no over- or undercompensation will result. Those individuals who contract cancer will receive full insurance benefits for their costs, while the lucky individuals who avoid cancer will ultimately receive no net award beyond the security offered by insurance. If the individual declines marketed insurance coverage, he or she is simply self-insuring and assuming a risk. As explained:

Although ex ante compensation (given before the harm materializes) may appear quite different, requiring defendants to provide insurance coverage to those at risk (or cash with which to pay the premiums) is functionally no different from making a payment once the injury has materialized. Logically, no difference exists between compensation for an unrealized risk and compensation of those ultimately harmed when the risk materializes. Given smoothly functioning markets, compensation for the risk is equivalent to paying for insurance, which in turn is equivalent to ex post liability.[39]

The proposed system depends on an effectively functioning private market in insurance, the current presence of which is somewhat debatable. The shortcomings in private insurance, however, are far less than those inhering in *post facto* recoveries in the tort system. If insurance is unavailable for the particular toxic risk suffered by a plaintiff, he or she should still be able to purchase some standard disability or death policy of roughly comparable value.

A second criticism of recovery for future risk involves the fear of overburdening the trial courts with cancer risk claims. In truth, each of the current 200,000,000 + Americans has suffered some enhanced cancer risk from environmental exposures, and the courts are rather obviously incapable of adjudicating so many claims. It is quite unlikely, however, that risk recovery will encourage an explosion of cancer litigation.

For the vast majority of individuals, the increased cancer risk from environmental exposure is quite small. Consequently, their proportional recovery would be very small and would be unlikely to be worth the litigation costs of pursuing a remedy. After analyzing the economics of plaintiffs' litigation, Professor Rosenberg of Harvard concluded that "the proportionality rule would clearly not increase the volume of such cases."[40]

If we want to permit small recoveries, it is a simple matter to provide administrative compensation or "small claims courts" for future risk claims below some certain threshold. Allowing recovery for a risk might also unburden trial courts to some extent. Problems of proof and complexity of litigation will be reduced by permitting suit at the time of exposure, rather than decades later. Reduced uncertainty about judgments could also encourage increased settlement of toxic tort litigation.

In any event, the fear of burdening courts provides a weak reason for denying compensation to worthy plaintiffs who have suffered legally cognizable injuries. Making recovery impossible for such plaintiffs is a poor answer to overburdened courts. Should this problem arise, procedural remedies such as administrative compensation could be employed to protect the courts.

The disadvantages of permitting probabilistic recovery for future risk of cancer are far outweighed by the benefits of this approach. Risk of cancer recovery provides plaintiffs a reasonable opportunity to recover for toxic torts. Most significantly, recovery for a risk overcomes the causation paradox inhering in the preponderance of evidence standard for *post facto* recovery. Risk assessment is admittedly inexact, but it provides a far more accurate and scientifically supportable measure of harm than do current *post facto* procedures for proof of cancer causation. Plaintiffs would need no longer assume the virtually impossible task of proving the precise cause of a particular cancer.

Allowing recovery for risk of future cancer also helps overcome the other leading barriers to plaintiffs in toxic tort cases. By permitting recovery at the time of exposure, the statute of limitations problem is largely cured. While plaintiffs must still prove exposure and defendants' violation of a liability standard, the contemporaneity of plaintiff's lawsuit significantly reduces the difficulties of proving these issues. Witnesses will be more available and current government monitoring records will provide valuable or even conclusive evidence on these issues. Defendants are much less likely to escape warranted liability through insolvency. Allowing recovery for a risk of future cancer is no panacea for plaintiffs, but it does eliminate many artificial barriers to justified compensation.

Allowing recovery for proportional future risk also has some benefits for defendants. Liability should be more even and predictable. The plaintiff who has not yet suffered cancer is less likely to evoke the sympathies of jurors, and defendants may avoid some exorbitant judgments founded in such sympathy or jury whims or ignorance. Greater predictability may enhance the insurability of potential defendants' activities. Defendants will also be better able to avoid vexatious litigation. At the present time, "complexity, coupled with the extraordinary expense attendant to defending these [toxic tort] cases, may motivate defendants to settle unmeritorious claims."[41] Proportional recovery may also promote horizontal equity among defendants, apportioning costs to responsible parties rather than to those parties who happen to be the most solvent or identifiable.

In addition to improving victim compensation, the more immediate recovery for future cancer risk contributes to the objective of deterring tortious conduct by those who create risks. When defendants are forced to bear the costs of the external public health harms that they cause, defendants are provided a financial incentive to prevent such harms, to the extent that prevention is less likely than compensation. Any improvement in the accuracy of identifying valid claims and compensating these claimants will improve the efficiency of the deterrence process. By improving accuracy, proportional recovery for future risk can improve the deterrence function of tort law.

The timing of litigation under the recovery for future risks also improves deterrence. Potential defendants may be somewhat blithe about imposing external health harms under the present system. Secure in the knowledge that cancer claims cannot be brought for decades after commission of a tort, and that future plaintiffs face almost insurmountable barriers to litigation, these potential defendants have relatively little incentive to mitigate present risks. Should the worst come to pass, bankruptcy is always an alternative to avoid future liability. If companies must bear the costs of toxic torts more immediately, presumably under the watchful eye of their insurance companies, the companies are more likely to scrutinize their operating behavior and prevent many controllable risks of cancer.

Allowing proportional recovery for creation of a future risk thus advances the two primary objectives of the tort system—compensation and deterrence. This proposed approach can improve the functioning of toxic tort litigation. As I have suggested in the context of liability for residential radon contamination:

> The remedy for radon contamination will often be limited to the costs of home repair, future medical surveillance, and possibly some small percentage of future cancer costs. If so, the tort system will be operating at its best, serving to correct a major public health problem at reasonable cost to defendants.[42]

Proportional recovery for risks of future cancer does not cure all the problems of toxic tort litigation, however, and some procedural reform is also required.

Procedural Reform—An Administrative Role

While proportional recovery for future cancer risks goes far to remedy the most difficult toxic tort problems, serious shortcomings remain. The remaining problems are largely evidentiary. The difficulty of proving a given level of cancer risk remains, as does the complexity of this proof and the failings of the court system in resolving the issue.

Proving or disproving a given level of cancer risk under the current system involves the hiring of expert witnesses and considerable expense. The opposing party will have its own expert witnesses and evidence. The dispute over risk will then be settled by inexpert juries or judges who may be susceptible to sophistic or demagogic appeals or simple confusion. Courts have acknowledged this, and one Texas decision complained that "[i]f the experts cannot predict probability in these situations, it is difficult to see how courts can expect a jury of laymen to be able to do so."[43]

Not only do courts provide an incapable tribunal for cancer risk assessment, but the cost of preparing such a case may itself deter many deserving plaintiffs. For toxic tort recovery to function accurately and equitably, change is required in the way that cancer risks are assessed.

Reform is also in the institutional interest of the judiciary. Courts not only must devote considerable resources to trying toxic tort cases, they must replicate every costly step in the next toxic tort case that comes along,

ENVIRONMENTALLY INDUCED CANCER

even if that case involves identical risk assessment issues. "Litigating in court, which is expensive in any circumstance, is particularly wasteful when the same scientific issues must be retried over and over again every time a case is brought."[44] Relitigation also creates horizontal injustice among plaintiffs or defendants, because it is extremely unlikely that two different juries will reach the same risk assessment conclusions, even if they were confronted with identical facts and testimony. Inconsistencies in resolution of the numerous occupational asbestos cases amply demonstrate this point.

Problems of expense, inaccuracy, and inefficiency can be substantially mitigated by granting administrative experts a role in toxic tort adjudication. Some administrative authority should be empowered to develop and publish potency assessments for the most common environmental carcinogens. These assessments would then be imported into toxic tort compensation. Such assessments would not only be admissable, but they also would be invested with some degree of presumptive validity. Once a plaintiff proved a certain level of individual exposure to a carcinogen and the source of that exposure, calculation of the plaintiff's risk would be a simple matter.

EPA would be well-suited to this task and has already developed risk assessments for many relevant carcinogens. These existing risk assessments generally should not be used in toxic tort adjudication, however. Risk assessment for policymaking purposes can properly employ conservative assumptions to produce an upper bound of risk and has typically done so. For compensation purposes, however, society needs the most accurate estimate possible, and this requires a central, most likely estimate of risk. EPA should be producing these most likely estimates anyway and is surely capable of doing so.

The administratively-produced potency assessments should provide a presumptive measure of cancer risk in toxic torts. Due process may require courts to allow parties to attempt to rebut the administrative assessments, but this rebuttal can be limited to unusual cases where a party can produce strong evidence that unique characteristics of the individual exposure make the more general administrative potency assessment inapplicable.

Conjoined with permitting recovery for future cancer risks, greater reliance upon expert administrative potency assessments promises greater accuracy and efficiency in the resolution of toxic torts. These benefits in turn offer greater fairness to both plaintiffs and defendants.

CONCLUSION

The substantive and procedural reforms proposed above could be incorporated into existing judicial adjudication of toxic tort claims with relatively little difficulty. Given the practical difficulties attendant to radical reform in victim compensation systems, this revision in the tort system may be the best option feasible. More significant structural change, however, would offer greater promise for achieving the equitable compensation and deterrence objectives of the system.

The Superfund Section 301(e) report proposed a two-tier compensation containing both administrative and judicial forums for compensating victims of hazardous wastes. While some of the group's recommendations, such as the rebuttable presumptions, should be rejected, the two-tier concept has promise. An administrative solution is most promising for compensation of relatively small risks of cancer.

For very small risks, such as 1 in 1,000,000, no compensation may be necessary. Courts are ill suited to remedying even larger risks, such as 1 in 100 or 1 in 1,000, however. These risks are relatively large and worthy of compensation, but the costs of litigation make judicial trials impractical for most plaintiffs suffering such risks.

Creation of an administrative "small claims court" for these relatively small risks can offer compensation at reasonable cost for defendants. Compensation here could be a relatively simple matter in which plaintiffs demonstrate their approximate exposure, compute their risk based on administratively prepared potency assessments, and recover the resultant percentage of future cancer risk, based on administratively established compensation schedules. The administrative apparatus would prepare these compensation schedules, based upon the costs of insuring for such relatively small future risks. A plaintiff could elect this simple administrative recovery or choose to use the judicial system.

Plaintiffs with greater exposure and cancer risk might still choose a judicial forum for compensation. This judicial remedy would offer greater compensation for larger risks, as well as recoveries for emotional distress, medical surveillance and punitive damages when appropriate. Even in this forum, administrative potency assessment would take the place of the current "battle of the expert witnesses."

The above two-tier system should further the interests of plaintiffs, defendants, and society as a whole. Plaintiffs would be offered a more certain, less arbitrary promise of compensation. Defendants would benefit from smaller individual awards and greater certainty. Society would benefit from a reduction in the transaction costs of compensation. This proposal does not cure every problem of compensating victims of environmental carcinogens, but it should go a long way toward improving the equity and efficiency of toxic tort recoveries.

NOTES

1. Statement of Leslie Cheek, III, Vice president-Federal Affairs of Crum & Forster Insurance Companies, printed in *Should Producers of Hazardous Waste Be Legally Responsible for Injuries Caused by the Waste*, 98th Cong., 1st Sess. (1983), 387.

2. Richard Marcus, *Apocalypse Now?*, 85 MICHIGAN L. REV. (1987): 1261, 1281.

3. Marcus, 1281.

4. National Association of Radiation Survivors v. Turnage, 115 F.R.D. 543 (N.D. Cal. 1987).

5. *New York Times*, August 21, 1988, p.14 (national edition).

6. Brantley v. Phoenix Insurance Co., 536 S.W. 2d 72 (Tex. Civ. App.—Houston 1976).

7. Vitants Gulbis, *Cancer as Compensable Under Workers' Compensation Acts*, 19 A.L.R. 4th 639 (1987).

8. Daniel Farber, *Toxic Causation*, 71 MINNESOTA L. REV. (1987): 1219, 1258 n. 158.

9. John Forstrom, *Victim Without a Cause: The Missing Link Between Compensation and Deterrence in Toxic Tort Litigation*, 18 ENVIRONMENTAL LAW (1987): 151, 174.

10. Note, *Administrative Remedies for Hazardous Waste Victims: Prospects for U.S. Action in an International Perspective*, 12 NORTH CAROLINA JOURNAL OF INTERNATIONAL LAW AND COMMERCIAL REGULATION (1987): 277, 297.

11. Forstrom, 175.

12. Section 301(e) Study Group, *Injuries and Damages From Hazardous Wastes—Analysis and Improvements of Legal Remedies (September 1982)*.

13. Section 301(e) Report, 213–214.

14. Kenneth Abraham, *Individual Action and Collective Responsibility: The Dilemma of Mass Tort Reform*, 73 VIRGINIA L. REV. (1987): 845, 888.

15. Cheek, 388.

16. 428 U.S. 1 (1976).

17. 428 U.S. at 25.

18. Mullins Coal v. Office of Workers' Compensation, 56 U.S.L.W. 4044 (1988).

19. J. B. Browing, *Public Compensation: A Chemical Industry Perspective* (1983), 9.

20. Note, *Developments in the Law: Toxic Waste Litigation*, 99 HARVARD L. REV. (1986): 1458, 1643.

21. Section 301(e) Report, 220.

22. Section 301(e) Report, 216.

23. Anderson v. Minneapolis, St. Paul, and Sault Ste. Marie Railway Co., 179 N.W. 45 (Minn. 1920).

24. W. P. Keeton, *Prosser and Keeton on the Law of Torts* (West Pub., 5th ed. 1984), 267.

25. Ora Harris Jr., *Toxic Tort Litigation and the Causation Element: Is There Any Hope of Reconciliation*, 40 SOUTHWESTERN L. J. (1986): 909, 956.

26. Harris, 956 n. 318.

27. Steve Gold, *Causation in Toxic Torts: Burdens of Proof, Standards of Persuasion, and Statistical Evidence*, 96 YALE L.J. (1986): 376, 395.

28. Gold, 395.

29. Gold, 395 n. 96.

30. Gold, 395.

31. Allen v. United States, 588 F. Supp. 247, 428 (D. Utah 1984).

32. Richard Delgado, *Beyond Sindell: Realization of Cause-In-Fact Rules for Indeterminate Plaintiffs*, 70 CALIF. L. REV. (1982): 881, 897.

33. David Rosenberg, *The Causal Connection in Mass Exposure Cases: A "Public Law" Vision of the Tort System*, 97 HARVARD L. REV. (1984): 851, 882.

34. Dwight Harvey, *Epidemiological Proof of Probability: Implementing the Proportional Recovery Approach in Toxic Exposure Torts*, 89 DICKENSON L. REV. (1984): 233.

35. Farber, 1240.

36. Robert Bush, *Between Two Worlds: The Shift From Individual to Group Responsibility in the Law of Causation of Injury*, 33 UCLA L. REV. (1986): 1473, 1491.

37. Richard Brooks and Edwin Jacob, *Responses to Robert L. Rabin*, 24 HOUSTON L. REV. 58, 62 (1987).

38. Farber, 1241.

39. Farber, 1241 n. 98.

40. Rosenberg, 895.

41. Richard Faulk, *Strategic and Scientific Considerations in Toxic Tort Defense*, 26 SOUTH TEXAS L.J. (1985): 513, 513 n. 2.

42. Frank Cross and Paula Murray, *Liability for Toxic Radon Gas in Residential Home Sales*, 66 NORTH CAROLINA L. REV. (1988): 687, 739.

43. Parker v. Employers Mutual Liability Insurance Co. of Wisconsin, 440 S.W. 2d 43, 49 (Tex. 1969).

44. Glen Robinson, *Probabilistic Causation and Compensation for Tortious Risk*, 14 J. LEGAL STUDIES (1985): 779, 802.

BIBLIOGRAPHY

Administrative Conference of the United States. *Federal Regulation of Cancer-Causing Chemicals.* Washington: Administrative Conference of the United States, 1982.

Alderson, M., ed. *The Prevention of Cancer.* London: Edward Arnold, 1981.

American Cancer Society. *Cancer Facts and Figures.* New York: American Cancer Society, 1983.

Anton-Guirgus, Hoda, and Henry Lynch. *Biomarkers, Genetics, and Cancer.* New York: Van Nostrand Reinhold Co., 1985.

Bailey, Martin J. *Reducing Risks to Life: Measurement of the Benefits.* Washington: American Enterprise Institute, 1980.

Becker, F. F., ed. *Cancer: A Comprehensive Treatise.* New York: Plenum, 1975.

Birnbaum, Sheila, and Paul D. Rheingold. *Toxic Substances Litigation 1982.* New York: Practicing Law Institute, 1982.

Bollier, David, and Joan Claybrook. *Freedom from Harm: The Civilizing Influence of Health, Safety and Environmental Regulation.* Washington: Public Citizen and Democracy Project, 1986.

Bowman, Malcolm. *Handbook of Carcinogens and Hazardous Substances.* New York: Marcel Dekker, Inc., 1982.

Burish, Thomas, Sandra Levy, and Beth Meyerowitz. *Cancer, Nutrition and Eating Behavior.* Hillsdale, N.J.: Lawrence Earlbaum Assoc., 1985.

Cairns, John. *Science and Society.* San Francisco: W. H. Freeman & Co., 1978.

Cairns, John, and S. Palmer. *Symposium on Food and Cancer.* New York: Columbia University Press, 1982.

Callahan, Daniel, and Bruce Jennings. *Ethics, The Social Sciences, and Policy Analysis.* New York: Plenum, 1983.

Campen, James T. *Benefit, Cost, and Beyond: The Political Economy of Benefit-Cost Analysis.* Cambridge, Mass.: Ballinger Publishing Company, 1986.

Chaganti, R. S. K., and James German. *Genetics in Clinical Oncology.* New York: Oxford University Press, 1985.

Clark, Timothy B., Marvin H. Kosters, and James C. Miller, eds. *Reforming Regulation.* Washington: American Enterprise Institute, 1980.

Clemmesen, J., D. Conning, D. Henschler, and F. Desch. *Quantitative Aspects of Risk Assessment in Chemical Carcinogenesis.* Springer-Verlag: Carl Ritter & Co., 1980.

Council On Environmental Quality. *Toxic Substances.* Washington: U.S. Government Printing Office, 1971.

Covello, V. T., L. B. Lave, A. Moghissi, and V. R. R. Uppuluri, eds. *Uncertainty in Risk Assessment, Risk Management and Decision Making.* New York: Plenum, 1987.

Crandall, Robert W., and Lester B. Lave., eds. *The Scientific Basis of Health and Safety Regulation.* Washington: Brookings Institution, 1983.

Currie, Graham, and Angela Currie. *Cancer: The Biology of Malignant Disease*. London: Castlefield Press, 1982.

Day, Stacey. *Cancer, Stress and Death*. New York: Plenum, 1986.

Deisler, P. F., Jr., ed. *Reducing the Carcinogenic Risks in Industry*. New York: Marcel Dekker, Inc., 1984.

Deisler, P. F., Jr., ed., *Risk in the Technological Society*. Boulder, Colo.: Westview Press, 1982.

Delong, M. *Practical and Legal Concerns of Cancer Patients and Their Families*. Durham, N.C.: Duke University Medical Center, 1984.

DeVita, V. T., S. Heilman, and S. A. Rosenberg, eds. *Cancer, Principles & Practice of Oncology*. Philadelphia: J. B. Lippincott Co., 1985.

Doll, Richard, and Richard Peto. *The Causes of Cancer: Quantitative Estimates of Avoidable Risks of Cancer in the United States Today*. Oxford: Oxford University Press, 1981.

Doniger, David D. *The Law and Policy of Toxic Substances Control: A Case Study of Vinyl Chloride*. Baltimore: Johns Hopkins University Press, 1978.

Douglas, Mary, and Aaron Wildavsky. *Risk and Culture: An Essay on the Selection of Technical and Environmental Dangers*. Berkeley: University of California Press, 1982.

Efron, Edith. *The Apocalyptics: Cancer and the Big Lie; How Environmental Politics Controls What We Know About Cancer*. New York: Simon and Schuster, 1984.

Epstein, Samuel S. *The Politics of Cancer*. San Francisco: Sierra Club Books, 1978.

Ferguson, Allen R., and Judith H. Behn. *The Benefits of Health and Safety Regulation*. Cambridge, Mass.: Ballinger Publishing Company, 1981.

Food Safety Council. *Proposed System for Food Safety Assessment*. Washington: Food Safety Council, 1983.

Fortuna, Richard C., and David J. Lennett. *Hazardous Waste Regulation: The New Era*. New York: McGraw-Hill, 1987.

Fraumeni, J., ed. *Persons at High Risk of Cancer: An Approach to Cancer Etiology and Control*. New York: Academic Press, Inc., 1975.

Graham, John D., Laura Green, and Mark J. Roberts. *Seeking Safety: Science, Public Policy and Cancer Risk*. Cambridge, Mass.: Harvard University Press, 1988.

Griffin, A. C., and C. R. Shaw., eds. *Carcinogens: Identification and Mechanisms of Action*. New York: Raven Press, 1979.

Hadden, Susan G., ed. *Risk Analysis, Institutions, and Public Policy*. Port Washington, N.Y.: Associated Faculty Press, 1984.

Hammond, E. Cuyler, and Irving J. Selikoff. *Public Control of Environmental Health Hazards*. New York: The New York Academy of Sciences, 1979.

Hiatt, H. H., J. D. Watson, and J. A. Winsten, eds. *Origins of Human Cancer*. Cold Spring Harbor, N.Y.: Cold Spring Harbor Laboratory, 1977.

Holleb, A. I., ed. *The American Cancer Society Cancer Book*. Garden City, N.Y.: Doubleday & Co., Inc., 1986.

Hutton, Gerald L. *Legal Considerations On Ionizing Radiation*. Springfield, Ill.: Charles C. Thomas, 1966.

Kates, Robert W. *Risk Assessment of Environmental Hazards*. New York: John Wiley & Sons, 1978.

Kates, Robert W., Christoph Hohenemser, and Jeane X. Kasperson. *Perilous Progress: Managing the Hazards of Technology*. Boulder, Colo.: Westview Press, 1985.

Keeton, William P. *Prosser and Keeton on the Law of Torts.* 5th ed. St. Paul, Minn.: West Publishing Co., 1984.

Kessler, Irving. *Cancer Control.* Baltimore: University Park Press, 1980.

Klein, G. and S. Weinhouse, eds. *Advances in Cancer Research.* Vol. 35. New York: Academic Press, 1981.

Krimsky, Sheldon, and Alonzo Plough. *Environmental Hazards: Communicating Risks as a Social Process.* Dover, Mass.: Auburn House Publishing Company, 1988.

Laszlo, John. *Understanding Cancer.* New York: Harper & Row, 1987.

Lave, Lester B. *The Strategy of Social Regulation: Decision Frameworks for Policy.* Washington: Brookings Institution, 1981.

———. Quantitative Risk Assessment in Regulation. Washington: Brookings Institution, 1982.

Lave, Lester B., ed. *Risk Assessment and Management.* New York: Plenum, 1987.

Levenson, Frederick. *The Causes and Prevention of Cancer.* New York: Stein and Day, 1985.

Litan, Robert E., and William D. Nordhaus. *Reforming Federal Regulation.* New Haven: Yale University Press, 1983.

Lowrance, William O. *Of Acceptable Risk: Science and the Determination of Safety.* Los Altos, Calif.: William Kaufmann, 1976.

MacMahon, B., and T. F. Pugh. *Epidemiology: Principles and Methods.* Boston: Little, Brown & Co., 1970.

Magnus, Knut. *Trends in Cancer Incidence.* Washington: Hemisphere Publishing Co., 1982.

Marks, Paul. *Genetics, Cell Differentiation, and Cancer.* Orlando: Academic Press, Inc., 1985.

McCaffrey, David P. *OSHA and the Politics of Health Regulation.* New York, Plenum, 1982.

Melnick, R. Shep. *Regulation and the Courts: The Case of the Clean Air Act.* Washington: Brookings Institution, 1983.

Mendeloff, John. *Regulating Safety: An Economic and Political Analysis of Occupational Safety and Health Policy.* Cambridge, Mass.: MIT Press, 1979.

———. *The Dilemma of Toxic Substance Regulation.* Cambridge, Mass.: MIT Press, 1979.

Miller, James C. III, and Bruce Yandle. *Benefit-Cost Analysis of Social Regulation: Case Studies from the Council on Wage and Price Stability.* Washington: American Enterprise Institute, 1979.

National Academy of Engineering. *Hazards: Technology and Fairness.* Washington: National Academy Press, 1986.

National Academy of Sciences/National Research Council. *Drinking Water and Health.* Washington: National Academy of Sciences Press, 1977.

———. *Regulating Pesticides.* Washington: National Academy Press, 1980.

———. *The Effects on Populations of Exposure to Low Levels of Ionizing Radiation.* Washington: National Academy Press, 1980.

———. *Risk Assessment in the Federal Government: Managing the Process.* Washington: National Academy Press, 1983.

———. *Toxicity Testing: Strategies to Determine Needs and Priorities.* Washington: National Academy Press, 1984.

————. *Regulating Pesticides in Food—The Delaney Paradox*. Washington: National Academy Press, 1987.

National Cancer Institute. *Cancer Control Objectives for the Nation: 1985–2000*. Washington: U.S. Government Printing Office, 1986.

Nicholson, William, ed. *Management of Assessed Risk for Carcinogens*. New York: New York Academy of Sciences, 1981.

Nicolini, Claudio. *Biophysics and Cancer*. New York: Plenum, 1986.

Nyhart, J. D., and M. M. Carrow, eds. *Law and Science in Collaboration*. Lexington, Mass.: Lexington Books, 1983.

Office of Technology Assessment. *Cancer Testing Technology and Saccharin*. Washington: U.S. Government Printing Office, 1977.

————. *Assessment of Technologies for Determining Cancer Risks from the Environment*. Washington: U.S. Government Printing Office, 1981.

————. *Identifying and Regulating Carcinogens*. Washington: U.S. Government Printing Office, 1987.

Oppenheimer, Steven B. *Cancer: A Biological and Clinical Introduction*. Boston: Allyn & Bacon, Inc., 1982.

Pitot, Henry. *Fundamentals of Oncology*. New York: Marcel Dekker, Inc., 1981.

Rabe, Barry G. *Fragmentation and Integration in State Environmental Management*. Washington: The Conservation Foundation, 1986.

Rheingold, Paul D., Norman J. Landau, and Michael M. Canavan. *Toxic Torts: Tort Actions for Cancer and Lung Disease Due to Environmental Pollution*. Washington: The Association of Trial Lawyers of America, 1977.

Roberts, Leslie. *Cancer Today: Origins, Prevention, and Treatment*. Washington: Institute of Medicine/National Academy Press, 1984.

Rushefsky, *Making Cancer Policy*. Albany: State University of New York Press, 1986.

Shapo, Marshall S. *A Nation of Guinea Pigs*. New York: The Free Press, 1979.

Shimkin, M. *Science and Cancer*. Washington: Silvergirl, Inc., 1980.

Simone, Charles. *Cancer & Nutrition*. New York: McGraw-Hill, 1983.

Slovic, Baruch, Paul S. Fischoff, and Sarah L. Lichtenstein, eds., *Societal Risk Assessment*. New York: Plenum, 1980.

Smith, V. Kerry, ed. *Environmental Policy Under Reagan's Executive Order: The Role of Benefit-Cost Analysis*. Chapel Hill: University of North Carolina Press, 1984.

Smith, Wrynn. *A Profile of Health and Disease in America: Cancer*. New York: Facts on File Publications, 1987.

Swartzman, Daniel, Richard A. Liroff, and Kevin G. Croke, eds. *Cost-Benefit Analysis and Environmental Regulations: Politics, Ethics and Methods*. Washington: The Conservation Foundation, 1982.

Tardiff, R. G., and J. V. Rodricks, eds. *Toxic Substances and Human Risk*. New York: Plenum, 1987.

Thompson, James, and Barry Brown. *Cancer Modeling*. New York: Marcel Dekker, Inc., 1987.

Toxic Substances Strategy Committee. *Toxic Chemicals and Public Protection*. Washington: Council on Environmental Quality, 1980.

Travis, Curtis, ed. *Carcinogen Risk Assessment*. New York: Plenum, 1988.

U.S. Department of Health and Human Services. *The Health Consequences of Involuntary Smoking*. Washington: U.S. Government Printing Office, 1986.

Upton, Arthur, Roy Albert, Fredric Burns, and Roy Shore. *Radiation Carcinogenesis*. New York: Elsevier, 1986.

Vanio, H., M. Sorsa, and K. Hemminki. *Occupational Cancer and Carcinogenesis*. Washington: Hemisphere Publishing Co., 1979.

Vessey, M. P., and Muir Gray. *Cancer Risks and Prevention*. Oxford: Oxford University Press, 1985.

Vogel, David. *National Styles of Regulation*. Ithaca, N.Y.: Cornell University Press, 1985.

Wellington, Dorothy, Eleanor Macdonald, and Patricia Wolf. *Cancer Mortality: Environmental and Ethnic Factors*. Academic Press, 1979.

Whelan, Elizabeth. *Toxic Terror*. Ottawa, Ill.: Jameson Books, 1985.

Whipple, Chris, ed. *Risk in the Technological Society*. Boulder, Colo.: Westview Press, 1982.

———. *De Minimis Risk*. New York: Plenum, 1987.

White, Lawrence J. *Reforming Regulation: Processes and Problems*. Englewood Cliffs, N.J.: Prentice-Hall, Inc., 1981.

Williams, C. *All About Cancer*. New York: John Wiley & Sons, 1983.

Weidenbaum, Murray, and R. DeFina. *The Cost of Federal Regulation of Economic Activity*. Washington: American Enterprise Institute, 1978.

Wildavsky, Aaron. *Speaking Truth to Power: The Art and Craft of Policy Making*. London: Transaction Books, 1979.

———. *Searching for Safety*. London: Transaction Books, 1988.

Wilson, James Q. *The Politics of Regulation*. New York: Basic Books, 1980.

INDEX

About the Author

FRANK B. CROSS is Associate Professor of Business Law at the University of Texas and Associate Director of the Center for Legal and Regulatory Studies. His numerous articles have appeared in publications such as the *Emory Law Journal, Vanderbilt Law Review, Administrative Law Review, Harvard Environmental Law Review,* and *Environmental Affairs Law Review.*